Contents

THE NEW DIALECTIC AND MARX'S *CAPITAL*

BY

CHRISTOPHER J. ARTHUR

BRILL
LEIDEN · BOSTON · KÖLN
2002

This book is printed on acid-free paper.

Library of Congress Cataloging-in-Publication Data

Arthur, C.J. (Christopher John), 1940-
 The new dialectic and Marx's *Capital* / by Christopher J. Arthur.
  p. cm. — (Historical materialism, ISSN 1570-1522 ; 1))
 Includes bibliographical references and index.
 ISBN 9004127984
 1. Marx, Karl, 1818-1883. Kapital. 2. Dialectical materialism.
 I. Title. II. Series.

 HB501.M37 A75   2002
 335.4'112—dc21   2002018616

Die Deutsche Bibliothek – CIP-Einheitsaufnahme

Arthur, Christopher J.:
The new dialectic and Marx's *Capital* / by Christopher J. Arthur.
 - Leiden ; Boston ; Köln : Brill, 2002
 (Historical materialism ; 1)
 ISBN 90–04–12798–4

ISSN 1570–1522
ISBN 90 04 12798 4

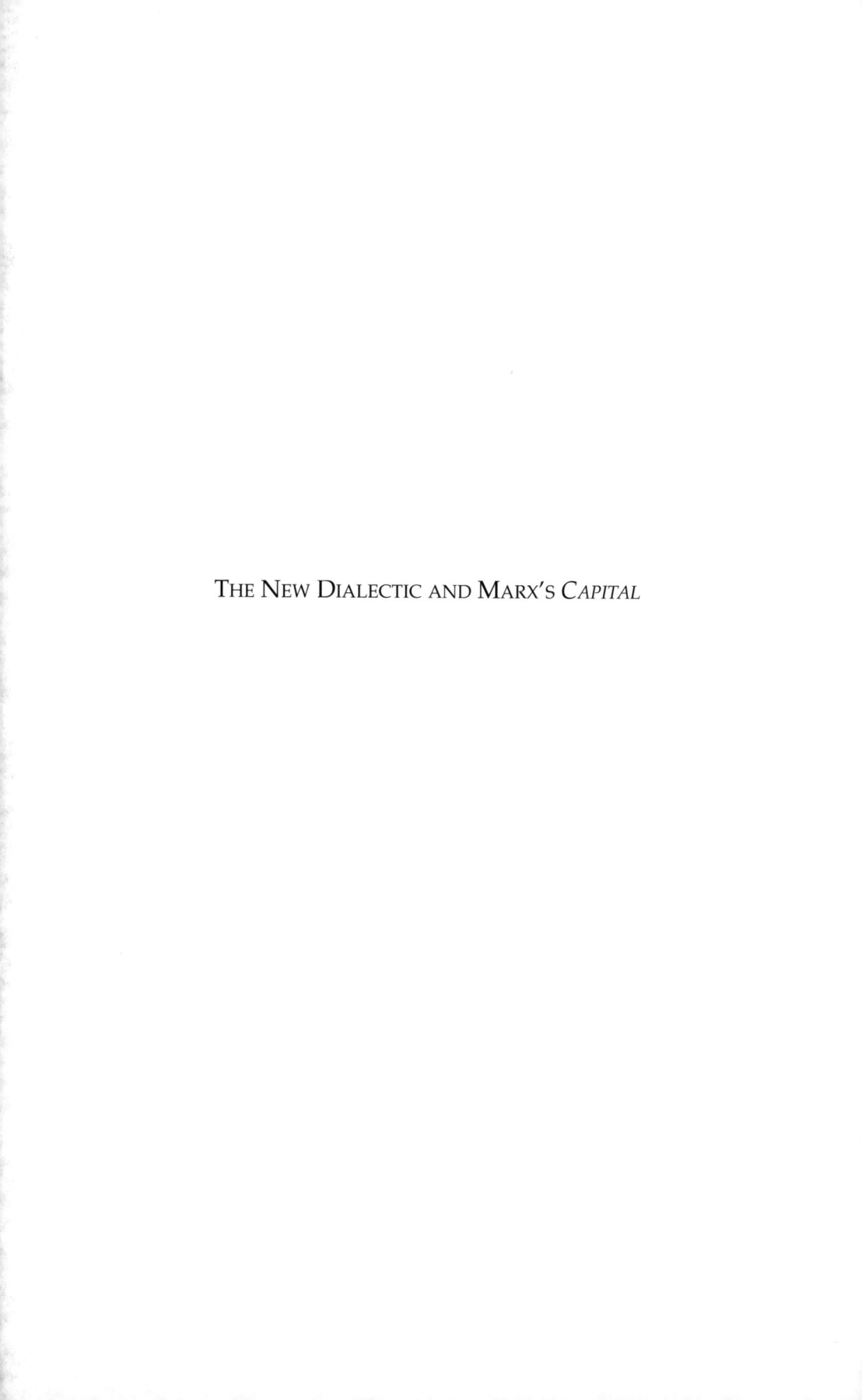

THE NEW DIALECTIC AND MARX'S *CAPITAL*

HISTORICAL MATERIALISM BOOK SERIES

Preface and Acknowledgements

The chapters of this book each address a specific issue, and they can be studied separately. However they are arranged in the most helpful order for developing an understanding of the general position of the book – at least, as far as the first eight are concerned. References in the footnotes are given in short form; full details of the edition used are given in the Bibliography at the back.

In the course of thinking about the issues addressed here I have had the benefit of presenting the ideas for discussion at many conferences and seminars. Earlier versions of the arguments advanced in the chapters below have sometimes appeared in associated conference publications. I am most grateful to those who organised such meetings and invited me to address them.

I thank for their support and constructive criticism at various points: Tony Smith, Geert Reuten, Patrick Murray, Riccardo Bellofiore, Fred Moseley, Martha Campbell, Mark Cowling, Mario Robles Baez, Joe McCarney, Sean Sayers, Geoffrey Kay, Bertell Ollman, Mike Williams, Filio Diamanti and Hillel Ticktin.

Chapter 2 is a thoroughly revised version of 'Against the Logical-Historical Method: Dialectical Derivation versus Linear Logic' in *New Investigations of Marx's Method*, edited by F. Moseley and M. Campbell (Humanities Press, 1997).

Chapter 3 is a revised version of 'Value, Labour and Negativity', in *Capital & Class* 73, (Spring, 2001).

Chapter 4 is an extended and rewritten version of a paper of the same name that appeared in *Science & Society*, (Fall, 1998).

Chapter 5 is a thoroughly revised and rewritten version of 'Hegel's *Logic* and Marx's *Capital*' in *Marx's Method in 'Capital': A Reexamination*, edited by F. Moseley (Humanities Press, 1993).

Chapter 6 is a somewhat extended and revised version of a paper of the same name that appeared in *Rethinking Marxism* (Winter, 1993).

Chapter 7 is a revision of a paper of the same name that appeared in *Studies in Marxism* 5, (1998).

Chapter 8 is a slightly shorter version of 'The Spectral Ontology of Value', which appeared in *Radical Philosophy* 107, (May-June, 2001) and in *Critical Realism and Marxism* edited by A. Brown et al. (Routledge, 2002).

Chapter 9 is a revision of 'Hegel's Theory of Value', which appeared in *Value, Social Form and the State*, edited by M. Williams, (Macmillan, 1988).

Chapter 10 is a slightly shortened version of 'Epitaph for the USSR: A Clock without a Spring' which appeared *Critique* 32–33 (2000).

Chapter 11 is a slightly revised version of a paper of the same name that appeared in *Studies in Marxism* 8, (2001).

Chapter One
Introduction: The New Turn to Dialectic

This book consists in part in a study of dialectical motifs in Marx's work, and in part in further developing these themes in the context of a new tendency that has emerged in recent years, which is variously labelled 'the New Dialectic', 'New Hegelian Marxism' or 'Systematic Dialectic'. It consists of a number of chapters linked by this approach, and hence supporting each other, in that their cumulative weight is intended to demonstrate the fruitfulness of the philosophical standpoint from which they are written. The term 'the New Dialectic' in the title was originally coined by me in a review, and it has since been widely used in the sense I intended, namely to refer to literature sharing certain common themes, but which does not take the form of a definite 'school'. Rather it is a convenient way of grouping together thinkers of independent spirit, clearly doing something rather distinctive in the present intellectual conjuncture.[1] It has already been made the occasion of robust criticism from John Rosenthal, who labelled it 'new Hegelian Marxism'. As we shall see, many of the most active researchers believe they are working within a new paradigm they call 'Systematic Dialectic', but the tendency I label 'new' is more comprehensive and includes those who still think Hegel's philosophy of history has something to offer (e.g. Joe McCarney).

What is involved in the first place is simply a return to *sources*, making a serious study of what Hegel and Marx really achieved with respect to dialectic. But the New Dialectic has not only recovered much of this indispensable original work, it is characterised by new thinking about the issues, and it has *reconstructed* the inheritance of Hegel and Marx in various ways. Amazingly, Fredric Jameson predicted what would happen. In his Adorno book of 1989, he wrote: 'Any number of straws in the wind point to an impending Hegel revival, of a new kind, likely to draw a revival of capital-logic along with it. . . . But the Hegel who emerges from this reading will be an unfamiliar . . . one who comes *after* the *Grundrisse*. . . .'[2]

The New Dialectic is indeed especially marked by a reevaluation of Hegel. Joan Robinson, in her *Open Letter to a Marxist*, asked rhetorically what business had Hegel putting his nose in between her and Ricardo. The answer is that Marx's concepts are different from Ricardo's and it is unlikely that Marx would have been able to rethink such questions as the concept of capital without his background in Hegel's philosophy, albeit that for tactical reasons he tried to diminish the evidence in his published texts. The whole question of the influence of Hegel on Marx is very complex. It cannot easily be settled by studying such explicit acknowledgements of it as are made by Marx; for these are in general very cryptic. Furthermore there is a problem about the interpretation of Hegel, which also involves the issue of what Marx's interpretation of him was, and whether it was fair. In the literature we see two tendencies. One, represented most strikingly by Herbert Marcuse, reads Hegel as materialistically as possible so as to claim his ideas may be readily resituated in a Marxian framework. The other, represented best by Lucio Colletti and Louis Althusser, argues that Marx struggled to leave behind this influence because Hegel was idealist through and through and hence could only be a bad influence. The very same words are interpreted entirely oppositely by such commentators. Hegel says in his *Science of Logic* that finite things must perish and hence give way to the infinite. Marcuse situates this as an anticipation of Marx's historical materialism, whereas Colletti finds this is the gateway to religion.[3]

As Jameson acutely foresaw, the new interest in Hegel is rather different from that of earlier Hegelian Marxism which was (rightly or wrongly) called 'historicist'. The new interest in Hegel is largely unconcerned with recovering the grand narrative of Hegel's philosophy of history and relating it to historical materialism; rather it is focussed on Hegel's *Logic* and how this fits the method of Marx's *Capital*. The point is usually put by saying the effort is to construct a *systematic* dialectic in order to articulate the relations of a *given* social order, namely capitalism, as opposed to an historical dialectic studying the *rise and fall* of social systems. (I will come back to the notion of a systematic dialectic.)

What, then, is 'new' about this dialectic? What is implicitly referred to here as the 'Old Dialectic' is the Soviet school of 'Diamat', rooted in a vulgarised version of Engels and Plekhanov. It was presented as a universal 'world outlook' and universal method. Engels was especially influential in drawing attention to Marx's use of dialectic and in elaborating his own version. He put forward 'three laws' of dialectic.[4] The point of the paradigm was the effort to fit everything into these three laws. It consisted of a set of *examples* and lacked *systematicity*. Lenin, in his philosophical notebooks, complained that dialectic had been reduced to 'the sum total of examples ("for example, a seed", "for example, primitive communism")' and he noted that Engels' work lay at the origin of this tendency.[5] This lifeless formalism proceeded by applying abstract schemas adventitiously to contents arbitrarily forced into the required shape. Even the great pan-logicist Hegel warned against this sort of procedure. Speaking of the 'triadic form', he said that 'when it is reduced to a lifeless schema, a mere shadow', it is not scientific. Science, he said, 'demands surrender to the life of the object' as opposed to that 'formalism which imagines it has comprehended something when it has attached some determination of the schema' to it.[6]

However, Hegel himself may be fairly charged with such a formalism in much of his 'applied' philosophy. Certainly, in his 1843 critique of Hegel's political philosophy, Marx characterised the Hegelian method as one which seeks 'a body for the logic'; he rejected it in favour of a scientific method based on 'the logic of the body'. A science must adopt the logic proper to the peculiar character of the object under investigation (*'die eigentümliche Logik des eigentümliche Gegenstandes'*).[7] If, then, it turns out that *Capital* is a veritable treasure of dialectic, this is not because of the application of an abstract universal method, but because the movement of the material itself requires expression in such logical categories.

Diamat ran out of steam in the 1950s. In the West this was followed by a recovery of the work of historicist Marxists such as Lukács, Korsch and Gramsci. But then came the high tide of structuralism and post-structuralism, analytical Marxism, discourse theory, etc., which rejected Hegel altogether, and generally had a skeptical attitude to dialectic. It was Althusser's strident anti-Hegelianism that opened the way for paradigms completely alien to Marxism to absorb it; thus there was the rise of so-called analytical Marxism, which relied on axioms that were essentially generalisations of neoclassical economics; this was vitiated by the same inability to explain the social forms that structured the supposed 'choices' of agents as its model (see chapter 9 below). But there were always people who refused to follow the fashion. Now we see a number of Hegelian inspired reappropriations of the dialectic; and, like Jameson, I predict this tendency will gather strength.

The particular variant of the New Dialectic to which I adhere is known by its exponents as systematic dialectic (beside my own work, see that of Geert Reuten, Michael Williams, and Tony Smith). So let me now expand on a systematic – as opposed to a historical – dialectic. There are two different type of dialectical theory in Hegel. First is a dialectic of history. Hegel believed there is a logic of development underlying world history. But there is a second sort of dialectical theory found in writings such as the *Science of Logic* and *Philosophy of Right*. This may be termed 'systematic dialectic' and it is concerned with the articulation of categories designed to conceptualise an existent concrete whole. The expositional order of these categories does not have to coincide with the order of their appearance in history. Hegel says: 'But it should be noted that the moments, whose result is a further determined form [of the concept], precede it as determinations of the concept in the scientific development of the Idea, but do not come before it as shapes in its temporal development.' And again: 'What we obtain in this [systematic development] is a series of thoughts and another series of existent shapes, in which it may happen that the temporal sequence of their actual appearance is to some extent different from the conceptual sequence.'[8] Exactly the same point is made by Marx: 'It would be unfeasible and wrong to let the economic categories follow one another in the same sequence as that in which they were historically decisive'.[9] There is very little in the secondary literature on how to do systematic dialectic even though Hegel's and Marx's major works are not historical but systematic. Moreover Marx himself never wrote

his threatened brochure on dialectical method; although he did leave its outcome in the shape of *Capital*.

I attempt now a general characterisation of systematic dialectic (emphasising that not all the thinkers I cite would accept everything in the following
paragraph). At the philosophical level it is a way of working with concepts
that keeps them open and fluid, and above all systematically interconnected.
At the methodological level it puts the emphasis on the need for a clear order
of presentation, which, however, is not a linear one, for the starting point is
not empirically or axiomatically given but in need of interrogation. Epis-
temologically it insists on the reflexivity of the subject-object relation.
Ontologically it addresses itself to totalities and thus to their comprehension
through systematically interconnected categories, which are more or less
sharply distinguished from historically sequenced orderings. Textually it pre-
fers to look at Hegel and Marx afresh, setting aside sclerotic received tradi-
tions of interpretation. Substantively it reexamines or reconstructs Marxian
theory in the light of the above protocols.

As to the last point, it is striking that those who have attempted such a rigorous dialectical systematisation of Marx's work have generally found it necessary to *reconstruct* it to some degree. Again, those of us who have attempted
it have motivated the transitions between the categories in rather different
ways. For Tony Smith it is a matter of discerning the structural tendencies
of the form under consideration. Once these are identified it is possible to
infer the character of a new social form comprehended with a new category.
Since the necessary structural tendencies impinge on social agents and give
rise to new behaviour, his approach amounts to a virtual phenomenology of
capitalism. However, Smith believes it is also in order to motivate a transition simply on the ground that it is required in order to reconstruct in thought
all essential determinations of the existent totality. For Reuten and Williams
it is a matter of transcending contradictions discovered in a given form,
through identifying the conditions of existence that sustain it; all the problems stem from the original dissociation between agents in a market economy. An interesting feature of their work is that they stress that at the more
concrete levels of investigation various solutions may be tried by agents, such
as the State, so at that point empirical contingency enters the study. Tom
Sekine attempts to model exactly Hegel's logic through excluding from the

'pure theory of capital' all disruptions to capital's drive to accumulate and to complete itself as a self-sustaining totality. My own view starts from the premise that theory faces an existent totality, that therefore in comprehending it through analysing it into its moments it is denatured; when the moments are abstracted from the whole they are inadequately grounded; hence transitions in the argument spring from the effort to *reconstruct* the whole, through identifying the inability of the category under consideration at each stage to comprehend itself; hence the dialectic moves to a more comprehensive one. (I develop my view on the method of systematic dialectic in chapters 2 and 4.)

Now I want to explore in more detail what is involved in the new reading of Hegel. Half a dozen Marxist writers in the last ten years dared to dissent from Marx in his verdict on Hegel, e.g. that in the *Grundrisse*: 'Hegel fell into the illusion of conceiving the real as the product of thought.'[10] Tony Smith, Ali Shamsavari and others explicitly contest this. Tony Smith's books are the clearest defence of a 'non-metaphysical reading' of Hegel. He rejects the reading of Hegel that sees human history as a field of action for some super-subject, namely the World Spirit. He rejects the reading of Hegel that sees reality reduced to thought. And he rejects the reading of the *Logic* that sees in it the self-development of the Idea. The textual evidence for such readings he dismisses as metaphor, at the level of what Hegel called 'picture thoughts' (*Vorstellungen*), rather than in terms of the pure concept (*Begriff*). More specifically Smith claims that Hegel's historical situation meant he had to dress up his philosophy so as to ease a Christian audience into it. So for Smith Hegel's real mistakes are said to occur at the level of substantive social analysis; in particular the presentation of bourgeois society as a realm of freedom. On his account the true Hegelian would be a communist. On Smith's non-metaphysical reading of Hegel the *Logic* is simply the progression of categories that we need to make sense of object-domains of increasing complexity. For Smith the most important lesson of the *Logic* is not so much to do with its specific results but to do with its *systematicity*. In addressing any object-domain our categories must be ordered according to systematic principles and their dialectical relations explicated. Smith holds that this is also Marx's method: *Capital* is unified through a systematic progression of socioeconomic categories reconstructing the capitalist mode of production in thought, beginning with the simplest abstract category and dialectically advancing to the concrete whole. Smith's appropriation of Marx's *Capital* does not involve any one-to-one mapping of logical categories onto those of capital. Indeed he always polemicises against such mapping because capital as a material system cannot literally be a logical structure. Rather he takes a meta-rhythm from Hegel's dialectic, its movement from a category of unity, to one of difference, to one of unity-in-difference. Others who may be characterised as new Hegelian Marxists in a similar sense to Smith include Reuten and Williams, except that they consider their systematic science to be a 'development from' Hegel's *Logic* rather than an 'application' of it.[11]

It is interesting to notice that, for Smith, Reuten and McCarney, the Hegel/Marx confrontation should, then, be staged at the level of substantive social theory, specifically *Capital* versus Hegel's *Philosophy of Right*. Reuten objects in principle to Hegel's idealisation of the capitalist state as the self-comprehending Idea. Smith characterises capitalism as a 'structure of essence', because riven by dualities; for him only communism would have the logical structure of Hegel's 'Concept'.

I belong to a different group, which also includes Patrick Murray, Moishe Postone, Tom Sekine, and Robert Albritton. By contrast with the previous group we stage the Hegel/Marx confrontation at the level of ontology. We all hold that Hegel was indeed an idealist, not only in his idealisation of bourgeois conditions but also in the *Logic* itself. The sort of language Marx reacted against cannot be dismissed as metaphorical. Speaking for myself, I believe it is patent that the movement of the *Logic* is indeed that of the self-acting Idea. We merely 'look on' says Hegel, and copy it down more or less successfully. What we can see, however, is a striking *homology* between the structure of Hegel's *Logic* and Marx's *Capital*, or, at least, a homology given some minor reconstructive work on either or both. Moreover, since the human bearers of this structure are reduced to personifications of its categories, we find the same kind of *self*-acting forms as those in Hegel's logic. Admittedly, they cannot be forms of *thought* as they are in logic. So the people mentioned need to account for this. For Postone, and also I believe for Sekine and Albritton, this is mainly explained ideologically, that Hegel eternalises the dialectical movement of capital by transforming it from an historically determinate system to the timeless realm of logic, through replacing the concrete terms with abstractions of themselves, so that instead of self-valorisation is put absolute negativity.

I myself believe that the capitalist system does indeed consist in part of logical relations. This is because I lay great stress on the way exchange abstracts from the heterogeneity of commodities and treats them as instances of a universal, namely value. This parallels the way the abstractive power of thought operates; and it gives rise to an homologous structure to logical forms, namely the value forms. I shall say more in detail in the relevant chapters of this work about the homology, but here I stress that I go further than just drawing attention to methodological lessons from Hegel's systematic ordering of categories. I draw also on his ontology. Hegel is the great expert on how an ideality would have to build itself up, moment by moment, into a self-actualising whole. If then, as I believe, capital has in part an ideal reality, then if it can be shown to incarnate Hegel's blueprint it can claim to be self-sustaining. My own approach aims to reconstruct the ontological ground of capitalism through interrogating the founding category of value and demonstrating it can be actual only as the result of the totality of capitalist relations. My view is that Hegel's logic can be drawn on in such a study of capitalism because capital is a very peculiar object, grounded in a process of real abstraction in exchange in much the same way as Hegel's dissolution and reconstruction of reality is predicated on the abstractive power of thought (see chapters 5 and 8). It is in this sense that it may be shown that there is a connection between Hegel's 'infinite' and Marx's 'capital' (see chapter 6).

At this point it is worth mentioning Rosenthal's book, *The Myth of Dialectics*. This started out as a critique of historicist Marxian thinkers written from a semi-Althusserian point of view. But at a late stage he realised he had to throw in a chapter against what he calls 'new Hegelian Marxism', much of which is avowedly non-historicist. The peculiar thing is that he himself accepts in part the homology thesis, but he calls it a 'fortuitous isomorphism'; in his view the annoying thing about this 'isomorphism' is that it might encourage people to become Hegelians.[12] In my view the isomorphism is so real that Hegel's logic is of definite use in exploring the reality of capital. But one has to mark very precisely the limits of its relevance. And of course the normative implication are immense. For a true Hegelian, if capital could be shown to embody the logic of the concept this would be a splendid thing. But for me the very fact that capital is homologous with the Idea is a reason for criticising it as an inverted reality in which self-moving abstractions have the upper hand over human beings (see chapter 8).[13]

The complaint is often addressed to dialectic that it simply plugs reality into ready-made pigeonholes. The pigeonholes are logical notions like universality, particularity, and individuality and so on. Bits of reality are then said to embody this or that logical category. But, if a perfectly adequate account of things and their relations can be given without reference to any such logical schemes, why try and fit them into such schemes? This effort is especially dubious if the claim is made that reality is as it is *because of* the logic (see chapter 6).

There are two possible answers to this complaint. For Tony Smith the logical categories are not themselves supposed to be efficacious in their own right. But it is useful heuristically to sort out the various conceptual frameworks that our thought about reality employs into a logical order such that we can grasp a real domain at its appropriate level of complexity. But nothing can be read off from logical form as such; genuine knowledge requires scientific work on the content, but the question to be asked may well be informed by the logical apparatus. For Hegel, however, I believe, contrary to Smith, that something stronger is claimed. For an idealist ontology the logic is indeed to be taken as efficacious on its own account. I believe this too but only in a special case, a case where for good material reasons an objective reality has the shape of an ideality. For this ideality, even though it is embodied from the start in commodities and their relations, logical categories are effective because the signalling devices that regulate the market are indeed abstractions, real abstractions not thought abstractions of course. Thus money (to take the most obvious case) stands in a *logical*, rather than *material* relation to commodities. It 'stands for' their universal aspect, their identity with each other as values ideally posited through exchange. Capital itself is in part 'conceptual' in nature (as Adorno saw), albeit that as an *objective* ideality it must inhere in material practices and structures. The 'idea' of capital articulates reality in dimensions of a logical sort. This is why it is possible to model it on Hegel's logic of the concept (see chapter 5). Marx may have taken Hegel's logic simply as an aid to exposition but for me the *logical* framework has *ontological* import.

Both Hegel and Marx produced dialectical social theories, believing rightly that the bourgeois epoch, especially, required this. But in my view neither of them understood just how 'peculiar' a money economy is. However, they had a better idea of it than any later thinkers; and in that sense their work is the most important point of reference for my own. This book takes seriously the question of how Marx's critique of political economy benefited, in its presentation at least, from his appropriation of Hegel's logic. It is my belief that Marx himself was not clear about the answer to this question; and the relatively sketchy, and enigmatic, methodological remarks in his Prefaces may be a sign of this. When Marx acknowledged the influence of Hegel's dialectic on his *Capital* he failed to explain how an idealist logic could assist a materialist science. He left the impression that one could preserve a logic while inverting its ontological presuppositions. But this introduces a dichotomy between form and content which is itself undialectical. Conversely it encourages the belief that the dialectical logic of *Capital* could be extracted and applied in other sciences (see E. V. Ilyenkov for example).[14] Here, in this book, I show that there is indeed an affinity between Hegel's 'Idea' and the structural relations of commodities, money and capital, but only because of certain very peculiar properties of a money economy.

As far as I am aware, there are only two worked-out versions of this 'homology thesis', establishing in detail the parallels between the categories of Hegel's logic and the social forms presented in Marx's *Capital*. Beside my own (see chapter 5) there is only that of Tom Sekine and his Canadian followers. What Sekine does in explicating 'the pure theory of capitalism' is to spread the categories of Hegel's *Logic* over the whole three volumes of Marx's *Capital*.[15] My objection to this is that it pays insufficient attention to the material basis of the claimed homology. In my view this has to do with the abstractness of exchange relations.

It is worth remarking that the logic is only *part of* Hegel's system of philosophy, and it is precisely that part in which, because thought deals only with itself, there are no obstacles to its free movement; it is in its native element. But this is certainly not true of the other domains Hegel attempts to 'logicize'; here there is always to be reckoned with otherness, contingency, finitude, alienation. The Absolute wins its freedom *in the real world* (not in self-contemplation), and it does so only *through* overcoming obstacles. It must undergo the seriousness, the suffering, the labour, of the negative, says Hegel. If one maps Marx's *Capital* on the *whole* of Hegel's philosophy, the obvious first move is to ask: where does value move freely in its own element? If there is such a sphere this is where the pure forms of logic are likely to find their homomorphs. The answer is surely the sphere of circulation; in such phenomena as price, and the metamorphoses of commodities and money, value deals only with itself in its various expressions. The crucial turning point in Marx's *Capital* is when we see the general formula of capital includes the category of a monetary increment, but where circulation alone cannot explain its source. Then, Marx says, we must leave the sunlit sphere of circulation and enter the hidden abode of production. In other words capital must transform use-values, and for that it needs labour, which remains capital's 'other' even under conditions of 'real subsumption' (see chapter 3). In my opinion this turn to production in the exposition of the dialectic of capital is parallel to Hegel's move from the perfect freedom of thought to spirit's engagement with the real world in which it becomes lost to itself, alienated, but becomes what it is only through emerging from this otherness having recognised itself in it.

In this book, where the appropriation of Marx's *Capital* is concerned, we draw upon a relatively new tendency in Marxian theory, which puts at the centre of its critique Marx's notion of 'value form'. It is necessary then to say something briefly now on value form theory. In value form theory it is the development of the forms of exchange that is seen as the prime determinant of the capitalist economy rather than the content regulated by it; thus some theorists postpone consideration of the labour theory of value until the value form itself has been fully developed. Hegel is an important reference for value form theorists because his logic of categories is well suited to a theory of form and of form-determination. Moreover Hegel's systematic dialectical development of categories is directed towards articulating the structure of a totality, showing how it supports itself in and through the interchanges of its inner moments. I argue capital is just such a totality.

The most important single influence on the value form approach to *Capital* was the rediscovery of the masterly exegesis of Marx's value theory by I. I. Rubin, namely his *Essays on Marx's Theory of Value* (1923/28).[16] Rubin stresses that all the material and technical economic processes are accomplished within definite historically specific *social forms*. Things, such as commodities, are assigned a social role as *mediators* of production relations. This is how a category such as value must be understood. The value form is the characteristic social form of commodity capitalist relations. He shows that the category of *form-determination* is often used by Marx to refer to the way things acquire definite social functions. Marx develops increasingly complex form-determinations corresponding to increasingly complex production relations.

Closer to the present is a seminal figure in current value form theory namely H.-G. Backhaus. (Unfortunately not much of his work is in English.) The interesting thing about Backhaus is that he came out of Frankfurt school *critical theory*. So for him the relevance of Marx for empirical research takes second place to the systematic demystification of the objective irrationality of the value form. For him the theory of value is not about deriving prices – a waste of time – but criticising this value form as an inverted crazy apparatus of alienation and fetishism. Much of this book develops such insights.

To come right up to date, what is striking about current value form theory is the enormous importance assigned to money. This is especially evident in the work of Reuten and Williams. This is the value form *par excellence* for them. Because they see it as 'pure transcendental form' as they put it, which is imposed on the material side of the economy, they argue that money need have no material bearer, electronic dots will do; they argue that money is the only measure of value, albeit that they continue to regard labour as its source.

Both neo-Sraffian theory, and neo-classical theory, fail to grasp the fact that capitalist social relations appear as monetary relations in the first place. It is an essentially monetary system; hence this form must be central to any adequate theory of capital.

Now as to my own work presented here. One thing which I see as consequent on value form theory is that, if it is predicated on analysis of *exchange forms* in the first place, it should not be in too much of a hurry to address the content. It is notorious that Marx dives down from the phenomena of exchange value to labour as the substance of value in the first three pages of *Capital* and people rightly complain they do not find any proof there. So I argue in several places here that we must first study the development of the value form and only address the labour content when the dialectic of the forms itself requires us to do so (e.g. chapter 5).

Finally, let us pre-empt some more or less misplaced criticisms that may be addressed to value form theory.

(i) The claim that if value is constituted in exchange, and measured in money, then it cannot be distinguished from *price* is a common criticism. (These critics do not grasp value as mediator between labour and price, so, when they notice value form theory distances value from labour, they of course jump to the conclusion value is intended to be identical with price.)

(ii) Moreover, similar complaints are also made with respect to abstract labour. If this is predicated on the exchange abstraction then how can it be a category of production?

(iii) Finally, since the theory necessarily pays most attention to *forms*, then it is a *qualitative* analysis. So the complaint is that it cannot handle the problems associated with determining the *magnitude* of value.

Our response to these criticisms is as follows.

First of all, when it is said that value is predicated on exchange, it is important to distinguish two sense which might be meant. This is the way Rubin tackles the issue. He points out that in some places Marx seems to assume value and abstract labour must already be given *to* exchange; and in other places Marx says they *presuppose* exchange. In resolving this conundrum he says: 'We must distinguish exchange as a social form of the process of reproduction from exchange as a particular phase of this process . . . alternating with the phase of direct production.' So what Rubin emphasises is that, if production is production *for* exchange, this 'leaves its imprint on the course of the process of production itself'.[17] This is why value and abstract labour are forms arising from a process of production *oriented to exchange;* but if exchange is taken *narrowly,* in opposition to production, they may be posited as prior to it. This is at one level very obvious. If value and labour are commensurated *in* exchange, then anyone organising production *for* exchange is forced to 'precommensurate' (to borrow a term from Reuten), assigning an 'ideal value' to be tested against actuality in exchange and competition. Of course the producer may not be aware that socially necessary labour time has just changed, but in the long run exchange mediates supposedly autonomous production units so as to constrain them accordingly.

In chapter 3 I argue for a new concept of abstract labour that gives a more definite sense to this idea that production *for* exchange is form-determined *by* exchange. I argue that, if production is orientated to value and surplus-value, then the material character of production, and the various concrete labours, are teleologically subsumed by this goal; hence capital counts as an abstract totality, not as the heterogeneous mass of use values in which it happens to embody itself at any given moment, and labours too count as abstract insofar as capital exploits all indifferently. So abstract labour is constituted in the capital relation as well as in commodity exchange.

The next accusation is that, simply because the theory stresses that value is actual only under the money-form, therefore no distinction can be drawn between value and empirically given prices. This does not hold water at all. Rubin and the other form theorists insist, not only on the importance of the social form of production generally, but on a careful accounting of the specifically *different* social forms that interlock in the bourgeois economy, the need to sort them out, and to present them in a definite order. In this approach there is no difficulty in principle in assigning the value category to the most fundamental of these social forms, the capital relation, while allowing that relations *between* capitals, and with landed property etc., come on the scene subsequently in the chain of relations that are finally embodied in price. Price is a hugely over-determined phenomenon. That should go without saying.

Finally, since form is a *qualitative* notion, is it going to occlude the *quantitative* problem of assigning magnitudes and the tendencies of these magnitudes to change? It must be admitted that the 'Konstanz-Sydney' group of value form theorists (viz. M. Eldred, M. Hanlon, L. Kleiber, M. Roth) did end up being very skeptical of 'economic science' if this was supposed to be quantitative. Or rather, for them, quantitative concepts are always monetarily determined. Hence the labour theory of value as a (causal) theory of price determination is dispensed with.

So there may be skepticism that any quantitative correlations are feasible. But it can be argued that, while the forms impose themselves on the content, they in turn necessarily have to reflect in their quantitative dimension changes *in the content*. Rubin argued as follows: 'The *social* equality of labour expenditures in the form of *abstract* labour is established through the process of exchange. But this does not prevent us from ascertaining a series of quantitative properties, which distinguish labour in terms of its material-technical and its physiological aspects, and which causally influence the quantitative determination of abstract labour before the act of exchange and independent of it.'[18]

To summarise this introductory chapter: this book combines two mutually supportive new trends in Marxist theory, that of systematic dialectic and that of value form theory. The investigations of the various topics treated in its chapters will aim to vindicate in detail the fruitfulness of the general approach sketched here.

The chapters of this book owe their origin to previously published work but, in most cases, the material has been entirely rewritten and expanded for this volume. The result is that the chapters, while capable of being studied individually, are linked by a common concern to explore Marxist theory in the light of the above-discussed paradigm. The following seven chapters address in this light various aspects of Marx's *Capital*. In all cases the argument, while starting from Marx's own words, presses forward to develop an original methodological framework for resituating it. Then follow three chapters that stand more on their own. Since a theme of the book is that Marx drew on Hegel, a special chapter looks at what Hegel himself thought about the key questions of political economy. Then one of the central concepts of the book, social form, is applied to the Soviet Union to provide an original account of its economic framework and the reason for its collapse. The final chapter of the book stands somewhat apart from the others in that it is an exercise in historicist Marxism, rather than systematic dialectic; but none the worse for that I think; *both* these variants of Marxism have their strenths and should be fruitfully combined.

---

[1]   See Bibliography entries for the following: R. Albritton; C. J. Arthur; J. Banaji; R. Bhaskar; M. Eldred; I. Hunt; M. Lebowitz; J. McCarney; P. Murray; R. Norman (and S. Sayers); B. Ollman; M. Postone; G. Reuten; T. Sekine; A. Shamsavari; F. C. Shortall; T. Smith; H. Williams; M. Williams.

[2]   Jameson, F. 1990 *Late Marxism*, p. 241.

[3]   Marcuse, H. 1954 *Reason and Revolution*, pp. 136 ff.; Colletti, L. 1973 *Marxism and Hegel*, pp. 7–8. It may be doubted whether Colletti understood Hegel; for on p. 49 he cites as a 'profession of idealism' by Hegel something (from his *Encyclopaedia Logic* §76) which is clearly not his view, and which turns out to be a paraphrase of Jacobi and Descartes. This same error occurs in the work of Colletti's master Galvano Della Volpe: 1980 *Logic as a positive science*, p. 50.

[4] Engels, F. 1954 *Dialectics of Nature,* p. 62.

[5] Lenin, V. I. 1961 'Philosophical Notebooks', p. 359.

[6] Hegel, G. W. F. 1977 *Phenomenology of Spirit,* pp. 29–32.

[7] Marx, K. 1975 'Contribution to the Critique of Hegel's Philosophy of Law', p. 91.

[8] Hegel, G. W. F. 1991 *Elements of the Philosophy of Right,* § 32 and Addition.

[9] Marx, K. 1973 *Grundrisse,* p. 107.

[10] Marx, K. 1973 *Grundrisse,* p. 101.

[11] Reuten, G. and M. Williams 1989 *Value-Form and the State,* pp. 26–7; Reuten, G. 2000 'The Interconnection of Systematic Dialectics and Historical Materialism' p. 142 n. 15.

[12] Rosenthal, J. 1998 *The Myth of Dialectics,* p. 139.

[13] See Arthur, C. J. 2000 'From the Critique of Hegel to the Critique of Capital'.

[14] Ilyenkov notices that value is the objective universal form of all commodities, infers (wrongly) such a conception 'cannot be explained by the specificity of the subject-matter of political economy' and therefore tries to find analogies in other sciences, with pretty absurd results e.g. biology is all about 'proteins': Ilyenkov, E. V. 1982 *The Dialectic of the Abstract and the Concrete in Marx's 'Capital'* , p. 224.

[15] Problems with such a 'pure theory' are discussed in Arthur, C. J. 2003 'The problem of Use Value for a Dialectic of Capital'.

[16] It is interesting to see that Rubin too cited Hegel favourably. See Rubin, I. I. 1972 *Essays on Marx's Theory of Value,* p. 117; Rubin, I. I. 1994 'Abstract Labour and Value in Marx's System', pp. 49–50, 58, 66–69.

[17] Rubin, I. I. 1972 *Essays on Marx's Theory of Value,* p. 149.

[18] Rubin, I. I. 1972 *Essays on Marx's Theory of Value,* p. 155.

Chapter Two

Dialectical Development versus Linear Logic

In the *Afterword* to the second edition of *Capital* Marx rightly said that his method had been little understood; but this second edition was not understood either, not least because the *Afterword* raised more questions than it solved, especially with regard to some notoriously ambivalent and opaque remarks on dialectic.

In the first part of this chapter the views of Engels are examined; he put forward what came to be known as the 'logical-historical method', according to which the logical structure of *Capital* is simply a corrected reflection of the historical stages of development of the capitalist system of production, in which each moment is exhibited at the stage when it attains its 'classical form'. This interpretation influenced the understanding of *Capital* even by those cautious enough not to rely on the historical claims made by Engels; for they replaced the historical story with what Meek described as 'mythodology', or with what Sweezy designated the 'method of successive approximations'. It will be shown below that the structure of the argument in Engels, Sweezy, and Meek, is logically the same. It is based on a *linear* logic (treated in the first section below). I counterpose to this (in the second section) a *dialectical* method, and argue that the latter is required because Marx's object of study is a *totality*, characterised by a set of internal relations.

This feature of my approach also has an important bearing on the debate over the reading of the initial chapters of Marx's *Capital*. The orthodox tradition, from Engels, through Sweezy, through Meek, to Mandel, understood these chapters not to be about capitalism but to be about a putative mode of production termed by them 'simple commodity production'. But, in truth, right from its first sentence the object of Marx's *Capital* is indeed *capitalism*. This issue in turn raises the problem of Marx's *method of presentation*; for it has to be acknowledged that the early chapters of *Capital* do not even mention wage labourers, capitalists and the like. Why not? The orthodox understanding of Marx's method explains this by arguing that he presents his theory through a sequence of *models*, that a model of simple commodity production as a one class society allows him to give a complete account of the law of value, and that the subsequent introduction of a model of capitalism as a two class society allows him to demonstrate the origin of surplus-value through the specific inflection capital gives to this law of value; subsequently more complicated models, including landed property and the like, introduce still further distortions of the operation of the law of value. In opposition to this reading the position taken here is that the order of Marx's presentation is not that of a sequence of models of more and more complex objects, but that of a progressive development of the forms of the *same object*, namely capitalism, from a highly abstract initial concept of it to more and more concrete levels of its comprehension.

This chapter has as its main problem the consequences of taking seriously this understanding of Marx's method. The results presented arise from an insistence on the dialectical interpenetration of these levels of abstraction such that no concept can attain its finished form at its original introduction but retains a *fluid* character, gaining a more comprehensive determinacy as it is systematically brought into relation with richer content.

Linear Logic

It is clear that Marx was influenced in his work by Hegel's method of developing concepts from one another in accord with a logical principle. However, what exactly was the lesson that Marx learnt from Hegel? A distinction can be drawn between systematic dialectic (a method of exhibiting the inner articulation of a given whole) and historical dialectic (a method of exhibiting the inner connection between stages of development of a temporal process). Examples of both are to found in Hegel; the problem with Engels's account is that he conflated the two. Thus for Engels, Marx's mode of exposition, while 'logical', was yet 'nothing else but the historical method', only stripped of 'disturbing fortuities'. Specifically, with this logical-historical method each moment can be examined 'at the point of development of its full maturity, of its classic form'.[1] However, at what point *is* a moment in 'its classic form'? In answering this question with respect to the commodity, Engels claimed that at the beginning of Volume One of *Capital* 'Marx takes simple commodity production as his historical presupposition, only later, proceeding on this basis, to come on to capital': the advantage of this was that he could proceed 'from the simple commodity and not from a conceptually and historically secondary form, the commodity as already modified by capitalism'.[2]

This is in fact a *misreading*: the truth is that *Marx never used the term 'simple commodity production' in his life*. Likewise, it is certain he never referred to the capitalistically produced commodity as a secondary derivative form.[3] The only occurrence of the term 'simple commodity production' in the whole three volumes of *Capital* occurs in Volume Three, but this is in a passage given to us subsequent to Engels's editorial work, as he himself warns us in a note.[4] It is now possible to check this against the manuscript itself, which has been published in the new *Marx-Engels Gesamtausgabe*. It is clear that the entire paragraph was interpolated by Engels (as, indeed, was the one on the next page about capital's 'historical mission').[5] Generations of students have been taught Marxist economics on the basis of a distinction between capitalist production and 'simple commodity production'. Yet this approach descends from Engels, *not Marx*.[6] But, since the authority of Engels gave this idea credence, it influenced Marxist economists right down to the late Ernest Mandel.[7]

It behoves us therefore to take this theory on its own terms before addressing Marx's method itself. However, I shall not enter into a discussion of the historicity of 'simple commodity production'; for there is a more interesting question from a theoretical point of view. Does the model work conceptually? Could the law of value really obtain its 'classical form' at such a postulated stage of development of commodity exchange?

In truth, it does not make sense to speak of value, and of exchange governed by a law of labour value, in a pre-capitalist society, because in such an imagined society there could be no mechanism to enforce such a law; price in such a case would simply be a formal mediation, allowing exchange to take place, but without any determinate value substance being present. According to Marx the law of value is based on exchange in accordance with socially necessary labour times, but in the case of simple commodity production there is no mechanism that would *force* a given producer to meet such a target or be driven out of business. When all inputs, including labour-power itself, have a value form and production is subordinated to valorisation, then an objective comparison of rates of return on capital is possible and competition between capitals allows for the enforcement of the law of value. The point of simple commodity production and exchange is to produce a good in the hope of exchanging it for a different one. While there are constraints, consequent on limit conditions, to such exchanges, there is no possibility of precise determination of the ratios of exchange concerned. Capitalist commodity production is production of a value in the hope of exchanging it for the purpose of acquiring more value; therefore capital is forced to pay close attention to all the value determinations such as socially necessary labour times. 'The product wholly assumes the form of a commodity only as a result of the fact that the entire product has to be transformed into exchange value and that also all the ingredients necessary for its production enter it as commodities – in other words it wholly becomes a commodity only with the development and on the basis of capitalist production.' (Marx)[8]

Any attempt to try to ground value in 'simple commodity production' must covertly rely on Adam Smith's original argument that the only consideration affecting the choices of individuals is avoidance of 'toil and trouble': equal quantities of labour are always 'of equal value to the labourer' he claimed.[9] This *subjective* hypothesis has little to do with Marx's argument that there exists in capitalism an *objective* law which makes exchange at value necessary. 'If the value of commodities is determined by the necessary labour-time contained in them', said Marx, 'it is capital that first makes a reality of this mode of determination and continually reduces the labour socially necessary for the production of a commodity.'[10] Thus starting *historically* with the commodity would *not* mean starting historically with value in Marx's sense, because under the contingencies operative in underdeveloped forms of commodity exchange we would have price, to be sure, but not yet labour values (unless one means something relatively indeterminate by value) for, as Marx says, 'the full development of the law of value presupposes a society in which large-scale industrial production and free competition obtain, in other words, modern bourgeois society'.[11]

Problems remain even in presentations of the argument more sophisticated than that of Engels. R. L. Meek, for one, thought the way to proceed was 'to begin by postulating a society in which . . . the labourers still owned the whole produce of their labour'. Next, 'having investigated the simple laws which would govern production, exchange and distribution in a society of this type, one ought then to imagine capitalism suddenly impinging upon this society.' This reference back to a supposed pre-capitalist society of simple commodity production, Meek said, was 'not a *myth* . . . but rather *mythodology*'.[12]

One thing Meek correctly pointed out was that 'the analysis of economic categories ought so far as possible to be conducted in terms of, rather than in abstraction from, "relations of production" in Marx's sense'.[13] Yet Meek clearly abstracted a stage too far in leaving out the key relation – the capital relation – and expecting that the 'essence' of capitalism (namely value production) could remain.

The problem about the actuality of value remains even for those who abjure any talk of a real or supposed *historically* prior stage of simple commodity production, and instead treat it as a 'logical' stage in the derivation of prices, if they cling to the view that in a *non*-capitalist model true value relationships obtain, and that adding capitalist competition to the model changes nothing essential about value, but merely 'moves it around' in accordance with the complications induced by the effects on prices of the tendency to equalise the rate of profit for capitals of different composition. Because of the lack of familiarity with dialectic of thinkers since Marx, it is not surprising that other methods have been employed. And what better than the kind that had proved so successful in Newtonian science? Methodologically sensitive Marxists such as Grossman and Sweezy put forward the method of 'successive approximations'. This depends on the notion that in order to exhibit value in its pure form a number of simplifying assumption may be made. After this simplification of the forms, a model of value relationships may be outlined in which the law of value would be perspicuous.

This is a perfectly respectable scientific procedure; but it works only if it really is true that the reality concerned *can* be grasped by a linear logic such that nothing essential is changed when the more complex model is built on the basis of the simple one. For example it is clear that no one has ever seen a body moving in a straight line at the same speed forever, because the forces Newton abstracted from in formulating his law of rectilinear motion are always present. Yet the law continues to hold in the more complex case, as one of a concatenation of circumstances that combine to give rise to the phenomena observed.

According to Paul Sweezy, the method of successive approximations 'consists in moving from the more abstract to the more concrete in a step-by-step fashion', removing simplifying assumptions at successive stages of the investigation so that theory may take account of an ever wider range of actual phenomena. Thus a series of models of greater complexity may be introduced which demonstrate both that the phenomena might look different but that the essential relationships established in the pure case still are operative in and through these complexities.

As Sweezy said, this leaves the problem of 'what to abstract from and what not to abstract from'.[14] At first, it seems that the capital relation was to be isolated as essential; but then he concluded that since this is 'in form' an exchange relation it is 'clearly a special case of a large class of such relations which have a common form and structure'; therefore a beginning should be made with 'analysis of the general phenomenon of exchange'.[15] Sweezy, however, could think of no way this could be done except on the assumption that 'Marx begins by analysing "simple commodity production",' and that this analysis was 'later on adapted to capitalism'. Of course 'to apply our theory of value to the analysis of capitalism it is first necessary to inquire carefully into the special features which set this form of production off from the general concept of commodity production'.[16] But notice that the theory is merely 'adapted' or 'applied' to capitalism because we have already the 'essentials' in the 'general' account, which assuredly apply also to the 'special case'.

What is wrong with this is the way the problem is set up as a movement from the 'general concept' to the 'special case' which, in spite of its 'special features', shares with the generality of cases 'a common form and structure'. This is decidedly *not* what Marx's development of the value form shows; on the contrary: the C-C' (C=commodity) structure is thoroughly *transformed* when C-M-C' (M=money) is developed, *transformed* again with M-C-M', *transformed* again with M-C-P-C'-M' (P=capital in the phase of production), and *transformed* again with the formation of an average rate of profit.

The 'general phenomenon of exchange' (in Sweezy's locution), *just because* it is general, is too indeterminate in its effectivity to ground a determinate realm of values; only when commodities are products of capital is the 'empty' form of value infused with a determinate content under the force of valorisation. As with Meek, Sweezy has undertaken 'an abstraction too far', and instead of deriving the actuality of value he has illegitimately built it in from the start.

Engels, Meek, and Sweezy, all (wrongly) believed *Capital* starts with a stage of 'simple commodity production' – however they characterised its status. (For Sweezy the virtue of 'simple commodity production' was its theoretical clarity as the starting point for a linear derivation, not its supposed empirical reality as part of a 'corrected history' as it was for Engels.) But, in any case, 'simple commodity production' could not ground 'value', still less a law of value. So why did all these thinkers insist that it did? Because the only logical method of exposition they could think of was *linear*. If in the *first* stage value and a law of value obtained, then it could be presumed that the law continued to obtain (albeit in disguised form) in later stages no matter how complex they were.

The question is whether value relationships are conformable to such a linear logic in their development from simple forms of value to more complex ones, or whether, as I shall argue, value becomes a truth only with the full development of capitalism. In the latter case the exposition of value forms cannot be based on a linear logic where the initial model establishes value in its pure truth; rather at the outset we have a concept of value that is thoroughly inadequate and has to be substantiated in its further development. On this account the true form of value *results* from the exposition, and the original seen from this perspective is precisely the overly simple, utterly abstract, appearance of the concept, whose methodological validity as a starting point is only secured in the result.

To use Engels's own words, concepts such as value and capital 'are not to be encapsulated in rigid definitions, but rather developed in their process of historical or logical formation';[17] but unfortunately, in his application of this insight about the fluidity of such concepts, Engels himself did not put into question his original *concept* of value; he merely suggested that its apparent effect is modified in the more 'derived' forms. The same is true for Sweezy and Meek. All share a linear logic, in which each stage supposedly embodies value relationships in a perfectly adequate fashion and thus provides a ground for the next one to 'add on', so to speak, new external causes of variation. But over and over again Marx stated that only with capitalism is the value form fully developed. For example: 'the concept of value is antecedent to that of capital but, on the other hand, its pure development presupposes a mode of production based on capital';[18] thus 'the concept of value wholly belongs to the latest political economy, because that concept is the most abstract expression of capital itself and of the production based upon it'.[19]

If 'simple commodity production' is not what chapter one of *Capital* is about, what then is going on there? Marx is dealing with 'simple' determinations to be sure; but the abstract moment of the whole system that he analyses is that of *simple circulation* in which the origin of the products circulating is bracketed, commodities being taken as given. Only after developing the categories of circulation is it appropriate to turn to the relations of production that underpin exchange relations apparent in simple circulation. The key transition in *Capital* is not from simple commodity production to capitalist production, but from the 'sphere of simple circulation or the exchange of commodities' to 'the hidden abode of production'.[20] Once this turn is taken circulation is grasped as the sphere in which production relations are reflected. But to begin with circulation is not comprehended as thus mediated; the exposition must therefore begin with it as the most immediate aspect of capitalism, but one which is at the same time abstract and indeterminate. The dialectical development of the argument further determines it until it is grasped in connection with the concrete totality. This is what is explained in the next section.

Dialectical Development

If we read Hegel and Marx it is clear that analysis of wholes through systematic dialectical argument is important in their work.[21] This is the issue when it is considered in what exactly does the logical development of the argument of *Capital* consist. It must be adequate to its object: but here, I suggest, the object is a *totality* where every part has to be complemented by others to be what it is; hence internal relations typify the whole. A thing is internally related to another if this other is a necessary condition of its nature. The relations themselves in turn are situated as moments of a totality, and reproduced through its effectivity.

The problem is that such a totality cannot be comprehended immediately; its articulation has to be exhibited. This methodological problem is not at all that of finding a pure or simple case isolated from concrete complexity; it is a matter of how to articulate a complex concept that cannot be grasped by some sort of immediate intuition. In doing so we have to make a start with some aspect of it. But the exposition can reconstruct the whole from a particular starting point because we can move logically from one element to another along a chain of internal relations; in strict logic if the very *meaning* of an element is at issue (which I shall argue is the case in the value forms commodity-money-capital, each of which requires the others to complete its meaning or develop its concept), or with a fair degree of confidence if *material* conditions of existence are involved (as with the relation of valorisation to production).

Thus in a dialectical argument the meanings of concepts undergo shifts because the significance of any element in the total picture cannot be concretely defined at the outset. If the significance of each element is determined by its place in the totality, yet the exposition is forced to start with some isolated (and hence to that extent falsified) relation, then this initial moment can be characterised only in a provisional under-determined way; as the presentation of the system advances to more complex, and concrete, relationships the originating definition of a concept shifts accordingly, normally towards greater determinateness. Instead of foreclosing on reality, the dialectical method remains open to fundamental reorganisations of the material thus far appropriated, as it gets closer to the truth of things.

Since the concept of 'capital' as 'self-valorising value' is far too complex a concept to be introduced immediately Marx started with commodity value as such; not because value pre-existed capital, but because 'value . . . is the most abstract expression of capital itself and of the production resting on it'.[22] However, just because it is thus abstracted from the capitalist totality, no finished definition of value can be given at the start; for it is to be understood only in its forms of development. It acquires greater concreteness and determinacy when these later developments are *reflected back on it*, as it were.

The reason a linear logic is inappropriate is that capitalism is constituted as a *totality*, which forms its elements in such a way that taken apart from it they are denatured. If value depends for its reality on the full development of capitalist production, then the concepts of Marx's first chapter can only have an abstract character, and the argument as it advances develops the meanings of these concepts, through grounding them adequately in the comprehended whole. The exposition of the system, in starting with some simple yet determinate relation (such as the commodity form), is thereby forced to abstract it violently from the other relations that in reality penetrate it and help to constitute its effectivity; thus it is necessary at the end to reconceptualise the significance of the beginning. Because this starting-point is severed from the whole, as abstracted thus it is necessarily inadequately characterised. However, insofar as this abstracted element has no meaning outside the structure to which it belongs, the exposition can then proceed precisely by questioning its status. The same dialectic applies to intermediate stages in the derivation. Only at the end of the reconstruction of the totality is its truth unfolded: truth is system from an expositional point of view.

It is noticeable in the linear logic that there is no genuine development from the posited stage of simple commodity production to capitalist commodity production. Rather, simple commodity production and capitalist commodity production are counterposed and compared on the assumption that the capital relation impacts on the simpler model because the theorist introduces it. There is no immanent dynamic in the presentation; the shift from one 'level of analysis' to another is due to a decision to add a further determination, e.g., 'let money be invented', 'let labour-power be a commodity', 'let different organic compositions prevail'. But in a dialectical argument successive stages are introduced because they are demanded by the *logic of the exposition*, and they are so demanded because the exposition itself conceptualises the internal relations and contradictions essential to the totality.

In dealing with a totality, the problem is how to articulate its inner nature systematically in such a way that a move from a suitable starting point may be made to the result that the totality is now grasped as the unity of its internal relations. There are, then, two things to settle: the choice of starting point, and the method of advance from it.

Postponing for a while the second question, let us address the first. As Marx said, it is necessary to employ 'the power of abstraction' to arrive at the 'cell-form' equivalent of the body of the capitalist totality. The sequence of thought in carrying through this abstraction must be such that it arrives at a starting point that is sufficiently *simple* to be grasped immediately by thought and yet sufficiently historically *determinate* to lead to the other categories that structure this specific society, namely, bourgeois society based on the capitalist mode of production. Furthermore, the starting point should presuppose as little as possible, so as not to assert dogmatically what has not been established; and it should itself eventually be grounded as a necessary result of the reproduction of the system.

What is required, then, is that the movement of abstraction retain in the proposed immediacy of the beginning some sign of its origin in a historically determinate set of relations of production. This is possible if, instead of taking the shape of a process of elevation to a more generic level, it seizes upon some particular aspect of the whole under consideration which, while simple, is also so implicated in the whole from which it is separated out that it still bears this trace of its origin.

With these considerations in mind, let us now reconstruct the sequence of Marx's thought. He is faced with capital; he cannot start with that because even if its concept is stripped to its bare essentials it still has the complexity of self-valorisation, whose immediate appearance is an increment in the reflux of money. So he abstracts from this complex relation the figure of money. But what is money? It is clear that money is essentially an incomplete idea, having no sense except in its various relations with commodities, such as medium of their circulation. It is not a suitably simple beginning.

It seems clear that the commodity is, as he himself stated, the 'cell-form' Marx needed.[23] The research program therefore took the form of deriving from the commodity first money and then capital. But what precisely are we starting from? – and how do we advance? To begin with, it may very well seem to be the case that the commodity cannot be a suitable starting point because it is disqualified for failing to meet both the criteria just given, namely simplicity and historical determinacy.

– The first because, upon analysis, it turns out the commodity itself embodies a puzzling dichotomy: it is a good in that it serves as a use value, and on the other hand a different, even contrary, determination is found in it, that of exchangeability.

– The second because this commodity form attaches to things that are not even products of labour, and, even if these are excluded by fiat,[24] it is still obvious enough that commodity exchange of some sort appears in pre-capitalist epochs.

However, to deal with the second point first, when we examine Marx's work more closely we see that in chapter one implicitly, and in other writings explicitly, Marx so determines the commodity taken as the starting point as to exclude any such pre-capitalist formations. The key point to grasp is that the simple category of *universality* is built into the starting point. Over and over again he explicitly excludes as relevant to the theory social formations in which only *surpluses* appear on the market. This is stated implicitly in the first line of *Capital* where it is specified that wealth takes the form of commodities where the capitalist mode of production prevails. More explicitly, Marx says that while, on the one hand 'the production and circulation of commodities . . . by no means require capitalist production for their existence, on the other hand it is only on the basis of capitalist production that the commodity first becomes the general form of the product.'[25]

Thus the starting point is not some vague notion of 'commodity' but the commodity as the characteristic form in which the product appears in capitalism. In a word, 'capital produces its product as commodity, or it produces nothing.'[26] Given this starting point the way is open to derive capitalism; for, in Marx's own words: 'a highly developed commodity exchange and the *form of the commodity as the universal necessary social form of the product* can only emerge as the consequence of the capitalist mode of production.'[27] (my emphasis) The phrase underlined is the historically determinate beginning of *Capital*, therefore. But only in one sense. For it turns out that in order to proceed Marx focuses on that aspect of the commodity betraying its social origin, namely exchange value.[28] (It will be recalled that the commodity is itself a unity of use value and exchange value.) Should it not therefore be stated that Marx's *true* starting point was *value*, something suitably simple and universal which we can show to be grounded in capitalism?

However, while simplicity and universality are certainly advantages for a starting point, another still more important is lacking here, namely *immediacy*. How do we *know* that we are dealing with value? Value is in truth something posited in exchange (though not yet *grounded* in its production of itself) only through the mediation of the totality of relationships of the commodities exchanged one with another. Faced with this ceaseless movement of exchange, the idea arises that some *identity* in essence is present behind the heterogeneous appearances of commodities. Such an analytical reduction of the observed phenomena may be mistaken, but it suggests the following research program: on what conditions of existence can value be shown to ground itself, so as to validate itself as this universal property of commodities? As we shall see shortly, a dialectical derivation of capital may be undertaken to answer this. The upshot establishes that if the commodity is the product of capital it instantiates value.

So what *is* the starting point then? The commodity has immediacy in our experience (popular consciousness is aware that in this society practically everything is bought and sold) yet it is susceptible of further analysis into use value and exchange value. Value is a simple universal but, while an immediacy for thought, is so only as a mediated immediacy, a thought arising from the contemplation of a systematic, regular, reproduced set of exchanges which give rise to the hypothesis of some ordering principle such as value. On the other hand, this 'value' is clearly something which, in virtue of its problematic status as an abstraction from the heterogeneity of the shapes in which commodities appear, cries out for a grounding movement.[29]

We find just such a dual starting point in Hegel. He says about his own logic: 'The beginning, in the sense of immediate being, is taken from [sense] intuition and perception: this is the beginning of the analytical method. . . . And in the sense of universality, being is the beginning of the synthetic method.' He explains further why the beginning of the *Logic* is both synthetic and analytical.[30]

In *Capital* Marx himself supplied a somewhat ambiguous characterisation of his starting point: he stated that just as the microscope resolved the body into cells so 'the power of abstraction' reveals that 'for bourgeois society the commodity-form of the product of labour [*die Waarenform des Arbeitsproduckts*] or the value form of the commodity [*die Werthform der Waare*] is the economic cell-form'.[31] But 'the' economic cell-form is here defined in seemingly different ways. However, Marx identifies them as follows:

> The product of labour in its natural form brings with it into the world the *form of a use value*. Therefore it requires further only the *value form* in order for it to possess the *commodity-form*, i.e. for it to appear as a unity of the opposites use value and exchange value. The development of the value form is hence identical with the development of the commodity-form.[32]

In these circumstances we endorse Jairus Banaji's ingenious suggestion that *Capital* has a *double* starting point: the commodity form of the product is the *analytical* starting point, from which we separate out value and use value, while this value forms the *synthetic* point of departure for developing more complex relationships in the course of seeking how to ground it as the pure universal essence of the commodity.[33]

It is clear to all Marxists that in its formal definition capital is a monetary form, money which breeds money; it is also clear that money essentially mediates commodity exchange; thus it is concluded that a beginning must be made with the commodity. What is not often realised is that, if these forms are to be forms *of value*, the reverse sequence of internal relations must also hold. For, as was demonstrated above, the concept of value cannot be convincingly posited as objectively grounded at the level of simple commodity relations alone, but must be grasped as the most abstract expression of capitalist production.

The method of advance in systematic dialectic is based on observing whether or not the characteristic provisionally identified, in this case value as a universal property of commodities, can be objectively grounded in the stage of development (here of exchange) under review. It may well turn out to be the case that the determination (here of value) imputed to such relations gives rise to a contradiction. This in turn gives rise to the immanent necessity to transcend the contradiction and thereby produce a more complex set of relations to which a more adequate actualisation of value may be imputed; thus in systematic dialectic the presentation develops itself by the transcendence of contradiction and through providing ever more concrete *grounds* – conditions of existence – of the earlier abstract determination.[34]

Once the commodity has been *posited* as a form of value through being linked as such necessarily to money and capital, we have a very different commodity under discussion than that originally grasped in the immediacy of experience merely as an aspect of an *uncomprehended* totality. In order to illustrate the point let us say something briefly about the value form as it develops from commodities to money to capital.

With respect to Marx's handling of these crucial transitions between value forms, his best is that in chapter one, from commodities to money; here he shows that value cannot be actualised in an accidental exchange but requires the unification of the world of commodities through the establishment of a universal equivalent. Marx starts with the simple relationships of commodities and demonstrates the 'defects' or 'deficiencies' involved in the attempt to present as a universal property of the commodity something that is only immanent in their relations.[35]

This contradiction is solved by the doubling of the value form into commodities and money whereby the value implicit in commodities appears explicitly in money; for as a mere immanence this abstraction of value from commodity relations must be grounded in something explicitly positing it, i.e. money, which, Marx notes in his *Grundrisse*, is 'value for itself'.[36] Money in turn, however, runs into the contradiction that to actualise the concept of value in autonomous form it must be somehow counterposed to circulation of commodities as value 'for itself' as distinct from merely relating these values 'in themselves' to each other. But if it is withdrawn from circulation and hoarded to preserve itself as autonomous value then it ceases to be money, it reverts to its gold shape as a mere natural object; gold is only money if it is gold *used* in circulation. Thus money cannot realise the concept of value because of the contradiction that in striving to be value for itself it must be alienated but cannot be. The solution to this contradiction is to alienate for the sake of realising *more* money, by making *itself* the object of its entry into circulation. That is to say, through a dialectical development the money form gives rise to a new form of value, surplus-value as the aim of exchange in the capital form.

'The ceaseless augmentation of value, which the miser seeks to attain by saving his money from circulation, is achieved by the more acute capitalist by means of throwing his money again and again into circulation.' Here there is no 'antagonism' between value in the shape of money and of commodities, as in the case of hoarding.[37]

Finally the key move from circulation to production is motivated for Marx by the search to ground satisfactorily the regular production of surplus-value. For a new contradiction presents itself: the source of surplus-value must arise in this circulation form, yet cannot on the working assumption of equivalent exchange. In *Capital* he points to the contradiction that 'capital cannot arise from circulation, and it is equally impossible for it to arise apart from circulation'.[38] The solution is stated to lie in the purchase and consumption of the value-producing agent labour-power. The very chapter title is 'Contradictions in the General Formula for Capital'. It hardly needs pointing out that the development and resolution of a contradiction has nothing in common with a method of successive approximations. Marx does not say 'let us complicate matters by treating labour-power as a commodity'; rather he argues the *concept* of capital demands that labour-power be available as a commodity.

Thus if capital as self-valorising value is to realise itself the movement of value must appear 'in a much more complex form' than in pure circulation; it must be 'the movement which simultaneously creates, produces, exchange values as its own premiss'. The phenomenon of circulation may now be viewed in a new light; as an immediacy it is 'pure semblance'; but as grounded in production it is the necessary form of appearance of capitalist relations of production.[39] Although it is correct to start with a simple immediacy, the commodity, the overriding moment in the system is industrial capital, for this is the site of its reproductive drive. Although in the derivation it necessarily must appear as result, it is really the presupposition, and the starting point must be characterised in such a way as to drive us to this identification of the result as the true ground. But, although industrial capital lies at the heart of the matter, it is important to grasp circulation as a developed totality, *before* turning to production; for the latter cannot be studied in *determinate* form, and its existing law of motion comprehended, unless the *intentionality* it is infused with, i.e. valorisation, is understood as deriving from these forms. Once the value form of capital, viz. M-C-M', is comprehended as *constituting* production as capitalist production, we can *then* see production as key in so far as it is the material potential of the productive forces to increase the productivity of labour that explains actual accumulation. The *form* of capital explains the *drive* for valorisation; but it cannot in itself, i.e. as pure form, bring it about, *produce* it. Thus Marx concludes that it is best to see production as the 'overriding moment';[40] but this is not production as a 'factor' external to, and causally effective upon, other 'factors', it is production as *mediated* by circulation whose form it internalises. Hence, methodologically, the exposition describes a circle: commodity circulation (form of value) – circulation reflected *into* production (valorisation) – circulation as a moment *of* production (realisation of value).

Let us now consider the dialectical derivation as a whole. As Marx pointed out, when we derive the concept of value from exchange we must worry about whether this is just 'our abstraction'.[41] But, after its detailed grounding, Marx said: 'In the course of our presentation, it has become evident that value, which appeared as an abstraction, is possible only as such an abstraction as soon as money is posited. On the other hand, money circulation leads to capital; and in general, it is only on the basis of capital that circulation can draw into its sphere all the moments of production.'[42] Through this argument a dialectical derivation is presented of value as the outcome of production. To sum up: value, abstractly implicit in commodity relations, is explicitly posited in money, taken as its own aim in capital, and becomes self-grounded in capitalist production.

Conclusion

No simple definition of value can be given; for it is understood only in its forms of development, through their dialectical positing. The key point is that no proof of the existence of value is established at the first stage of simple commodity relations (reference to barter or simple commodity production – whether as historical or as a model – is quite inappropriate to such a task), but only when the later developments are *reflected back on it*, as it were. The law of value is not something lying at an *origin*, whether logical or historical, it is something that *comes to be* in the form-determinations of the capitalist totality.[43]

Rather than treating the starting point of *Capital* as a historical presupposition, or as a simple model, it should be considered as a provisional immature abstract moment of a complex totality. The commodity as the starting point of the exposition then has to be reconceptualised at each stage of the argument. As an abstraction from the reality that produced it, it is not *known* adequately when given immediately. The first stage of the reconceptualisation is its presentation as a form of value; then it is characterised as a product of capital; as such it is posited as a container of surplus-value; and therefore a necessary moment in the cycle of capital accumulation; and finally it is differentiated into a mass of products whose complementarity (some, means of production, and some, means of consumption) assures the reproduction of the total social capital. Its concept is complete only when it is grasped as reproduced through the immanent drive of the capital system; in other words it requires the whole three volumes of *Capital*! Such an unfolding of form, revealing deeper essential determinations at each stage, requires, not the fixed definition of terms, but an *exposition* through which this system of forms is grasped as a totality, not as a set of independent stages. Grounded in the totality and its law of reproduction, 'the commodity form of the product of labour' acquires the character of necessity, rather than just being contingently present in experience,[44] and the 'value form of the commodity' becomes actually established as a concretely universal determination.

[1] Engels, F. 1969 'Karl Marx, *A Contribution to the Critique of Political Economy*' [1859], p. 514. For a discussion of this review of Marx's 1859 *Contribution to a Critique of Political Economy* see Arthur, C. J. 1996 'Engels as Interpreter of Marx's Economics', pp. 179–187. In that attention is drawn (p. 184) to Engels's seizing on the double exposition in Marx's book where the substantive discussion is followed at the end of each section by a review of the literature of economic thought: this led Engels to claim that the historical development of the literature is a guiding thread to the logical development of the theory. It should have been pointed out that Engels here followed Hegel's claim about the history of philosophy: 'The succession of philosophical systems in history is the same as their succession in the logical derivation of the categories of the Idea.' (Hegel, G. W. F. 1985 *Hegel's Introduction to the Lectures on the History of Philosophy*, p. 22).

[2] Marx, K. 1981 *Capital* Volume III, p. 103.

[3] In his *Anti-Dühring* (1962), pp. 225–26, Engels claimed to have found in *Capital* a discussion of the historical transition of commodity production into capitalist production. He cites at length a passage in which Marx presupposes the worker owned his own product (Marx, K. 1976 *Capital* Volume I, pp. 729–30). He does not notice

that passage is written in hypothetical mode. I argue it is counter-factual in character in chapter 6.

4   Marx, K. 1981 *Capital* Volume III, p. 370 and p. 371n.

5   Compare the version of Volume III in Marx-Engels *Werke, Band 25*, pp. 271–73, with the 1863–65 manuscript in MEGA II 4.2 (1992), pp. 334–36.

6   It is true that Engels was able to cite a passage from the manuscript of the third volume in which something like the content of the idea of a stage of simple commodity production was discussed by Marx. Seizing enthusiastically on this, Engels claimed that 'if Marx had been able to go through the third volume again, he would undoubtedly have elaborated this passage significantly' (Engels, F. 1981 'Supplement to Volume 3 of Capital', p. 1034; the full passage from Marx 1981 is on pp. 277–78.); however, it is just as possible he would have decided it was a false trail and eliminated it! Certainly, odd references in *Capital* to pre-capitalist production are not used with any *systematic* intent, and there is no such reference whatsoever in the first three chapters of *Capital*.

7   Ernest Mandel composed the article on 'Karl Marx' in *The New Palgrave: A Dictionary of Economics*, 1987. This multi-volume work contained the distilled wisdom of the economics profession, and it included enough articles on Marxism to enable a separate volume on it to be extracted and published, *The New Palgrave: Marxian Economics*, 1990, in which Mandel's overview has pride of place. He referred to 'what Marx calls "simple commodity production" – "*einfache Waren-produktion*".' (Mandel 1990, p. 4) In this, quasi-official expression was given to the most enduring myth of Marxology. The truth is that Marx never called anything '*einfache Waren-produktion*'. The occurrence of the term on p. 370 of *Capital* Volume Three (1981) is part of an insertion by Engels; Engels also inserted the phrase 'and commodity production in general' on p. 965.

8   Marx, K. 1989 'Economic Manuscript of 1861–63', p. 265.

9   Smith, A. 1976 *The Wealth of Nations*, pp. 34–37. For Marx's criticism of Smith on this point see his 1859 *Contribution*, Marx, K. 1987, p. 299.

10 Marx, K. 1981 *Capital* Volume III, p. 180.

11 Marx, K. 1987 *A Contribution to the Critique of Political Economy* [1859] p. 300.

12 Meek, R. 1973 *Studies in the Labour Theory of Value*, pp. 302–04.

13 Meek, R. 1973 *Studies in the Labour Theory of Value*, p. 317.

14 Sweezy P. M. 1970 *The Theory of Capitalist Development*, pp. 12–13.

15 Sweezy P. M. 1970 *The Theory of Capitalist Development*, pp. 16–17.

16 Sweezy P. M. 1970 *The Theory of Capitalist Development*, p. 23, p. 53, p. 56.

17 Marx, K. 1981 *Capital* Volume III, p. 103.

18 Marx, K. 1986 'Economic Manuscripts of 1857–58', p. 183.

19 Marx, K. 1987 'Economic Manuscripts of 1857–58', pp. 159–60.

[20] Marx, K. 1976 *Capital* Volume I, p. 280, p. 279.

[21] For a detailed exposition of the method of systematic dialectic see chapter 4.

[22] Marx, K. 1973 *Grundrisse*, p. 776.

[23] Marx, K. 1976 *Capital* Volume I, p. 90. Marx also pointed out in *On Wagner* that starting with the commodity has the advantage of starting with a '*Koncretum*': Marx, K. 1989 'On Wagner', p. 538.

[24] I differ from Marx in that I believe it is possible, through the power of abstraction, to push back the beginning beyond 'the commodity form of the product' to the world of commodity exchange as such, because I hold that the dialectic of the 'value form of the commodity' of itself reaches the required result. The 'synthetic' movement, i.e. the search for the systematic grounding of value, is sufficiently powerful to derive from it the necessity of capitalist production *without* introducing as an initial restriction that the commodities considered at the start be products. For my attempt at this dialectical derivation see chapter 5.

[25] Marx, K. 1988 'Economic Manuscript of 1861–63', pp. 312–13.

[26] Marx, K. 1988 'Economic Manuscript of 1861–63', p. 313.

[27] Marx, K. 1976 *Capital* Volume I, Appendix *Results . . .*, p. 949.

[28] In the circulation of commodities, 'physical matter appears as the actual content of the movement, the social form only as a fleeting mediation for the satisfaction of individual wants'. (Marx, K. 1987 'Original text of *A Contribution to a Critique of Political Economy*', p. 484) Value is 'the social form as such' from which we now proceed, said Marx. (Marx, K. 1987 'Original text of *A Contribution to a Critique of Political Economy*,' p. 490. See also Marx, K. 1987 *A Contribution to the Critique of Political Economy*, p. 270.)

[29] It is an interesting fact that during November 1858 (Marx, K. 1987 *A Contribution to the Critique of Political Economy*, p. 547 n. 95) Marx changed his chapter plan from Value-Money-Capital (Marx, K. 1987 'Economic Manuscripts of 1857–58', p. 421) to Commodity-Money-Capital.

[30] Hegel, G. W. F. 1991 *The Encyclopaedia Logic*, §238.

[31] Marx, K. 1983 *Das Kapital Erster Band 1867*, p. 12; Marx, K. 1976 *Capital* Volume I, p. 90.

[32] Marx, K. 1983 *Das Kapital Erster Band 1867*, p. 639; Marx, K. 1994 '*Capital First Edition* Appendix on the Value Form', p. 24.

[33] Banaji, J. 1979 'From the Commodity to Capital: Hegel's Dialectic in Marx's *Capital*', pp. 28, 36, 40.

[34] Reuten, G. and M. Williams 1989 *Value-Form and the State*, p. 22.

[35] Marx, K. 1976 *Capital* Vol. I, pp. 154, 156, especially.

[36] Marx, K. 1986 'Economic Manuscripts of 1857–58', p. 388. Also Marx, K. 1987 'Original text of *A Contribution to a Critique . . .*', p. 441.

[37] Marx, K. 1976 *Capital* Volume I, pp. 254–56.

[38] Marx, K. 1976 *Capital* Volume I, p. 268.

[39] Marx, K. 1986 'Economic Manuscripts of 1857–58', pp. 186–87. Marx, K. 1987 'Original text of *A Contribution to a Critique . . .*', p. 479.

[40] Marx, K. 1986 'Economic Manuscripts of 1857–58', p. 36.

[41] Marx, K. 1987 *A Contribution to the Critique of Political Economy*, p. 285.

[42] Marx, K. 1987 'Economic Manuscripts of 1857–58', p. 159.

[43] In general, although its elements (commodity, money, capital) preexist capitalism, they did not – precisely because they were not formed by the totality – have the same nature, function and law as they subsequently gained within it. For my discussion of this issue see Arthur, C. J. 1996 'Engels as Interpreter of Marx's Economics', pp. 195–98, or Arthur, C. J. 1998 'Engels, Logic and History', pp. 12–14.

[44] Marx, K. 1989 'Economic Manuscript of 1861–63', p. 301.

Chapter Three
Labour, Value and Negativity

This chapter takes particular positions on several of the key debates in the theory of value. While the mainstream position in Marxist theory has read concepts such as value, socially necessary labour time, and abstract labour, largely in a technical sense, I adhere to the growing minority that centralises the idea of *social form,* insisting that all such categories have to be explicated within an account of specifically capitalist social forms of production and exchange. Here the rediscovery of the Soviet scholar I. I. Rubin's masterly exegetical work *Essays on Marx's Theory of Value* (1923, 3rd ed. 1928) in the 1970s was an important influence on us. However, it has to be said that Rubin concentrated very much on the forms of *exchange.* Here I deepen the category of social form to include the bearing of the form of the capital relation, as essentially conflictual, on the primary value categories.

Rubin stands at the origin of the 'value form' paradigm of Marxist theory. Much mainstream Marxism ignores Marx's warning that previous labour theories of value had failed to grasp the significance of the value *form* as the social appearance acquired by capital's products. Many Marxists still simply collapse value into labour. Rubin pointed out that this leaves no mediation between labour and price. He rightly insisted that value is distinct from both labour and exchange value: value is related to the concept that precedes it, abstract labour, as its content, and, through its form, with the concept that follows it, exchange value.[1] It will be important to my argument below to show that labour and value are not to be *positively* identified with each other, but rather are dialectically interpenetrating *opposites*.

This chapter draws on the new reading of *Capital* provided in the last. I there denied that *Capital* is structured according to a sequence of 'models', beginning in chapter one with so-called 'simple commodity production', a term invented by F. Engels after Marx's death; not only does the term not occur in *Capital*, its first sentence makes clear that the circulation of commodities and money discussed in the early chapters is that of *the capitalist economy*. From the start the object of investigation is the capitalist totality, and this is grasped first of all abstractly and then more and more concretely. Because this is so, all the concepts of Marx's first chapter have only an *abstract* character, and the argument as it advances develops the meanings of these concepts, through grounding them adequately in the comprehended whole. In the previous chapter I argued that value is concretely determined only when the commodity is a product of capital; here I look at the forms of labour constitutive of its value.

If the concepts of the first chapter are necessarily highly abstract it follows that something gets lost, the more concrete determinations are elided. Specifically, I claim that such central categories of value theory as 'abstract labour' (the solution to the so-called qualitative value problem) and 'socially necessary labour time' (the solution to the so-called quantitative value problem)[2] are necessarily inadequately conceptualised when articulated as presuppositions of value in the context of simple circulation prior to any discussion of the production process. They are insufficiently *determinate*. For example, at the start Marx assumes there is no problem about labour appearing as value. But later we discover that this is consequent only on the success of the struggle to subsume labour under capital. Since the circulation of commodities discussed in the early chapters is in truth the circulation of *capitalistically produced* commodities, their value, and the relevant determinations of labour, are concretely constituted only in the capital relation.

Finally, this chapter advances a novel interpretation of 'exploitation'. The orthodox interpretation founds its concept of exploitation on the expropriation of the surplus-value 'created' by labour. Even many who disagree strongly with the labour theory of value, as an account of price and profit, still accept that the existence of a 'surplus' may be assigned to the exploitation of labour. Both the orthodox view and 'the surplus approach', in this long-running debate, have in common an account of exploitation in the context of a struggle over the *distribution* of the surplus, however measured, 'after the harvest' so to speak. My argument will be that exploitation is primarily located in *production*; that it is capital which 'creates' value; but it does so only through the unremitting 'pumping out' of labour services throughout the working day; it will be shown that 'socially necessary exploitation time' determines the magnitude of value.

A New Concept of Abstract Labour

While it is a condition of a commodity being exchanged that it is a use value, it acquires in the value form the new determination of exchange value which abstractly negates all difference of use value between commodities and thereby declares them all identical as values. This value form inverts the relation between the particularity of commodities as concretely natural bodies and their general social determination as exchangeables, because now the body of the commodity counts only as the 'bearer' of its value (as Marx puts it).

Insofar as this is so, the labours related through the mediation of commodity exchange thereby are equally reduced to abstractions of themselves. However, if the commodities concerned are taken as products of capital, this theorisation implies a conception of labour as abstract within the capital relation itself.[3] But here there is a textual question to be considered. In *Capital* discussion of abstract labour is confined to the first chapter. There, the context of labour's determination as abstract is clearly that of the practice of *exchange*. Implicitly, this is considered as exchange of capitalistically produced commodities, but this does not alter the fact that it is the character of exchange as a 'real abstraction' from the existence of commodities as differentiated products issuing from concrete labours that is the relevant determinant. When Marx turns to discuss the capital relation, and such matters as the valorisation process, the term does not appear. However, textual support for my view can be found outside *Capital* in the following passage from Marx's *Grundrisse*:

As *the* use value which confronts capital, labour is not this or that labour, but *labour pure and simple*, abstract labour; absolutely indifferent to its particular specificity but capable of all specificities. Of course the particular labour must correspond to the particular substance of which a given capital consists; but since capital as such is indifferent to every particularity of its substance, and exists not only as a totality of the same but also as the abstraction from all its particularities, the labour which confronts it likewise subjectively has the same totality and abstraction in itself. For example, in guild and craft labour, where capital itself still has a limited form, and is still entirely immersed in a particular substance, hence is not yet *capital as such*, labour, too, appears as still immersed in its particular specificity: not in the totality and abstraction of labour as such, in which it confronts capital. That is to say that . . . capital . . . confronts the *totality* of labours potentially, and the particular one it confronts at a given time is an accidental matter. On the other side, the worker himself is absolutely indifferent to the specificity of his labour; it has no interest for him as such, but only in as much as it is in fact labour and, as such, a use value for capital.'[4]

Therefore, beside the abstraction constituted in the exchange of commodities there is also abstraction in the constitution of labour in the capital relation. The reason why labour is properly conceptualised as 'abstract' within the capital relation is that industrial capital treats all labours as identical because it has an equal interest in exploiting them regardless of their concrete specificity. So the qualitative identity of labours posited in the equation of products is complemented by a process that posits them as abstract in production itself. In the passage above it might seem that labour considered as 'capable of all specificities' is not 'abstract labour' but 'concretely general labour'. Taken 'in itself' this is so; but here we have to take it in the form capital takes it. Marx writes: 'This indifference towards the specific content of labour is not only an abstraction made by us; it is also made by capital, and it belongs to its essential character.'[5]

Capital as an abstract totality considers labour as its opposite, simply as the instrument of its valorisation. While it is forced to allocate labours to different tasks the point is that exploiting them yields a homogeneous product, the accumulation of capital itself. However, it is important to the 'practical truth' of the category 'abstract labour' that capital can exploit the 'concretely general' capacities of labour so as to reallocate it as and when necessary.[6] But there is an inversion inherent in the capital relation such that the different concrete labours count merely as instances of their abstract identity with each other in their potential for valorisation – hence, as an abstract totality. Similarly whenever workers treat their labour instrumentally, as a wage-earning activity, they abstract from whatever concrete tasks they perform. Separated from the objective conditions of their activity the workers' subjectivity is thrown back into itself. Each becomes a mere 'work-man', looking for 'work' in general. Their use value for capital is simply the capacity for such 'work'. It is important that when one 'finds work' in a capitalist firm this is undertaken under the capital relation in which the object and instruments of production are the property of another; this does not therefore overcome estrangement between subject and object but rather preserves the alienated relationship, while allowing production to proceed.

It is a mistake is to *identify* the abstract labour that is the substance of value with the supposedly 'abstract' character of the modern labour process in its *physical* form. Marx himself apparently drew such a conclusion in the *Grundrisse* immediately after the passage earlier quoted:

> This economic relation – the character which capitalist and worker have as the extremes of a single relation of production – therefore develops more purely and adequately in proportion as labour loses all the characteristics of art; as its particular skill becomes something more and more abstract and irrelevant, and as it becomes more and more a *purely abstract activity*, . . . a merely *physical* activity, activity pure and simple, regardless of its form. Here it can be seen once again that the particular specificity of the relation of production . . . becomes real only with the development of a particular material mode of production and of a particular stage in the development of the industrial productive forces.[7]

Notice that in the earlier passage capital confronted a set of specific labours, *totalised* abstractly, but here it is the *members* of the set that supposedly lack specificity: two very different notions. To postulate the reality of the latter is in fact very dubious, because it relies on a contestable empirical claim that simply cannot be sustained. Even if the labour process could be said to have a somewhat abstract character in a material sense, this would make no difference because the conceptual mistake remains. This mistake consists in conflating the concept of abstract labour, which is a determination of *social form*, with a peculiar kind of concrete labour, a material simplification of the labour required of the worker. This simplification may well be a consequence of its social form but it is to be understood as merely an approximation to the 'content' of the concept of 'abstract labour'. The simplification of labour refers to an impoverishment of its quality. But even the simplest motion still has *some* quality, it can never be abstraction as such.

Harry Braverman used the term 'correspondence' to cover the case when he wrote: 'Labor in the form of standardised motion patterns is labor used as an interchangeable part, and in this form comes ever closer to corresponding, in life, to the abstraction employed by Marx in analysis of the capitalist mode of production.'[8] The value content thereby shadows the value form through the agency of capital organising the labour process in such a way that labours do not merely *count* formally as abstract but *become* more abstract in the material sense of generically homogeneous.[9]

However, it remains the case that the labour employed by capital is formed as 'abstract' *no matter* what degree of 'correspondence' exists. For the *opposition* between concrete and abstract remains just as long as that between use value and exchange value. When capital organises the production process so as to maximise valorisation the real object aimed at is money returns. Money is the existent form of 'abstract wealth' (Marx) and this means that the activity producing it is itself posited as abstract; hence the living labour employed in the capitalist production process counts only as a passage of working time. The worker becomes *'time's carcase'*, in Marx's phrase.[10] Thus 'abstract labour' is so posited by the social relations within which production goes on.

Of course it is convenient for capital if the concrete forms of labour are simple enough to make an ideal 'precommensuration' of the labour time determining the value it hopes to realise on the market. In this respect Braverman was quite right to say with respect to time and motion studies that 'this abstraction from the concrete forms of labour . . . which Marx employed as a means of clarifying the value of commodities . . . exists as well in the mind of the capitalist, the manager, the industrial engineer.'[11] The more labour becomes simple motions in time the more it approximates to how it is anyway 'cognized' ideally in valorisation.

But the distinction between abstract and concrete cannot be collapsed. There may well be pressure in the factory to make the labour process one in which capital moves as if in its own element, namely the universal time of production, but since it is always burdened with matter it is necessarily particularised in concrete labour processes. Conversely, insofar as value is produced capital has translated concrete into abstract more or less effectively. While immediately concrete labour, the work of each becomes socially posited as abstract in virtue of its participation in the capitalist process of valorisation. As abstract it is a question of how labours are counted, and not how they are concretely; it is a question of the social form living labour acquires within the valorisation process; as form-determined by capital it functions as a particularisation of its abstract essence, as abstract movement in time. As Marx says 'the different working individuals seem to be mere organs of this [socially abstract] labour.'[12]

In sum, the commodity form of the *product* embodies in dead labour an abstraction from the concrete heterogeneity of labours. Capitalist *production* posits living labour processes as abstract activity, pure motion in time. These must be grasped as informing each other.[13]

If anything, the constitution of labour as abstract in the capital relation is *more* fundamental than its constitution as abstract in exchange.[14] Since generalised commodity circulation exists only on the basis of capitalist production, value becomes determinate only with capitalistically produced commodities. Prior to competition between industrial capitals there is money and hence price; but without the aim of production being set by valorisation, and without the rigorous policing of labour time by capital, any value form implicit in earlier relations, for example merchant trade, is empty of content, and prices relatively contingent. It follows that any 'substance' of value, such as abstract labour, cannot exist prior to generalised commodity production on a capitalist basis.

Moreover this conception allows a solution to the following contradiction:

> On the one hand, commodities must enter the exchange process as objectified universal labour time, on the other hand, the labour time of individuals becomes objectified universal labour time only as a result of the exchange process.[15]

This statement of the problem comes from Marx's *Contribution to the Critique of Political Economy* (1859). There he solved it to his own satisfaction by the introduction of money.[16] But it might be thought that although money certainly posits the labour it represents, and hence by reflection the labour represented by all commodities, as abstract universal labour, the abstraction is still not posited *prior* to exchange. While abstract labour is no longer considered merely 'our abstraction'[17] but one really posited in and through the exchange of commodities for money, it may yet be true that this abstraction cannot be read back *into production*. It may still be the case that labour becomes 'abstract' only when products are priced. If this is so, it might be thought that the counting of labour only as an abstraction of itself is a social illusion, a 'shadow form' cast by monetary circulation. To put it in terms of our original problem, it seems the category is not yet fully determinate.

I. I. Rubin addressed the same 'contradiction'[18] and rightly pointed out that, if what happens prior to exchange is the capitalist production of commodities *for* exchange, this leaves its imprint on the process of production itself.[19] This is what was demonstrated above when it was shown that if production is value formed, that is, undertaken by self-positing capital, then living labour is treated as abstract *prior* to exchange precisely because it is treated as abstract *in* exchange.

In effect, abstract labour as a form-determination of the living labour of the wage worker, and abstract labour as the dead labour objectified in a commodity, are the same thing, in the one case looked at as activity, in the other as its result.

A New Concept of Exploitation

It is a feature of Marx's concept of 'abstract labour' – and of our extension of it – that it depends on a process of inversion to give it significance as a reality. In the value form, and in the labours set in relation to each other in it, 'the abstractly general counts not as a property of the concrete, sensibly real, but on the contrary the sensibly concrete counts as the mere form of appearance or definite form of realisation of the abstractly general.'[20] In truth this inversion in the relation of abstract and concrete is a result of the fact that the whole relation of production is inverted, that subject and object are inverted, that the producers are dominated by their product (value, capital) to the extent that it is doubtful whether the workers may be said to be producers at all, but rather they are reduced to servants of a production process originated and directed by capital. There is a close connection, therefore, between abstract labour and alienated labour; labour is alienated in part just because it is socially recognised as a source of 'wealth' only as abstract activity; conversely this social form of labour arises from the peculiar way in which the estrangement of workers from the objective conditions of their labour is overcome in the capital relation.

Marx speaks of 'this inversion, indeed this distortion, which is peculiar to and characteristic of capitalist production, of the relation between dead labour and living labour'.[21] This inversion inherent in the value form determination of production has definite material consequences. In capitalist commodity production there is an *inversion* of subject and object in that the real subject of the process is capital; it sets the agenda for production and *'employs'* in the most literal sense labour as its instrument. As Marx puts it: 'It is no longer the worker who employs the means of production, but the means of production which employ the worker.'[22]

Labour considered in itself is concretely universal, being able to expend itself in a wide variety of concrete specifications on demand. Moreover ideally the labour process would proceed in the manner outlined in *Capital*, in which the worker is said to be like an architect in conceptualising the product before producing it. But, with the real subsumption of the labour process under capital, the adaptability of labour is taken advantage of to redraw labour so as to make the workers more like bees, supplying their efforts to the collectivity of production but without attaining any meaningful individual relation to the enterprise as a whole, which is beyond their ken, being put together by the representatives of capital on the basis of the technical specification of labour, machinery and materials. The subjectivity of the mass of workers is reduced to a matter of understanding simple instructions. Anyone less like an architect than the assembly line worker would be hard to imagine. Even skilled workers operate only as fragments of the collective labourer. Since all – whether skilled or unskilled – contribute piecemeal to the process of production, the whole is not constituted as their productive power but as that of the capital hiring them. This means not only that each individual does not produce a commodity but that since the collective labourer is set up under the direction of capital it is hard to say that the collective does either. It seems more reasonable to say that capital produces the commodity than that labour does.

There is certainly warrant in Marx's texts for this claim that capital, not labour, embodies the forces of production. Let us review three important passages. Firstly a lengthy passage from Marx's *Grundrisse*:

> The transformation of labour . . . into . . . capital is, in itself, the result of the exchange between capital and labour, insofar as it gives the capitalist title of ownership to the product of labour (and command over the same). This transformation is *posited* only in the production process itself. Thus the question whether capital is productive or not is absurd. Labour itself is productive only if absorbed into capital, where capital forms the basis of production, and where the capitalist is therefore in command of produc-tion. The productivity of labour becomes the productive force of capital. . . . Labour, such as it exists for itself in the worker in opposition to capital, that is, labour in its *immediate being*, separated from capital, is *not productive*. . . . Therefore, those who demonstrate that all the productive force ascribed to capital is a *displacement* [*verrückung*], a *transposition of the productive force* of labour, forget precisely that capital itself is essentially this *displacement, this transposition*, and that wage labour as such presupposes capital, so that, from its standpoint as well, there is this *transubstantiation*, the necessary process of positing its own powers as *alien* to the worker. . . . Others say, e.g. Ricardo . . ., that *only labour* is productive, not capital. But then they do not conceive capital in its specific character as *form* [*spezifischen Formbestimm-theit*], as a relation of production reflected into itself. . . .[23]

Secondly he gives a neat formula in *Results of the Immediate Process of Production*:

> Thus capital [is] *productive*:
> (1) as the *compulsion to* [do] *surplus labour*. Now if labour is productive it is precisely as the agent that performs this surplus labour. . . .
> (2) as the *personification and representative*, the reified form of the "social pro-ductive forces of labour".[24]

Thirdly, in *Capital* Volume Three Marx speaks of:

that inversion of subject and object which occurs in the course of the production process itself . . . how all the [social] productive forces of labour present themselves as productive forces of capital.[25]

Striking as these quotations are, still more striking consequences may be
drawn from them. On the basis of passages like these, one important theorist, Claudio Napoleoni, concluded that it is meaningless to speak of 'productive labour' if labour is nothing but a reified factor of production, and all
'productive power' is an attribute of capital. If capital, not labour, produces
commodities then it seemed to Napoleoni that labour cannot be the source
of value, nor, *a fortiori*, surplus-value. It also follows, he thought, that it is
impossible to read into the capital relation an account of exploitation on the
basis that the capitalist expropriates some or all of what the workers have
produced; for it is capital which has to be taken as the effective producer.[26]
His view that exploitation in capitalism must be radically rethought follows
not so much from his rejection of the labour theory of value on technical
grounds as from this deeper material claim.[27]

From the premise that in capitalism a class of non-workers appropriate under
the form of value some of what the workers produce it might be concluded
that there is exploitation in much the same sense as in pre-capitalist formations. For example, Ernest Mandel argued that surplus-value has 'a common
root with all other forms of surplus product: unpaid labour'; this 'deduction
theory of the ruling classes' income', as he called it, is *ipso facto* 'an exploitation theory'.[28] So close is this theory to an ahistorical account of exploitation
that the same 'deduction' is postulated by some who reject Marx's value theory. Thus G. A. Cohen, in a well-known paper on exploitation, offers a refu-
tation of the labour theory of value; but he goes on: '[The workers] create the
product. They do not create *value*, but they create *what has value*. . . . What
raises a charge of exploitation is not that the capitalist gets some of the value
the worker produces, but that he gets some of the value *of what* the worker
produces.'[29]

These views are exactly those which Napoleoni opposed. Even if it is true
that in pre-capitalist exploitation the source of the surplus is a 'deduction'
from what the worker creates, it is not so in capitalism, he believed. Rather,
if capital is the true productive power a deduction has to be made from *what
capital creates* so as to provide subsistence for the workers.[30]

If the 'subject' of production is no longer labour but capital, how can a theory of exploitation specific to capitalism be provided that does not rely on the attribution of a surplus, whether surplus-value or surplus product, to the special contribution of labour? By a neat twist Napoleoni reintroduced the term 'exploitation' as the appropriate characterisation of the very alienating relationship that makes nonsense of the old definition! 'Capitalist exploitation is in reality that inversion of subject and predicate . . . by which man, the 'subject', is but the predicate of his own labour.'[31]

Let us return to the Marx passages cited earlier. As we saw, Marx thinks capital is productive both in the sense that it organises production and that it enforces exploitation. On the other hand it is able to do this only because it can rely on its 'agent', the working class, whose social productive powers are 'displaced' and 'transposed' to capital. Capital as value in motion is not distinct from matter in motion shifted by labour; labour acts *as* capital, not just at its behest. Marx says: 'Labour is not only *the* use value which confronts capital, it is *the use value* of capital itself.'[32] This labour is absorbed by productive capital and acts as *'a moment of capital'*, he claims.[33]

A genuine aporia emerges here: just whose productive power is this? Is it not the very same productive power that is ascribed both to labour and to capital?[34] This is indeed so. But this is not due to the ambivalence of the theorist, it arises from the contradictory interpenetration of the poles of the capital relation, within which 'labour becomes productive only by producing its own opposite' (Marx).[35]

Let us explore the notion of inversion employed both by Marx and by Napoleoni. It is often said that productive labour is the essence lying behind the appearances of value interchanges and capital accumulation. Even where such appearances are not disparaged as 'mere' appearances (as with socialist Ricardians) they are still often understood as secondary phenomena, at best the mediatory forms within which productive labours are related in this particular economy. However the passages in which Marx assigns productive power to capital could well lead in a contrary direction: that capital is the real subject of production and that in its drive to accumulate it necessarily must engage with labour and machinery, and that it *mediates itself in them* (as Marx said, labour is 'the mediating activity' by means of which capital valorises itself).[36] In sum the second view is an inversion of the first. Both views are in truth correct, although contradictory. What this means is that capitalism is characterised by a *contradiction in essence*. This does not involve formal logical contradiction because the concept of 'inversion' can be carefully located so as to allow the identification of the effectivity of each 'essence' separately, albeit in dependence and interaction. Capital is not so powerful as to abolish natural laws, thus much of what happens in the labour process cannot be fundamentally altered by its subsumption under the valorisation process. What does change is the social effectivity of the forms of the production relations, and the objective positions of the concrete and abstract aspects of the process. Labour and its objective social expression – or subject and object – become inverted, and thereby social form itself becomes autonomous. As a result of labour's alienation, and of its subsumption under capital, the objectivity of productive positing, become autonomous, reflects back on the labour process as its 'truth'. At the very same time as being still in some sense nothing but the objective social expression of labour it achieves dominance over labour; labour is reduced to a resource for capital accumulation.

This contradiction in essence means that the affirmation of the essence (whichever one) leads to its appearance in the mode of denial.[37] Thus labour's objectification coincides with its expropriation, its positing as a moment of capital; while capital's subjectification appears as its utter dependence on the activity of living labour.

The above diagnosis explains precisely why the same productive power 'counts twice'. The ontological inversion inherent in the value form means that production acquires an ideal reality in addition to its mundane material one. Under one description it is the combined power of labour and machines. Under another, equally valid, description it is the productive power of capital. Hence the necessary ambiguity in such phrases as 'the productive power developed by the workers socially is the productive power of capital'.[38]

Thus, if the 'principle' of production becomes valorisation, the exact relation between the 'principle' and what is 'principled' is puzzling. Since the workers are 'possessed' by capital and the material labour process is simultaneously a valorisation process, the same thing has two frames of reference. But this is not merely a matter of different ways of talking, or of the coexistence of alternative realities, it is also a matter of determination, of one side informing the other with its own purposes. Capital determines the organisation of production but the character of labour, natural resources and machinery limit it in this endeavour. Although capital is hegemonic in this respect,[39] its subsumption of labour can never be perfected; labour is always 'in and against' capital.

This is what Napoleoni overlooked when he ascribed 'productive power' only to capital. Albeit that the production process is really subsumed by capital, the problem for capital is that it needs the *agency* of labour. It is not really a matter of reducing the worker to the status of a mere instrument of production, like a machine, or like an animal whose will has to be *broken*. It is a matter of the *bending* of the will to alien purposes. In *Capital* Marx spoke of the producer employing the cunning of reason in the use of the means of production. But with the 'real subsumption' (Marx) of labour to capital the cunning of reason is turned against the erstwhile 'producer'. The former 'subjects' of production are treated as manipulable objects; but it is still a question of manipulating their activity, not of depriving them of all subjectivity. They act for capital, indeed *as capital*, but still in some sense *act*. Even in the limiting case in which they could theoretically be replaced by robots they still have to be induced to set themselves to *act as robots*.

Thus, even if Marx is right that the productive power of labour is absorbed into that of capital to all intents, it is necessary to bear in mind that capital still depends upon it. Moreover, the repressed subjectivity of the workers remains a threat to capital's purposes in this respect.

It is because of this that I do not follow Napoleoni in abandoning entirely the labour theory of value, or the possibility of a measure of exploitation in surplus-value. Rather, I present below a new theory of value determination founded precisely on the above discussion of capital's 'productive power'.

A New Theory of Value Determination

As we know, Marx insists that the secret of valorisation in production lies in the distinction between what is bought/hired, namely labour-power, which enters production under the wage-form, and living labour, the use of labour-power, employed during production. But of course the distinction between the value and the use of commodities is a general feature of them; it is possible, for example, to distinguish between the cost of machinery and 'machining', the more so with automatic machinery. Why is 'labouring' different from 'machining'? The obvious answer is that only labour is capable of 'teleological positing', namely working towards an end, albeit one set by capital here. However, the fact that labour is subsumed by capital such that its powers appear as those of capital throws doubt on this. The correct answer lies in something more subtle. With a standard commodity its value is set by its conditions of production, its use value is a known quantity, and the use made of it is of no concern to the seller. But labour is not a standard commodity because it fails on all three counts. The wage is set through class struggle in the context of the historically given level of 'subsistence'; the contract of employment does *not* guarantee in advance any specific supply of service;[40] on the contrary this too is the outcome of class struggle at the point of production; and, finally, so far from its employment being of no concern to the seller, the inseparability of the labourers from their labour-power means it is of very great importance to them. In these three ways, then, wage labour is peculiar and very different from a standard use value. Marx stresses that use value questions are of central importance to his theory: 'For money as capital, labour capacity is the immediate use value for which it has to exchange itself. In simple circulation, the content of the use value was a matter of indifference, dropped out of the form of economic determination. Here it is the essential economic moment.'[41] With wage labour we have not merely use value, nor merely use value socially transferred to another, nor merely a use value socially transposed onto its own opposite (capital as dead labour employs living labour), but a use value which is itself *inherently* at odds with its social determination as a moment of capital. This last means capital can constitute itself only in a contradictory way, through employing an agent that resists its use for alien purposes.

In its endeavour to organise production, and to maximise output, capital finds that it is confronted with a special difficulty: the residual 'subjectivity' of the worker poses unique problems for capital because it gives rise to a definite recalcitrance to being 'exploited' which the other factors do not possess. The other 'factors' of production, land, machinery, materials, enter with their productive potential *given*, known in advance; only with labour is productivity contestable and contested, known only in the *upshot* of the working day. So if capital has replaced labour as the 'subject' of production it certainly cannot produce under conditions of its own choosing. Capital is limited by the extent to which it can enforce the 'pumping out' (Marx) of labour services. The consequence of this special feature of labour is that the relation of capital and labour is intrinsically antagonistic and that in this sense there is reason to speak of waged labour not so much as 'productive labour' but as *counterproductive labour*' in that the workers are actually or potentially recalcitrant to capital's effort to compel their labour.

This is why, for a theory grounded on the *social form* of the economy, labour is to be correlated with value. New value is the successful reification of living labour. As Marx says, value 'is the product of alien labour, the alienated product of labour'.[42] Capital can produce value only through winning the class struggle at the point of production. As M. A. Lebowitz superbly states the case: 'In capitalism as a whole, the two-sided totality, capital does not merely seek the realisation of its own goal, valorisation; it also must seek to suspend the realisation of the goals of wage-labour. Capital, in short, must defeat workers; it must negate its negation in order to posit itself.'[43]

The distinction in *Capital* between the living labour employed and its representation as 'dead labour' in the value of the product, is put even more strikingly in Marx's *Grundrisse* where labour is defined as 'not-value', that which stands opposed to value but on which valorisation depends.[44] Value is not the social recognition of labour's success at producing a good, but of capital's success in producing a commodity through alienating labour to itself, producing value through exploiting 'counterproductive labour' during the working day. Thus, whereas at the start of *Capital* Marx assumes there is no problem about labour appearing as (reified in) value, we now discover that this is consequent only on the success (partial and always contested) of the struggle to subsume labour under capital.

My position is quite different from that of the orthodox tradition, which sees labour creating something *positive*, namely value, then expropriated (a position which is presupposed in any theory of value rooted in a model of 'simple commodity production' of course). Rather I hold that behind the positivity of value lies a process of *negation*. Capital accumulation realises itself only by negating that which resists the valorisation process, labour as 'not-value'. This new concept of valorisation allows a restatement of the labour theory of value as a dialectic of negativity.

Ernest Mandel went so far as to say 'For Marx *labour is value*'[45] – emphasising the point. Mandel is directly refuted by Marx's own text. Marx said that 'labour is not itself value'; although 'labour creates value' it 'becomes value' only in 'objective form' when the labour embodied in one commodity is equated with the labour embodied in another commodity.[46] Moreover labour is socially validated thereby only as 'abstract', and this in turn requires the presence of the money commodity to ground the universal dimension required. In brief, like the orthodox tradition generally, Mandel overlooked the importance of the value *form* in the labour theory of value.

Clearly, any theory that conflates labour and value is bound to consider their relation in an entirely *positive* light. The activity of labouring is immediately identical with a value stream; the critique of capital then has to take the form of a complaint that, while there is a reflux of value to the labourers under the wage-form, capital diverts part of the stream to its reservoir of accumulated value. Exploitation consists in expropriating this value. But, on my view, since expropriated labour is precisely the real content of value; it is *under the value form* that the specifically capitalist exploitation of labour occurs; value is *constituted* through the dialectical overcoming ('sublation') of living labour, which is both negated and preserved ('dead labour') as its 'substance'.

My new way of conceptualising the labour theory leads me to say that the magnitude of value is determined by '*socially necessary exploitation time*'. If labour time is the determinant of the magnitude of value it is nonetheless at the same time a determined determinant; for it is *capital* that perpetually strives to reduce the socially necessary time of production through compelling workers to increase their productivity. In the early chapters of *Capital* it is not yet clear to what exactly 'socially necessary labour time' refers; lacking any other information one takes it in a technical sense; but once this labour time is set in the context of the capital relation it has to be seen as primarily the necessity capital is under to extort labour from the exploited, something which is informed by the balance of class forces.

It is obvious here that this exploitation time to which I refer comprises the whole of the working day, not just the so-called 'surplus labour time'.[47] It is not the case in reality that the workers first supply themselves and then check into the factory to work the extra. On the contrary, the accounting of necessary and surplus labour time is the outcome of the struggle at the point of production over exploitation; and the unremitting pressure of capital's representatives on the workforce is present the whole day from the first minute. Since capital 'takes charge' of production, the 'pumping out' of surplus labour cannot be distinguished on the ground from the pumping out of labour generally because during the whole working day its use value is exploited. So there is a conceptual distinction hidden here, between exploitation in this sense, and the sense in which exploitation is identified with only the extension of the working day beyond its necessary part.

I would be inclined to reverse Marx's emphasis when he said: 'Capital is not only command over labour, as Adam Smith thought. It is essentially command over unpaid labour.'[48] Instead I would write: 'Capital is not only command over unpaid labour, as Karl Marx thought. It is essentially command over labour, i.e. of the entire working day.' (Of course Marx knew perfectly well that it is only because capital acquires 'command over labour' that this 'coercive relation . . . compels the working class to do more work than would be required by the narrow circle of its own needs'.)[49]

It is also obvious that I reject implicitly the labour theory of value where so-called 'simple commodity production' is concerned; and I do so just because I do not see how socially necessary labour time can be calculated and enforced where each is their own master.

My view allows for a 'traditional' measure of exploitation if we distinguish two kinds of exploitation. Exploitation in *production* is in effect not dissimilar to alienation in that it involves the subjection of workers to alien purposes; it goes on throughout the day. Exploitation in *distribution* arises from the discrepancy between the new wealth created and the return to those exploited in production. Interesting examples of *purely* 'distributional' exploitation are mentioned by Marx when he discusses forms *transitional* to capitalism. Where the actual producers fall prey to usurers and merchants, because of their lack of market power, they are reduced to a subsistence existence and forced to part with the surplus product. This is so in spite of the fact that the capitalists concerned have no control over the process of production (and cannot therefore develop it).[50] No capital relation takes charge of production. For this reason Marx says 'no capital exists yet in the strict sense of the word'. It is only 'formally' capital as yet, lacking an adequate ground in production.[51] In these transitional cases it makes perfect sense to say the workers create what is expropriated. But the tendency of exploitation within production under the *control* of capital is to substitute the productive power of capital for that of the erstwhile 'immediate producers'.

Accordingly, Napoleoni argues that this kind of exploitation has replaced what I call 'distributional' exploitation and thereby made redundant all calculations of value and surplus-value rooted in the 'special contribution' of labour.[52] To Napoleoni such a notion of surplus-value makes no sense if it is capital that creates the new value. But, on my account, if this value commensurates the expropriated labours out of which capital produces commodities, and reproduces itself, then it is still possible, *ex post*, to distinguish necessary and surplus labour within the working day.

Napoleoni's error is encapsulated in the following remark: 'The phenomenon of value takes place entirely at the level of capital, i.e. it starts when the transfer of productive powers from labour to capital has already been accomplished.'[53] We see here that Napoleoni treats 'transferred' labour as part of the technical conditions of production organised by capital, leaving value to be negotiated between capitals. But on my view the category of value should be rooted precisely in capital's struggle with labour to accomplish this 'transfer' of the said productive powers. Likewise, the actualisation of the form 'abstract labour' is rooted in the manner in which capital measures what it appropriates therewith and makes into its substance.

When I base the labour theory of value on the daily round of exploitation this does not mean I am motivated primarily by a moral or political concern, promoting an externally applied criterion of justice or fairness unconnected with a scientific theory. If class struggle is *ontologically constitutive* of capitalism then the labour theory of value is explanatory as well as critical. Value measures capital's success in this battle to appropriate labour to itself and as a first approximation each capital would be rewarded accordingly. Then a *different* relation supervenes, that between capitals themselves, so it is necessary to elaborate further categories to conceptualise this; but the *fundamental* relation is between capital and that which is its other and has to be subdued by it. It is through this relation to labour that capital *constitutes* itself as self-valorising value and it is therefore logically prior to any analysis of relations *between capitals*.

Conclusion

I have argued that the concepts of the first chapter of Marx's *Capital*, value, abstract labour, and socially necessary labour time, are posited *abstractly* at that point. As the argument proceeds, and the capitalist totality becomes comprehended in more complex and concrete terms, these original 'markers' require rethinking. New determinations come to light that must be integrated into the concepts concerned.

'Abstract labour', I have argued, must be seen as internal to the capital relation, although this is conceptually tied to its immediate appearance as the identity posited in the value equivalence of its products. Such an identity in its product flows from its position in the capital relation, in which both sides are constituted as 'abstract totalities' (Marx) confronting one another. Under the form of value production, labour counts only as an abstraction of itself, a bearer of the time for which it is employed.

On the ground of the separation of the worker from the object of productive activity there results the subordination of the worker to capital, and therewith the expropriation of their productive powers by capital which exploits them for its own ends; but we have derived from the essentially contested nature of this exploitation a new understanding of the labour theory of value as a dialectic of negativity. In short, capital is the subject of production, producing above all itself, while labour is negatively posited as its sublated foundation.

'Socially necessary labour time', considered as the determinant of the magnitude of value in the first chapter of *Capital*, must also be reconsidered in the light of the discovery that value is the shape in which labour as 'not-value' is reified. Once 'socially necessary labour time' is situated in the capital relation, it is seen to be the time during which labour services are 'pumped out' of the employee. Value is the result of abstract alienated labour, and its magnitude is determined by the time of such exploitation. It is the outcome of class struggle at the point of production.

In sum all the relations of the capitalist system determine one another from beginning to end.

1 Rubin, I. 1972 *Essays on Marx's Theory of Value*, p. 122.

2 Marx, K. 1987 *A Contribution to the Critique of Political Economy*, p. 305; Sweezy, P. 1970 *The Theory of Capitalist Development*, p. 25.

3 Claudio Napoleoni argued this and he was the first to draw attention to the important passage from Marx's *Grundrisse* quoted below: Napoleoni, C. 1975 *Smith, Ricardo, Marx*, pp. 104–6.

4 Marx, K. 1973 *Grundrisse*, pp. 296–7.

5 Marx K. 1988 'Economic Manuscript of 1861–63'. p. 55.

6 Marx, K. 1973 *Grundrisse*, pp. 104–05. This means that it is a precondition of the category 'abstract labour' having effectivity in a law of value that labours must be sufficiently adaptable to be potentially mobile between jobs. I have argued that this is an ontological precondition of the specification of labour as abstractly universal in commodity exchange in my paper 'Dialectics and Labour' 1979. In a private communication Ernest Mandel urged against my view that it would make the category meaningless where pre-capitalist simple commodity production was concerned. So far from this being an objection to my view it is a consequence I fully accept (as I think Marx does in the passage given at the start of this section).

7 Marx, K. 1973 *Grundrisse*, p. 297 – translation amended.

8 Braverman, H. 1974 *Labor and Monopoly Capital*, p. 182.

9 David Gleicher provides a sophisticated account of the development of the specifically capitalist division of labour in industry. He explicitly opposes this historical account of developing 'abstraction' to the so-called 'logical abstraction' derived from value form analysis. But in my view his discussion relates to the *consequences* of the latter. Gleicher D. 1994 'A Historical Approach to the Question of Abstract Labour'.

10 Marx, K. 1976 *Poverty of Philosophy* p. 127.

11 Braverman, H. 1974 *Labor and Monopoly Capital*, p. 181.

12 Marx, K. 1987 *A Contribution to the Critique of Political Economy*, p. 272.

13 See R. Bellofiore 1999 'The Value of Labour Value. The Italian Debate on Marx: 1968–1976' pp. 51–56; he concludes:

The successive determinations of abstract labour have led us from the *final* commodity market (where labour is *objectified* labour: the abstraction of labour as a real hypostasis actually going on in exchange, as analysed by Colletti), to the *initial* labour market (where labour is labour-power: the real hypostatization process now affects the worker who becomes a predicate of her/his own capacity to work), to the *centre* of the valorization process, the immediate process of production (where labour is the *living* labour of the wage worker as 'other-directed' work: the real hypostasis here is the worker becoming a predicate of abstract living labour as value in process).

[14] Using the quotation at the beginning of this section as an epigraph to their paper 'Capital, Labour and Time', R. Bellofiore and R. Finelli have already developed a position similar to mine here: 'The abstractness of labour in the process of exchange is the consequence . . . of the subjection to capital of wage workers' living labour.' Bellofiore, R. and R. Finelli 1998 'Capital, Labour and Time' p. 54.

[15] Marx, K. 1987 *A Contribution to the Critique of Political Economy,* p. 286.

[16] Marx, K. 1987 *A Contribution to the Critique of Political Economy,* p. 288–89, p. 307.

[17] Marx, K. 1987 *A Contribution to the Critique of Political Economy,* p. 285.

[18] Rubin I. 1972 *Essays on Marx's Theory of Value,* p. 147.

[19] Rubin I. 1972 *Essays on Marx's Theory of Value,* p. 149.

[20] Marx, K. 1994 *'Capital First Edition* Appendix on the Value Form' pp. 18–19.

[21] Marx, K. 1976 *Capital*: Volume I, p. 425.

[22] Marx K. 1994 'Economic Manuscript of 1861–63' p. 122; Marx K. 1976 *Capital,* Volume I, p. 425.

[23] Marx, K. 1973 *Grundrisse,* p. 308–9.

[24] Marx K. 1976 *Capital* Volume I, Appendix: *Results . . .* p. 1056. (Note the mistranslation: 'appears' should be 'is' as in Marx, K. 1994 'Results of the Direct Production Process' p. 459; I concede other cases of 'appears' in this translation of *Results . . .* are genuine.) Marx first arrived at this formula in the 1861–63 manuscript; see Marx, K. 1994 'Economic Manuscript of 1861–63' p. 128; the whole section pp. 121–29 is very instructive.

[25] Marx, K. 1981 *Capital* Volume III p. 136. Here I read 'social' with Marx's manuscript: Marx K. 1992 *Das Kapital. Drittes Buch. Die Gestaltungen des Gesamtprozesses,* p. 61. F. Engels changed it to 'subjective' in his edition of it.

[26] Claudio Napoleoni, 1991 'Value and exploitation: Marx's economic theory and beyond' in *Marx and Modern Economic Analysis,* pp. 232–36. I have commented on Napoleoni's views in my paper 'Napoleoni on Labour and Exploitation' (1999) given at the Napoleoni memorial conference, organised by R. Bellofiore, held at the University of Bergamo, 1998. The present paper draws on that but is somewhat more critical of Napoleoni.

[27] Thus, while he agrees with the neo-Sraffian approach to the calculation of prices and profits, Napoleoni attacks the residual Marxism of 'the surplus approach' promoted by I. Steedman which retains the category 'productive labour'. ('Value and exploitation: Marx's economic theory and beyond' p. 236, p. 237 n. 9.)

[28] Mandel, E. 1990 'Karl Marx' p. 20. It is worth remembering that Marx warned us that the expression 'unpaid labour' is scientifically worthless, no matter how attractive as a 'popular expression'. (1976 *Capital* Volume I, p. 671.) This has not stopped most Marxists using it without Marx's health warning! Why is 'unpaid labour' a fraudulent notion? – Because as the source of value labour cannot itself have a

value, and therefore there can be no question of its being 'paid' or 'unpaid'. What is paid for is labour-power. Marx's tremendous achievement was to show that even when the capitalist pays the full value of all the inputs to production a surplus-value can still emerge from it. It is misleading, therefore, to call this a 'deduction' theory. In his notes *On Wagner* Marx stresses that the capitalist 'not only "deducts" or "robs" but *enforces the production of surplus value,* thus first helping to create what is to be deducted'. (Marx, K. 1989 'On Wagner', p. 535) F. Engels showed great insight into the specificity of Marx's value theory when he illustrated it by using the analogy of the modern theory of combustion (see his Preface to *Capital* Vol. II). Whereas previously it was thought the element undergoing combustion *lost* something, the scientific revolution in this field occurred when it was understood that something was *added* to it. In the same way Marx's breakthrough was to see that capital gained surplus-value through *adding* a *new* value to those in play in its circuit. Engels may have drawn on Marx's own use of this analogy in *Capital* Volume III (Marx, K. 1981, p. 130).

29 Cohen, G. A. 1981 'The labour theory of value and the concept of exploitation' p. 218. Note that his approach means 'exploitation' loses much of its explanatory power, and is reduced effectively to a normative category.

30 See Napoleoni, C. 1991 'Value and exploitation' p. 236.

31 Napoleoni, C. 1991 'Value and exploitation' p. 235.

32 Marx, K. 1973 *Grundrisse*, p. 297; for the topic of this section Notebook III of Marx's manuscript is important esp. pp. 295–312, 331–334, 358–364.

33 Marx, K. 1973 *Grundrisse*, p. 364.

34 Napoleoni held it was not possible for the same thing 'to be counted twice' (1991 'Value and exploitation' p. 234); he also claimed *Marx* knew it too, but the text he relies on for this is corrupt; see my 1999 'Napoleoni on Labour and Exploitation', p. 155 n. 25 n. 26.

35 Marx, K. 1973 *Grundrisse*, p. 305.

36 Marx, K. 1973 *Grundrisse*, p. 305.

37 Richard Gunn thematizes 'existence in the mode of being denied' in his 1992 'Against Historical Materialism'.

38 Marx, K. 1976 *Capital* Volume I, p. 451.

39 Marx, K. 1973 *Grundrisse*, p. 693.

40 On the significance of the contract of employment see Screpanti, E. 1998 'Towards a General Theory of Capitalism'.

41 Marx, K. 1987 'Original text of *A Contribution to a Critique . . .*' p. 504.

42 Marx, K. 1973 *Grundrisse*, p. 638.

43 Lebowitz, M. A. 1992 *Beyond 'Capital'*, p. 85.

44 Marx, K. 1973 *Grundrisse*, pp. 295–96.

45 Mandel, E. 1990 'Karl Marx' p. 11.

46 Marx, K. 1976 *Capital* Volume I, p. 142.

47 'Exploitation should not be understood so much as the expropriation of surplus product or surplus labour, which are common enough phenomena in pre-capitalist social forms too, but rather as direct and indirect imposition and control that affects *all* labour.' Bellofiore R. and R. Finelli, 1998 'Capital, Labour and Time' p. 63.

48 Marx. K. 1976 *Capital* Volume I p. 672.

49 Marx. K. 1976 *Capital* Volume I pp. 424–25.

50 Marx. K. 1994 'Economic Manuscript of 1861–63' pp. 117ff.

51 Marx. K. 1998 'Economic Manuscript of 1861–63' p. 32.

52 An example of such a justification of the labour theory of value is that offered by Simon Mohun: 'Value is labour-time because of an essentialist ontology that what defines human existence as specifically human is purposive productive activity.' (1994 'Value, Value-Form and Money' pp. 215–16) But what if the labourers' 'purposes' are overwritten by capital?

53 Quoted in Rodano G. 1999 'The Economic Thought of Claudio Napoleoni' p. 20 n. 32.

Chapter Four
Systematic Dialectic

Earlier in this book I briefly sketched the difference between historical dialectic and systematic dialectic; in the present chapter I go on to elucidate the latter in more detail.

The distinction between historical and systematic dialectic should be obvious enough but unfortunately it is not often marked. Although most of Hegel's work (*Phenomenology of Spirit, Science of Logic, Encyclopaedia,* and *Philosophy of Right*) was systematic he frequently obscured this by using illustrations from different historical periods. As for Marx's great systematic work, *Capital,* this has suffered from a virtually universal misreading, originally sponsored by Engels, according to which its method is 'logical-historical', in other words the two dialectics get conflated. But in this it was clear that the historical is taken to be precedent, the 'logical' part consisting merely in tidying up the history by disentangling pure forms from contingent accretions. While it is true then that parts of these works of Hegel and Marx have been read in an historical key, I emphatically reject such readings. (In previous chapters of this book I explicitly argued against such a reading of *Capital*.)

In discussions of dialectic generally it is most often taken to be a *historical* process; indeed it is frequently reduced to a type of efficient causality. A contradiction is said to 'produce' a resolution in much the same way as a cause 'produces' an effect. Now it is clear that if the paradigmatic works by Hegel and Marx mentioned above are not historical works any such interpretation is irrelevant. What is characteristic of these works is that they treat a *given whole* and demonstrate how it reproduces itself: thus the ordering of the categories is in no way determined by the recapitulation of a historical chain of causation; it is articulated on the basis of purely systematic considerations.

Moreover, systematicity is of the essence where the object of investigation is a totality. Dialectic grasps phenomena in their interconnectedness, something beyond the capacity of analytical reason and linear logic. As Hegel argued, 'since what is *concretely* true is so only as . . . *totality*', science in treating such a totality must take the shape of *system*.[1] The system comprises a set of categories expressing the forms and relations embedded within the totality, its 'moments'. Since all 'moments' of the whole exist synchronically all movement must pertain to their reciprocal support and development. While this motion implies that moments become effective *successively*, the movement winds back into itself to form a *circuit* of reproduction of these moments by each other. Because of this character of a totality the appropriate theoretical system can trace a logic of mutual presupposition in the elements of the structure and hence of the *necessity* of certain forms and laws of motion of the whole under consideration.

The Science of System

Let us turn then to an account of the meaning of system.[2] While categories mark ontological unities, and are thus required to render actuality intelligible, they must themselves form a coherent whole, they must 'hang together' so to speak. Hegel's *Science of Logic* shows how the categories may be systematically related to one another in such a manner that their exposition, and 'reconstruction', provides a theory whereby each category gains systematic meaning by virtue of its positioning with respect to the other categories and the whole.[3] Taken in isolation, in abstraction from its systematic placing, a category is imperfectly grasped.

The task of systematic dialectic, then, is to organise such a system of categories in a definite sequence, deriving one from another logically. If such a systematic sequencing is to be undertaken, a method is required for making transitions from one category to another in such a way that the whole system has an architectonic. Now, I shall argue that, if a whole is built up in this way, the systematic ordering of its categories may be understood both 'forwards', as a progression, and 'backwards', as a retrogression. After explaining this, I will lay special emphasis on the merits of the retrogressive aspect of the architectonic and hence the possibility of a 'pull' from the culmination of the system for motivating dialectical transitions within the development of the categories; and I will then illustrate the point with examples from Hegel and Marx.

Although it is natural to read a systematic exposition as one in which later categories are developed from their antecedents – at least in the sense that the latter must be analytically presupposed – in Hegel's view this cannot be the whole story for he rejects any dogmatic founding category. The progressive development is therefore not securely established on a given presupposition. There is, however, another consideration. Since the categorial progression cannot be validated as a *deduction*, it can only be *reconstruction* of the totality; as such what it is heading for must be granted.

But have we not merely duplicated the problem of the foundation? If the beginning cannot justify the end is it not also the case that the end cannot justify the beginning? The answer is that there is indeed an asymmetry here. The end, as the most concrete, complex, and complete reality, does adequately support and sustain all the elements that make it up, and thereby retrogressively justifies the logical sequencing from this viewpoint. Insofar as Hegel's dialectics finish with something 'absolute', its absolute character grants validity retrospectively to all the stages of its exposition, and their dialectical relations, through integrating them into its architectonic; if 'the truth is the whole' the moments of the whole gain their validity within it. J. M. E. McTaggart understood this perfectly:

> The dialectic must be looked on as a process, not of construction, but of reconstruction. If the lower categories lead on to the higher, and these to the highest, the reason is that the lower categories have no independent existence, but are only abstractions from the highest. It is this alone which is independent and real.[4]

Tony Smith explains this retrogressive aspect of systematic dialectic as follows: 'If the theory culminates in a stage that is true "for itself", i.e. concretely and actually, then this shows that an earlier stage leading up to it must have been true "in itself", i.e. abstractly and potentially.'[5] The method required, then, is to develop categorial items in a sequence that is to be considered as 'grounding' of categories retrogressively, and as disclosure, or presentation, of further categories, progressively.

The fact that the logical progression is at the same time 'a retrogression' means that the beginning may be shown to be 'not something merely arbitrarily assumed' but itself grounded as an abstract moment of the whole.[6] The following key passage sums up Hegel's view:

> Each step of the *advance* in the process of further determination, while getting further away from the indeterminate beginning is also *getting back nearer* to it. . . . What at first sight may appear to be different, the retrogressive grounding of the beginning, and the progressive further determining of it, coincide and are the same. The method, which thus winds itself into a circle, cannot anticipate in a development in time that the beginning is, as such, already something derived . . . and there is no need to deprecate the fact that it may only be accepted *provisionally* and *hypothetically*.[7]

While every category depends on its antecedents for its constitutive moments, the problem of the beginning is resolved if the richness of the granted content presupposes analytically the simpler, more abstract, antecedent categories. To reiterate, the progressive introduction of new categories cannot be deduction (for the beginning is not to be taken as an axiom), it can only be a reconstruction of reality which takes for granted that what it is headed for is logically complete. So the sequence of categories has to be read in both directions, as a disclosure, or exposition, progressively, and as a grounding movement retrogressively. What constitutes progression is an arrangement of categories from abstract to concrete; successive categories are always richer and more concrete.[8] Indeed the basis of the advance is generally that each category is *deficient* in determinacy with respect to the next and the impulse for the transition is precisely the requirement that such deficiency must be overcome.[9] As McTaggart said, 'the really fundamental aspect of the dialectic is not the tendency of the finite category to negate itself but to complete itself'.[10] All stages are deficient with respect to the final fulfillment of the dialectic in a systematically ordered totality.

Indeed the progressive/regressive sequencing depends upon the presupposition that there is a whole from which a violent abstraction has been made so as to constitute a simple beginning, which, in virtue of this negation of its positioning in the whole, has 'lost its footing', so to speak; and thus there arises a contradiction between the character of the element in isolation and its meaning as part of the whole. The treatment of this moment as inherently in contradiction with itself, on account of this, is given if it is assumed throughout the dialectical development that the whole remains immanent or implicit in it. This provides the basis for the transitions in the development of the categorial ordering. There is an impulse to provide a solution to a contradiction – a 'push' one might say – and there is the need to overcome the deficiency of the category with respect to its fulfillment in the whole – a 'pull' one might say.

For the most part these elements exist in combination. Since dialectic is generally regarded in the former sense as the positing and resolving of contradictions I want here to stress the importance of the fact that the final goal is the fully comprehended whole and that any given stage *en route* is always deficient with respect to it. The impulse to move from one category to the next is the *insufficiency* of the existing stage to comprehend its presuppositions; while it is a necessary result of the previous stage it depends on conditions of existence that have yet to be developed; each stage 'takes care of', with the minimum of new elements, the problem perceived with the previous stage, but in turn is found insufficient. (It is important that the transition involves a 'leap' to a qualitatively new categorial level. A dialectical development has nothing in common with a vulgar evolutionism predicated on extrapolating an existent tendency.)

If it is presupposed that the whole system of categories is complete and internally self-sustaining, then it is possible to reconstruct its order precisely through moving sequentially from categories deficient in such respects (that is in being inclusive and self-sustaining) to ones less so, until the system as a totality is thereby exhibited as such. Moreover the method of presentation articulates the categories in such a manner as to show how the logic of the system tendentially ensures its completeness through 'positing' all its presuppositions. The presentation ends when all the conditions of existence needing to be addressed are comprehended by the entire system of categories developed.

Such a system is complete only when it returns to, and accounts for, its starting point. Because any starting-point is severed from the whole, as abstracted thus it is necessarily inadequately characterised. As Hegel put it of his own system: 'Because that which forms the beginning is still underdeveloped, devoid of content, it is not truly *known* in the beginning.'[11] Marx was therefore correct in the first place, having started with 'the commodity', to draft a final section entitled 'commodities as the product of capital'.[12]

I hold that much of Hegel's and Marx's work can be interpreted in this way, as informed by such a dialectical logic.[13] In the remainder of this chapter, then, I elucidate the points about systematic dialectic made in its first half by treating some case studies, one from Hegel and two from Marx. These are:

– the transition from right to morality in Hegel's *Philosophy of Right;*
– the derivation of money in *Capital;*
– the resolution of the contradiction in the general formula of capital in *Capital.*

The general aim in my interpretations of these examples will be, firstly, to demonstrate that 'contradictions' in the strict sense may be predicated of a given stage only in virtue of the systematic placing of that stage with respect to the totality in question, whether that of Right (in the first example following) or that of Value (in the examples from *Capital*); secondly, to show how the new stage is developed in virtue of a retrogressive grounding movement.

The System of Right

Hegel's overall objective in his political philosophy is to demonstrate that freedom is actualised in a system of 'right'. This system of right he articulates in a dialectical development from the supposedly basic right to property onwards to rights of citizenship and to the state organised so as comprehensively to underpin all the various spheres of right. At the end of the section on 'abstract right' he explains how right in the abstract is unable to maintain itself because, without morality, custom or law, everyone in defending their own property and honor against transgression may be 'asserting a right' but their purely personal actions are seen by the other party as themselves transgressive of their rights; hence a vendetta situation develops.

Now many philosophers address this problem by arguing that to keep the peace a superior force must come on the scene. Hegel does not take this route at all. He wants the *concept* of right itself to become more developed, more comprehensive in its scope. This higher form of right at the next level is the concern for right as such, not simply one's own rights, a concern to do right even where this might not seem immediately in one's interests. How is this idea to be dialectically developed? In the basic vendetta situation there is no contradiction at all, only conflict, and there is nothing contradictory about supposing such vendettas interminable. The contradiction arises only if the concern for *right as such* is brought to bear.

Clearly it is not possible for all parties to be 'in the right' all the time so a situation in which everyone is left free to claim and defend their own rights contradicts the demand of a system of right that right be actualised in reality. There is clearly a 'pull' to the next higher category of right: 'morality', as Hegel calls it. However, there is more to it than this; for if this concern is imputed to the agents involved in a vendetta then their own consciousness becomes contradictory (that is, if the whole is taken to be *immanent* in the moments of each stage rather than merely an external benchmark of progress). For if each claims to be avenging an infringement of right as such they are claiming that their cause is just, but justice is a universal which transcends the specific interest particular people have in prosecuting their own claims, while here each is acting as judge and jury in their own case and their attempt to pursue the criminal cannot be distinguished from the subjective motive of revenge. This may be viewed as giving a 'push' to resolve this contradiction, to sort it out by casting around for a solution. Hegel concludes as follows:

> The demand that this contradiction . . . in the manner in which wrong is annulled be resolved . . . is the demand for a justice freed from subjective interest. . . . This implies the demand for a will which, though particular and subjective, yet wills the universal as such. But this concept of *morality* is not simply something demanded, it has emerged in the course of this movement itself.[14]

The important thing to understand here is that, while dialectical development is *immanent* to the content under consideration, whether one thinks of the categorial structure as progressive or regressive in its architectonic the transitions are *conceptual* necessities. This is the sense here in which the concept of morality is *required*. As mentioned above such a move represents a qualitative leap. While there is a structural tendency for the categorial level of righting wrong abstractly to issue in vendetta, this tendency cannot of itself transcend this fate. It would be wrong to interpret Hegel's transition here as a quasi-causal story in which the agents involved in a vendetta are supposed to wake up to the requirements of morality as a result of its structural features. They may or may not. It is not relevant. What is relevant is that it is a requirement of reason that a new category come to life.

It is also a consequence of Hegel's systematic approach that both the claims of the individuals for their rights, and the concern of moral consciousness to do the right thing, are presuppositions of any coherent articulation of a legal system of right by the state. This illustrates also a general point about systematic dialectic: that nothing is *lost*, that every 'refuted' position is yet preserved within a more comprehensive form of realisation of the concept in question, here that of 'right'.

The Necessity of Money

For our first case from *Capital* of a retrogressive grounding movement, let us see how the contradiction between use value and exchange value gives rise to money. According to Marx this contradiction is present in the commodity as such and expressed already in the simple form of value. Yet if one thinks about such a relation of commodities as constitutive of barter there is a problem, for it is hard to see anything contradictory about the persistence of barter relations. There is a contradiction in the commodity *only* if it is claimed that it is imbued with a universal, namely value, as a result of its participation in a whole network of capitalist commodity production. Marx's argument in chapter one is that for value to overcome its contradiction with use value requires the development of money.

But, again I stress, there is no contradiction whatsoever in supposing that exchange can be carried on without money: barter is a well attested phenomenon historically and anthropologically. It has no *necessity* to develop into a money system. Yet Marx in *Capital* tries to demonstrate the necessity of money. He predicates it on the fact that 'exchange of commodities implies contradictory and mutually exclusive conditions'.[15] These contradictions arise only because it is *presupposed* in his discussion that the commodity is to be a bearer of value. It is only on this basis that the forms of value Marx considers in his first chapter are said to be 'defective' or 'deficient'. They are deficient in that the presence of value is not adequately expressed in the first three forms considered, but only in the money form. Thus the derivation of money is not based primarily on a 'forwards' argument but rather a 'backwards' dialectic, in which it is assumed that value is to be socially validated, and then money is shown to be (at this stage) the most adequate actualisation of value through an argument establishing the inadequacies of less developed expressions of commodity relations. Once the category of 'money' is granted then value is *better grounded* than it is in simple commodity relations.

If at the start one imputes value to a single commodity (through an analytical abstraction from the world of exchange relations) one immediately creates a contradiction between use value and value because value has a purely social reality.[16] Since in isolation commodities lack 'a form of value distinct from their natural forms'[17] such a commodity can appear only as a particular use value, yet at the same time is required to realise the universal *negation* of use value, for that is how value is socially constituted.[18] If value *cannot* appear in an isolated commodity, then, since 'essence must *appear*' (Hegel),[19] in effect it is not really present in such a case. Thus one can say a 'demand' has arisen for this contradiction to be superseded through the said commodity finding a way of distinguishing itself as a value from itself as a use value, to express this value as *other* than itself therefore. This it does in calling on another commodity to be its equivalent as value. In this simple relation Marx rightly saw the germ of money which as a special commodity excluded from all others is 'value for itself' and reflects back on them an adequate value form in their price.

It is important to notice that the whole argument is driven *conceptually*: for the concept of value to be meaningful money is required. There is no trace in Marx's presentation of a quasi-causal story about commodity exchangers having as a result of the structure of their situation a tendency to invent money.

If the validating of the value inherent in commodities is only accomplished in the dialectical movement to a higher category, to money, it is also true that the commodity as such retains its contradictory character. The resolution of contradictions does not abolish them, nor discard them, but *grounds* them, gives them 'room to move' as Marx puts it.[20] Furthermore money itself turns out to embody a contradictory unity of use value and exchange value at a higher level. And so does each further concretisation. The key question is this: is capitalism *finally* able to resolve this contradiction? Or does it remain prey to it however it adapts itself? Will it run out of 'room to move'?

Contradictions of Capital

The clearest example of the reading of *Capital* as a dialectic informed by the need to reconstitute the given whole is the transition to production which Marx makes in the chapter 'Contradictions in the general formula of capital'.

In the previous chapters he has dealt with simple circulation of commodities and the mediation of this in money. Now it is clear that there is no contradiction involved in the idea of simple circulation at value. There is indeed no contradiction in the idea that clever merchants are generally successful at selling dear and buying cheap. (But notice that it is contingent that an increment in value is gained at the expense of another through luck or judgment or cheating.) Why then does Marx find it *necessary* to turn to production in order to resolve *contradictions*? It arises only from the demand that the concept of capital be actualised. This demand is only supportable on the assumption that the object of the exercise is to explain capitalism as a going concern, trace its potential to reproduce itself together with all its conditions of existence, and identify any insurmountable contradiction. It is presupposed at this point in the argument that capital is defined as self-valorising value, in which surplus-value accrues to capital as a matter of necessity in virtue of its form. Only on this presupposition is Marx entitled to formulate the key contradiction: 'Capital cannot arise from circulation and it is equally impossible for it to arise apart from circulation'.[21] The solution is stated to lie in the purchase of the value-producing agent itself, labour. However, here there is an unexamined precondition, namely that there be a labour market. Yet nothing whatsoever is done by Marx to explain this at the point where it is introduced. This is not because he is unaware that he is making such an assumption;

he simply declares the origin of free labour to have no theoretical interest![22] Nothing could show more clearly the nature of Marx's dialectic. He does not derive free labour from the dialectic of circulation as its result. Rather he says the concept of capital demands its prior presence if the dialectic is to proceed. And he proceeds! But this issue is not left hanging forever. This condition of existence of capital which at the outset is taken as a premise (and shown to be historically a contingent result of the developments covered in the last part of *Capital*) is later itself grounded as a result of the development of the capital relation.[23] We see now why Marx has no interest in deriving the labour market *prior* to the capital relation; it is derived as its *consequence*; capital 'posits' its own preconditions.

Nothing could more clearly illustrate than this example that *Capital* is the exposition of the reciprocal conditions inherent in a whole and not a quasi-historical development from primitive conditions to advanced ones. Marx's development of the capital relation contains no argument of a quasi-causal character purporting to show how capitalism arose, such as the argument that given monetary circulation there will be a structural tendency for some people to start making money of money and then to subordinate the immediate producers to such aims. Rather his dialectic is about the necessity, if valorisation is to be secured, of the exploitation of labour. It is a *conceptual* link that is established.

An Organic System

Although the chronological origin of free labour has no interest from the point of view of systematic dialectic, which is concerned with the relation of synchronic elements, historically it is of interest, for Marx never tires of pointing out that the origin of capitalism cannot be explained on the basis of free labour as a natural premise. It is, rather, unnatural to separate the worker from the means of production, and this requires a special explanation in terms of an antecedent history. However this process vanishes in its result and systematically is of no interest, for the system itself reproduces this condition of its existence.

It was precisely in connection with the historical emergence of (doubly) free labour that Marx observed that dialectic must know its limits. Let us examine this interesting passage:

The free worker is the premiss for the emergence and even more for the being of capital as such. Its existence is the result of a lengthy historical process in the economic formation of society. It is made quite definite at this point that the dialectical form of presentation is right only when it knows its own limits. . . . The exposition of the general concept of capital does not make it the incarnation of some eternal idea, but shows how in actual reality, simply as a *necessary* form, it has yet to flow into the labour creating exchange value, into production resting on exchange value.[24]

Yet, as I have argued, there is no need to go into the pre-history of capitalism insofar as systematic dialectic explores the 'inneraction' of an organic whole. In this endeavour it demonstrates how all presuppositions of the system are also posited by the system. But I add now that there are two kinds of presuppositions thus to be determined. We can see that this is implicit in Marx's own insights into the capital totality. Here is a relevant paragraph from Marx's *Grundrisse*:

In the completed bourgeois system every economic relation presupposes every other in its bourgeois economic form, and everything posited is thus also a presupposition. . . . This organic system itself, as a totality, has its presuppositions, and its development to its totality consists precisely in subordinating all elements of society to itself, or in creating out of it the organs which it still lacks. This is historically how it becomes a totality.[25]

In considering this passage I stress the very real difference between 'subordinating' and 'creating'. These refer to very different 'conditions of existence' of capital. One can speak properly of 'creation of organs' where 'home grown' forms like the factory system (within which real subsumption of labour is ensured) are concerned. These capital brings forth as its own, so to speak. Quite different are those 'organs', necessary conditions of existence of capital, that it *encounters* and then subordinates to its purposes, subsuming them under peculiar value forms. Such conditions of existence are historically *given* to capital and then brought within it. Such an example of a historically given condition of existence of capital is the presence of doubly free labour. But once capital moves on its own basis such preposited labour is reduced to a moment of capital, at least in the sense that it participates in a sub-circuit of capitalist reproduction such that its doubly free character is reproduced immanently.

To sum up: what these cases show is that systematic dialectic, as employed by Hegel and Marx, investigates the conceptual connections between the inner forms of a given whole; a sequence of categorial levels is established in which more developed forms ground earlier ones. This logic does not depend in any way upon the historical development that first threw up the elementary preconditions of the system, for these are articulated and grounded *within* the logical ordering itself.[26] The logical ordering corresponds to the inner relations of the object, tracing the mutually affirming forms that ensure the reproduction of the totality.

Historical Illustrations in 'Capital'

I have argued for the separation of systematic dialectic from considerations pertaining to historical sequences; implicitly I have suggested a reading of *Capital* Volume One in which the last part, on 'Original Accumulation', as strictly historical, has a different status from the previous parts, organised according to a logic of categorial development. It might be thought to be evidence against such a reading of *Capital* that historical material is brought in even where, on my view, the motor of the argument is strictly logical. I account for this material in different ways.

Firstly, it is important to notice that almost the whole of the first three parts of *Capital* is a strictly systematic thematisation of circulation and valorisation. Only in chapter ten, on the working day, is there an extended historical discussion pertaining to struggles over the working day. In my opinion this is strictly illustrative and does not advance the argument. It can be deduced from the concept of the capital relation that there must be struggles over the length of the working day, but it was by no means necessary for Marx to illustrate it at such length.

The second substantial historical discussion is in part four on the 'Production of Relative Surplus-Value.' This has two aspects. One is that inherent to its concept is that capital must continually revolutionise the productive forces; but that in England at a certain time the power-loom transformed the cotton industry is purely illustrative of this tendency. The other is more important, because it involves the development of new concepts. It is the supplementation of formal subsumption of labour to capital with real subsumption of labour under capital.[27] This is the background to the transition from manu-facture to machinery, which is not explicable solely in technical terms.[28] I account for this by making a distinction between the truth of a concept and its actualisation. It is inherent to the concept of capital that it must reproduce and accumulate, and in this it seeks to overcome all obstacles and to make the material reality it engages with conform as perfectly as possible to its requirements. But it takes time to do this, namely to make a reality of its ideal world of frictionless circulation and growth. Its opposite pole, labour, is indeed recalcitrant much of the time to the demands capital imposes on it. Thus, although the category of 'real subsumption' is logically implicit in the con-cept of capital, being required to perfect it, in actual fact a whole series of revolutions in the capitalist mode of production were required to create the requisite conditions for capital's vindication of its hegemony.

Finally , the chapter on the 'General Law of Accumulation' finishes with some historical facts about England and Ireland, but this chapter is explicitly labelled by Marx: 'Illustrations'.

In sum, the argument of *Capital* is generally logical with historical material indicating how certain tendencies inherent to the concept were played out in reality.

Dialectics: Affirmative and Critical

I have said that every higher category is truer, because more comprehensive, than earlier, more simple and abstract, ones. It seems then that systematic dialectic necessarily has an *affirmative* character in which all categories con-sidered are granted validity in terms of their place in the whole system which itself guarantees its own truth in thus comprehending them.

Now Klaus Hartmann has argued that such a dialectic cannot be Marxian, because as Marx's argument develops the verdict on capital becomes more *negative*, that it is crisis-ridden, exploitative, and irrational. Tony Smith has responded to Hartmann that Marx's dialectic is of a new type which is 'at once affirmative and critical'.[29] I agree. It is quite possible to argue that money, for example, makes possible an enormous expansion of economic activity beyond that of barter, while at the same time arguing that the money system subjects us to the sway of alien forces.

A purely *affirmative* dialectic would show how capital subsumes under its forms all elements of economic life, becoming absolute in the sense of conquering and shaping the use value sphere itself. The *critical* aspect of the dialectic shows that on the use value side capital faces two 'others' of itself that it cannot plausibly claim – in Hegelian fashion – to be only aspects of it own self. Its external other is Nature which capital is degrading at frightening speed thus undermining its own material basis. Its internal other is the proletariat, capital's own creation, which is potentially capable of overthrowing it.

The points I made just now do not invalidate a method of exposition based on systematic dialectic. One can use the notion of a drive to overcome contradictions in order to motivate transitions from one category to another, whether one assumes, with Hegel, that a final resolution within the terms of capitalism is available, or whether, with Marx, that capital cannot overcome its contradictions.

[1]   Hegel G. W. F. 1991 *The Encyclopaedia Logic*, §14.
[2]   See the reading of Hegel's system provided by Klaus Hartmann (1972); and (within Marxism) Tony Smith (1990), Geert Reuten and Michael Williams (1989). They all argue that Hegel's great merit lies in his understanding of the necessity of categorial ordering, exhibited primarily in his *Logic*.
[3]   Hegel, G. W. F. 1969 *The Science of Logic*, p. 39.
[4]   McTaggart, J. M. E. 1922 *Studies in Hegelian Dialectic*, p. 3.
[5]   Smith, T. 1990 *The Logic of Marx's 'Capital'*, p. 49.
[6]   Hegel, G. W. F. 1969 *The Science of Logic*, p. 70.
[7]   Hegel, G. W. F. 1969 *The Science of Logic*, p. 841.
[8]   Hegel, G. W. F. 1969 *The Science of Logic*, p. 840; Marx, K. 1973 *Grundrisse*, p. 100.
[9]   Hegel, G. W. F. 1969 *The Science of Logic*, pp. 828–9.
[10]   McTaggart, J. M. E. 1922 *Studies in Hegelian Dialectic*, p. 9.
[11]   Hegel, G. W. F. 1969 *The Science of Logic*, p. 72.
[12]   Marx, K. 1976 *Capital* Volume I, p. 949.
[13]   I do not claim fidelity to Hegel or to Marx. I simply draw on these thinkers to help me elucidate what is a key methodological resource needed to make sense of the capitalist system. While I give examples of systematic dialectic from Hegel and from Marx, I do not claim all their arguments have this character.
[14]   Hegel, G. W. F. 1967 *The Philosophy of Right*, §103.
[15]   Marx, K. 1976 *Capital* Volume I, p. 198.

[16] Marx, K. 1976 *Capital* Volume I, pp. 138–39.

[17] Marx, K. 1976 *Capital* Volume I, p. 141.

[18] Marx, K. 1976 *Capital* Volume I, p. 128.

[19] Hegel, G. W. F. 1991 *The Encyclopaedia Logic*, §131.

[20] Marx, K. 1976 *Capital* Volume I, p. 198.

[21] Marx, K. 1976 *Capital* Volume I, p. 268.

[22] Marx, K. 1976 *Capital* Volume I, p. 273.

[23] Marx, K. 1976 *Capital* Volume I, pp. 723–24.

[24] Marx, K. 1987 'Original text of *A Contribution to a Critique . . .*', p. 505.

[25] Marx, K. 1973 *Grundrisse*, p. 278.

[26] Marx, K. 1973 *Grundrisse*, pp. 459–61.

[27] Marx, K. 1976 *Capital* Volume I, p. 645.

[28] Marx, K. 1976 *Capital* Volume I, pp. 490–91.

[29] Smith, T. 1990 *The Logic of Marx's 'Capital'*, p. 83.

Chapter Five
Marx's 'Capital' and Hegel's 'Logic'

Marx said that a science must adopt the logic proper
to the peculiar character of the object under investigation.[1] The question arises, therefore, what is the
appropriate logic for the critique of political economy? We know from numerous sources that Marx
characterised his presentation in *Capital* as 'dialectical'. Unfortunately, he never wrote his promised work
on dialectic. But we know that he found re-reading
Hegel's *Logic* a great help in the '*method* of treatment'.[2] Furthermore, in *Capital* itself he 'openly
avowed' himself 'the pupil of that mighty thinker'.[3]
In the first section of this chapter, therefore, I show
just how Hegel's logic, in spite of his avowed idealism, is indeed relevant – precisely to the 'peculiar'
character of a money economy. Thus our exploration
of the latter can draw on the parallel found in Hegel's
presentation of his logic. We shall show the movement from commodity exchange to value parallels
his 'Doctrine of Being'; the doubling of money and
commodities parallels the 'Doctrine of Essence'; and
capital, positing its actualisation in labour and industry, as 'absolute form' claims all the characteristics
of Hegel's 'Concept'. The bulk of the chapter offers
such a reconstruction of the analysis of the value
form initiated by Marx. It takes the shape of a *systematic dialectic of categories*. But in concentrating on
the value form I leave aside initially any labour content – in this way departing from Marx who analysed

both together. However, I conclude by providing a novel proof that Marx was indeed right in giving central importance to capitalistically produced commodities.

The Value Form and Hegel's Logic

Hegel's logic treated the fundamental categories of thought as pure categories independent of any contingent empirical instantiation. He presented them as systematically ordered, from simple abstract ones to more complex, hence more concrete, ones. This system of categories was said to be 'self-moving' in that meditating on one category drives us to introduce another contrary, or more comprehensive, one. Hegel was an idealist in that he seemed to think that he had thereby shown the necessity of such relationships arising and developing in the real world.

In order to establish the relevance of Hegel's logic to the critique of political economy, it is necessary to grasp the *ontological* foundation of the capitalist system.

This foundation is the *reality* of that abstraction in exchange predicated on the identification as 'values' of heterogeneous commodities. This 'material abstraction' has a substantive reality quite independent of any methodological points about abstraction in theory construction. It produces an 'inverted reality' in which commodities simply instantiate their abstract essence as values; and concrete labours count only as lumps of abstract labour. What is of great interest here is that this abstraction is not a mental operation; it is a *material abstraction*. Before the positing of labour as 'abstract' there is the positing of commodities themselves as bearers of their abstract identity as values.[4] It is implicit in this purely material process of abstraction that it is not necessary for the parties to the exchange to know what they are doing in this respect, or the logical form posited in their practical activity. As a consequence of this material abstraction from the specificity of the use-values concerned, which is 'suspended' for the period of exchange, the commodities acquire as a new determination the character of exchange values, and the particulars concerned play the role of bearers of this determination imposed on them while passing through this phase of their life-cycle. They become subject to the *value form*. Conversely, in actualising their use value, their exchange value is suspended, or vanishes altogether (although in productive consumption it may reappear in 'transferred' form).

In order to explain further why Hegel's logic is relevant to value theory let us provide now a preview of the presentation of the value form to come. Goods are brought to market because they are believed to be use values required by others, and if they are consumed eventually this actualises their original positing as use values. But along the way they are in a different phase of being; for while they are being exchanged they are not being used; furthermore this power of exchangeability has no evident basis in their use value as such. Occasionally such a comparison might occur if, say, two half-bottles of wine were to exchange against one full one, but in the main the commodities exchanged are incommensurable as use values because their particular qualities are adapted to different uses. What is going on is an abstraction from such particularity, and the negation of this difference of use value.

When goods are reduced to moments of a unifying form in commodity exchange they are taken as identical instantiations of their abstract essence (value). But in such an identity their particularity drops away and remains as such excluded from the further advance of the dialectic of forms. The value form of the commodity posits a split between value as the identity of commodities premised on an abstract universal posited through equivalent exchange and their enduring particularity, differentiating them from each other as use values. This is the key to our argument for the relevance of Hegel's logic; for he too starts with an abstraction from everything particular and determinate. Our point is that there is a strong parallel between Hegel's 'pure thoughts', i.e. the evacuation of contingent empirical instantiations to leave the category as such, and the same process in practical terms when a commodity acquires a value form which disregards its natural shape. In the value form there is not only a split between form and content, but the former becomes autonomous and the dialectical development of the structure is indeed form-determined. The value forms, 'commodity', 'money', and 'capital' initially are pure forms which subsequently gain a footing in material production. There is a sense in which the forms *apply themselves* to the material to be formed, rather than the form naturally being taken on by the content. However, this means that form and content are not fully unified but retain a structure of abstract contraposition: the content is inscribed in the form while retaining much that cannot be grasped in it. Because of this, I argue that capital is both real and ideal. Hence the categories of Hegel's logic can be drawn on, but in a critical way. Just as Hegel's logic follows the self-movement of thought as it traverses the categorial universe, so the dialectic of exchange sets up a *form-determined system*. Here the formal structures are indeed 'self-acting'; not just in the sense of being categorially connected by our thought process. Immediately, such form-determination posits a content that amounts to nothing more than the abstract possibility of place, a pure algebraic variable, a determinable with no particularly necessary determinate content. Although there is no *given* content that could express itself in exchange value the latter can reflect its form into itself, its form *as content*. So anything and everything can in principle become a bearer of value. At the same time the universal needs the particulars it subsumes. Whereas Hegel's pure thoughts posit merely potential extensions, the economic forms must be constituted materially in the relation of exchange. Thus all the way through its analysis we will find that a *doubling* into the abstractly universal, and the materially particular, is characteristic of the value form.

I think that the relationship between Hegel's logic and the value form is much closer than that of an external identification of its logical structure, or a methodologically motivated application of its norms of adequacy, or an expositional strategy that finds it convenient to move from simpler to more complex structures. I believe that in some sense the value form and Hegel's logic are to be *identified*; we are not simply applying Hegel's logic to an independent content. It is not that the value form happens to generate structures of a complexity mapped by Hegel in his logical categories; the forms are in effect of such abstract purity as to constitute a real incarnation of the ideas of Hegel's logic. Marx's claim that the *presentation* of the commodity-capitalist system is *at the same time a critique* of it[5] (it is so in itself – apart from the bringing to bear of any external criteria, e.g. the rather dubious one of justice) makes sense in our context when we observe that it is precisely the *applicability* of Hegel's logic that condemns the object as an inverted reality systematically alienated from its bearers, an object which in its 'spiritualisation' of material interchange and practical activities into the heaven of pure forms virtually incarnates the Hegelian 'Idea'.[6]

To sum up: the secret of the structure and development of the capitalist economy is to be found right at the start when the material abstraction of commodity exchange creates the reality of pure forms which then embark on their own logic of development (as in Hegel) and the entire system has to be grasped (within limits yet to be specified) as form-determined.

The Method of Exposition

Given my argument thus far, it can be understood why in what follows I feel able to draw on Hegel's method of exposition in analysing the value form, and the form-determined totality arising from it (see Chapter 4). The presentation is intended to articulate the inner structure, and law of motion, of a (relatively) self-subsistent whole. The method employed in the presentation of the forms of value below may be unfamiliar; it is therefore worth spelling out. What it is not: it is not an inductive method generalising from perceived instances a hypothetical law of the phenomena, to be further tested in experience; it is not a hypothetico-deductive system in which an axiom is made the basis of a sequence of inferences that formally follow from it, the result being, as it is said, already 'contained in' the premises; it is not a transcendental argument for the conditions of possibility of a form of experience taken as established. It is the logical development of a system of categories, or forms of being, from the most elementary and indeterminate to the richest and most concrete; it is self-evident that the result cannot be 'contained' in the premise, for the latter is poorer in content than the former. But this is precisely the key to the argument; the impulse to move from one category to the next is the *insufficiency* of the existing stage to prove its necessity and prevail against the contingencies to which it is subject. Upon examination, it is seen that the form under consideration is not able to sustain itself on its own basis; it depends on conditions of existence that seem to be contingent, such that it could easily vanish.

The movement of thought is thus from the 'conditioned' to the 'unconditioned'; each stage 'takes care of', with the minimum of new elements, the problem perceived with the previous stage, but in turn is found insufficient. The presentation ends when all the conditions of existence needing to be addressed are comprehended by the entire system of categories developed. The forms incorporate within themselves, and produce through their own effectivity, these conditions; this means that the totality so grounded is judged self-sufficient. The starting point is not an axiom or an empirical given upon which all else depends; rather the originating form gains actuality and truth only when grounded in the totality to which it gives rise through the dialectic outlined.

A number of points about this Hegelian method need to be added. First, because the development is from the poorer to the richer form, a transition cannot be so formally necessary that a computer could predict it. Rather a certain openness and creativity is present. Hegel speaks here of 'an upward spring of the mind'.[7] This allows Hegel to present what he takes to be a logically necessary development as at the same time a free self-production of spirit. Second, for Hegel's absolute idealism the major point of reference is not the individual thinking being. Instead of the ordinary mind solving problems with this method of advance, Hegel likes to think of the categories arising and dissolving out of their own instability; in so far as they are thought, it is by some 'objective mind'. This 'objectivist' tendency of his logic is further strengthened because its truth is meant ontologically as much as logically. The coherence of the logic is at the same time the coherence of reality. We, of course, are dealing from the start with forms of reality, of which the categorial equivalents drawn from Hegel are always to be interpreted in terms of a real system of commodity exchange. Finally, we must explain that a *specific* domain of reality, namely capitalist commodity exchange, can yet give rise to the most abstract categories, homologous with those of Hegel's logic, the most abstract part of his *universal* philosophy. Although our implicit starting point, namely 'the commodity produced by capital', appears as a concrete one, the real abstraction, imposed in exchange, from every given feature of it leads to a dialectic of 'pure form' homologous with the 'pure thoughts' of Hegel's logic. Whereas Hegel abstracts from everything through the power of thought, exchange abstracts only from what is presented to it, a delimited sphere of use values. So we have in the dialectic of capital one that is less general than Hegel's in its scope, but within its own terms equally *absolute* in so far as it is founded on all round abstraction to leave quasi-logical primitives.

So we will follow in the method of presentation a Hegelian procedure in ordering categories according to their relative abstractness, and in motivating transitions according to the criterion of the relative insufficiency of the currently established categorial framework to guarantee on its own basis the self-reproduction of the system. Essentially, then, the presentation is of a system of categories. These may be picked up from everyday discourse, or from existing bourgeois ideology, but some will have to be newly evolved because of the confusions of existing thought. The most general guideline in evolving these new categories, and in the presentation of the whole system of categories, is that the presentation should be able to establish a clear order of succession, from the simplest to the most complex, from the most abstractly indeterminate to the most concretely specific. Each category will unify a manifold. But in so far as it appears external and imposed on the elements, and they, conversely, appear only contingently available to it, the category is not securely grounded, and hence the real as it is grasped under this aspect appears unstable and liable to dissolution. In so far as the real is self-reproducing, the presentation should be able to exhibit its categorial articulation in such a manner as to show how this is achieved through certain inner necessities of its structure, in other words, how the logic of the system tendentially ensures its reproduction. It should also be possible to indicate the degree of dependence of the system on empirically given contingencies. Thus that money is a necessity for capitalist development may be demonstrated; but the role historically played by gold in this connection clearly presupposes the contingencies of its existence and suitability.

The most notable category to be picked up from everyday experience is that of commodity exchange. Like Marx we begin from the perception that 'the wealth of society in which the capitalist mode of production prevails appears as an immense collection of commodities.'[8] But I differ here from Marx in that I refuse to find it necessary to come to labour until after conceptualising capital as a form-determination. Bringing in labour too early risks giving the appearance of model-building and committing the exposition to a stage of simple commodity production.[9] To begin with we shall analyse the commodity-form itself and only at the end give grounds for picking out as systematically important those commodities which are products of labour. In this way by exploring to the full the dialectic of form, and letting the form itself reach the content it demands, we do something very different from the bulk of the Marxist tradition which is always in a hurry to address the material content. I hold that under definite historically emergent conditions the value form comes to acquire substance, or, conversely, labour comes to express itself in value. But here I shall be concerned solely with the derivation of the forms of value; I shall only indicate in a general way where and why the reconstruction will explore the category of labour.

The ultimate object of Marxist theory is the capitalist form of social material production; but it does not follow that in the presentation it is necessary to evolve general categories of production and then further specify these in terms of the form of capital. It is proposed here that, because of its importance in shaping the character and direction of social material production, the value form (as the germ of capital) should be analysed first; and the transition made to production in accordance with the determinations immanently required for the reproduction of capital according to the necessity of its concept. In other words the question of form is so crucial that the presentation starts with the form of exchange, bracketing entirely the question of the mode of production, if any, of the objects of exchange. This has the advantage that we begin with the same perception as that of everyday consciousness, namely, that in the bourgeois epoch nearly everything is capable of taking on commodity-form, and we avoid an appearance of arbitrariness in concentration from the outset only on products of labour. My approach will have the advantage of starting with commodities in general, while arriving through the dialectic of the systematic presentation itself at the justification for a focus on production as the prime site of economically significant relationships. Before embarking on the argument proper, let us contextualise it further by giving a general characterisation of the social form of the bourgeois epoch.

Social Form

The question of social form is central to the Marxian understanding of economic systems. It is only in virtue of differences in social form that Marx can insist that there is no such thing as 'economics' in general, but that each mode of production has its specific and peculiar laws of motion. Unfortunately the laconic opening sentence of *Capital* ('The wealth of society in which the capitalist mode of production prevails appears as an immense collection of commodities.') is far too brief a gesture towards the necessity of spelling out just what is peculiar about the social form of the bourgeois economy.[10] He goes immediately into the double determination of the commodity; and only in the last section of the chapter, in the interests of highlighting the uniqueness of the fetishistic form of the commodity, is there a fuller discussion of social form. It is true that Marx himself has a superb analysis of the forms of value in sections 3 & 4 of chapter one of *Capital* (and this is where the influence of Hegel is seen most clearly). He has a critique of form (fetishism) as well as a critique of content (exploitation); but in his anxiety to relate value to production he had already jumped – far too hastily – to labour as its substance. In expounding the logic of the bourgeois social form I draw on the terminology of Reuten and Williams (although I do not pretend to follow their definitions exactly), and employ the triad of categories: sociation, dissociation, and association.[11]

By *sociation* is meant the universal, ahistorical reality that in order to be active economically, people engage in social relationships and social practices. Outside of a Robinson Crusoe situation, production and consumption are immediately, or mediately, socially contextualised.

By *dissociation* (the negation of sociation) is meant the historically specific reality of the separation between economic agents predominant in the bourgeois epoch; 'separation' here does not mean a geographical distance of course, but a *social* barrier. Dissociation has three dimensions: first that useful objects are held by persons as their private property and hence are not immediately available for satisfying the needs of others; second that production is carried out in enterprises likewise in the hands of private owners; third that labour-power is separated from its object in that the most important means of production are held as the property of members of the capitalist class.

By *association* is meant that the opposition of sociation and dissociation is mediated in the form of exchange whereby consumers acquire the objects they require, production units acquire inputs and dispose of outputs, and through contracts of labour people find work and capitalist enterprises find workers. It is important to understand that when dissociation is negated through association this is on the same ground; that is to say, the basic element of privatised appropriation of goods is retained, but a form of mediation (properly called here sublation – *Aufhebung*) is found. Thus association does not replace dissociation; rather it replicates it through developing its conditions of existence; sociation now takes the contradictory form of their unity. I agree with Reuten and Williams that dissociation is the conceptual starting point of the presentation of the bourgeois epoch; and that the exchange relation provides the first moment of association. The presentation proper will thus start with exchange.

Since exchange is understood to mean a voluntarily undertaken transaction, which is not indicated by any central authority, and is rooted solely in the private purposes of the agents concerned, it is on the face of it extremely unlikely that any coherent economic order could emerge at all; still less one characterised by the beneficent 'hidden hand' of Smithian faith. Our problem is to determine the conditions of existence of a system in which goods take the form of commodities offered for exchange on the market. What is the form of social cohesion in a system in which all decisions to produce and to exchange are private? It is the forms of unity of this system which it is our task to explore, with a view to seeing just how much integration is possible.

Although the form of capital will turn out to be the overriding moment in the system, the drive which provides the impulse for reproduction, we could not possibly start with it right away, because it is far too complex a determination. Rather the presentation deliberately starts with the most indeterminate characterisation of the whole (namely exchange). The argument develops precisely because of the need to overcome the inadequacy of this characterisation, measured either immanently, e.g. by its self-contradictory implications, or by reference to its failure to be self-subsistent. In this way thought is impelled onward to reach a more concrete totality; only when the presentation reaches the whole is the starting-point grounded in its connection with the whole and thereby validated as a true determination in this relative sense of being inadequate on its own but valid as one of the determinations that come together in a mutually grounding interchange to constitute the concrete whole. The whole is grounded in its elements, and these elements mediate themselves in the whole. Commodities are the starting point; we do not at first raise the question of where commodities come from, whether they are produced or non-produced goods, or, if they are produced, under what relations of production; but the development of the argument itself eventually grounds them as results of capitalist production.

To sum up this introductory material: the sociation-dissociation contradiction is the presupposition of the entire epoch, and hence our presentation; it is association through exchange that gives this contradiction 'room to move';

the first concrete category is therefore this mediation, and we study its further development; this first category of *movement* determines goods as commodities, and hence the first *object* of analysis is the commodity, a unity of use value and exchange value; this doubling is a relation in which the form, the abstract universal, dominates the matter, the particular use values; the value form is therefore the *theme* of our categorial dialectic.

The Presentation of the Value Form

We have said enough to establish a general case for appropriating Hegel's logic in our value analysis, substituting for the movement of thought the movement of exchange. We presuppose at the outset that exchange is a primary mode of social synthesis in the bourgeois epoch – it constitutes and reproduces bourgeois relations such as the dissociation of production and consumption. The presentation will work through this in detail.

As a preliminary, let us lay out our plan (compare Hegel's *Logic* §83):

   i. exchange in its immediacy: value implicit in *commodities*.
  ii. in its mediation: the reflection and showing-forth of value in *money*.
 iii. in its return into itself (circulation) and its development of itself: value in and for itself as capital.

(For a more detailed comparison of Hegelian and Marxian categories see the Appendix to this chapter.) Categories from Hegel's logic are in **Bold** on their introduction below.

(i) *Commodity Exchange*

This first section thematizes the commodity. This is value in the shape of 'Being' – a category of Hegel's *Logic* – and the determinations below will also follow those in the *Logic*, namely: 'Quality, Quantity, and Measure'; to which correspond in our domain, it will be seen, 'exchangeability', 'amount', and 'exchange-value'. The dialectical exposition proper begins with the most abstract indeterminate notion, but nonetheless the essential and originating one, which initiates the process of social synthesis in the bourgeois epoch, that of exchange. The only presupposition made at the outset is that dissociation is overcome through commodity exchange. Goods therein take the form of commodities.

Given exchange, we can speak of commodities in terms of the elementary opposition between Being and Nothing treated by Hegel at the beginning of his *Logic*.[12] They have their **being** in the circuits of exchange; but as yet they reveal **nothing** about themselves that guarantees this status; indeed they regularly disappear from the space of exchange relations, perhaps to be consumed. Their **being** become **determinate,** and fixed in this sphere, is that of exchangeable commodities. Commodities are distinguished from being goods in general by the **quality** of being exchangeable. (The denotation of the category is of course historically variable. Water was once a free good; now it is an increasingly expensive commodity.) At the same time, exchangeability is still rooted in their utility. At this level the immediate motor of exchange appears to be the exchange of one commodity for another of a different kind having a different use. There is no conceivable point in exchanging effectively the same good. We do not exchange iron for iron, but iron for corn. Thus a condition of existence of exchange is the universe of use value.

The quality of exchangeability requires further determination. If exchange is to be possible, it is not enough for the goods to be specified as having properties that make them exchangeable in a general indeterminate sense; a determination is required that allows for discrete exchanges to occur; in other words a commodity must be specifiable as an item (a bakery does not in truth sell 'bread', it sells so many loaves of such and such weight). The good has to take on a determinate shape, and has to specify itself in discrete items, each of which announces itself as an instantiation in delimited form of the good concerned.

Through the notion of amount we make the transition to the category of **quantity**. To be a commodity a good offered for exchange must be delimited quantitatively, and presented as an amount of itself. The striking thing about this quantification is that, although each good has its own index of amount (weight or whatever) in terms of which haggling goes on, these amounts seem unable to refer to any common index because, *ex hypothesi*, as naturally diverse goods, their index of amount differs absolutely (no one would exchange two pounds of gold for two pounds of iron). Hence the **quantum**, the unit of exchange, does not appear as a unit of anything common; it is a pure **number**, or rather a **ratio** of such numbers: 'I'll give you six of these for four of those.' is the quantitative form of the offer for exchange.

Incommensurable as natural bodies, the commodities are bargained over in the abstract, where the haggling is in terms of pure quantitative variation. The contradiction is that the properties that give them the quality of exchangeability – their use values – are too particular to form the basis of a common measure; yet in a bargain a pure quantitative relation must be fixed in spite of such absolute difference. There appears no ground for such determinacy. This is no mere theoretical contradiction, but a practical incoherence. Perhaps, as Aristotle feared, we must accept its theoretical absurdity in the interests of practical expediency; or maybe we must accept the subjective approach of the neo-classicals; or, as here, we must press the objective tendency of the logic further.

As it stands the relation is unstable and insecure; there seems no reason why any particular pair of numbers should form the basis for the striking of a bargain. There is no necessity yet granted to this form in its character as quantitatively determinate. Someone, sometime, for some reason, might accept a certain amount of one commodity for a certain amount of another. Even if a commodity does achieve social recognition in an exchange, the ratio of exchange, the bargain struck, seems purely accidental – arising *ad hoc*, it may vary on the next occasion.

Yet the abstraction of quantity and quality from each other is not absolute. They are as much in unity as opposed. For, after all, one is not in the bargain settling for 'six', one is settling for six *something*; there is a qualitative determinant present as much as suspended in the haggling over amounts. But the 'something' varies in material terms with every transaction as much as the numbers quantifying it. It could be 'anything'. Can all these 'somethings' represent the same thing?

Exchangeable commodities can only actualise themselves in a bargain, that is, in quantitative form. Conversely, the quantitative ratio practically uniting them in the bargain actualises their common character as exchangeables, as having the potential to draw other commodities in exchange for themselves. The **ratio** of exchange is thus implicitly a **measure** of this potentiality, their value in exchange.

To recapitulate: goods entering the circuits of exchange become determined as commodities; their quality as exchangeables requires a complementary quantitative dimension if bargains are to be struck; the ratios of such quantities given in exchange suggest that we have here a measure of exchange-ability. But there are as many such exchange values as there are commodities; if a genuine 'measurable' is to be posited it must exist in a form that is **absolutely indifferent** to the way it is measured, to all the specific exchange values; this suggests that there underlies the relations of commodities to one another a common **essence**, a value in itself distinct from any particular relation that might be established between two commodities: it is thereby posited that what is measured externally in the ratio of exchange is an inherent dimension of the commodity just like its volume.

Such a move is in no way a 'proof' of value, as perhaps one reading of Marx's section one would hold. Rather it poses the problem of further grounding such a point. Marx skips over this transition astonishingly quickly. He simply declares that in the exchange relation of iron and corn there is a quantitative identity, which clearly cannot be assimilated to the natural properties of iron and corn, and must therefore represent some 'third thing' present, if not visible, in both: their value. Critics have been vociferous in denying the necessity for any such inference.

The meaningfulness of this transition therefore needs thorough elucidation. It involves grasping the relation with the other as mediatedly a *self-relation*. In the terms of the discourse of bargaining, it is marked by a shift from the simple demand 'offer me more of that other commodity' to the proposition that 'this is worth more than what you are offering' or even more precisely 'this is worth twice that'. Such formulae show the consciousness of 'this' being immediately, in itself, 'of worth', that value has an identity with itself, and thereby grounds some immanent measure which is merely expressed or reflected externally in a satisfactory bargain, one in which no one 'loses anything'. The relation of exchange between A and B is now grasped as no longer a conjunctural external relation but a self-relation in which each, in referring to the other as an embodiment of its value, is indirectly only referring to its own value as reflected in something equivalent to itself. Thus we now say 'A is worth B' or 'as values A=B'.

If the quantitative determination established in an exchange is not to be purely conjunctural, determined extrinsically in the contingencies motivating the agents bearing the goods to market (preference schedules, for example), it requires a dimension intrinsic to both commodities yet distinguishable from their appearance as immediately different. This dimension is such that, for each commodity, it obviously varies in proportion to its own index of amount; but it is itself, in so far as it no longer has anything to do with the particularity of use value, a single quantitative determination – that is value in itself.

It is just this notion of an intrinsic value that Samuel Bailey, and others since, objected to. For them, the value posited in exchange is illusory. There is, in truth, nothing lying behind the visible relation. 'A table is worth four chairs' resembles in grammatical form 'This shoe is as long as two of those put together'. But it is not the same; because extension is an inherent dimension of the shoes, whereas exchange value is a purely relative matter, an accidental external relation. Tomorrow, or in the next town, a table might be worth three chairs. We should not be misled by such relations into postulating any identity in the substance of the goods. There is no such thing as 'intrinsic value', only conjunctural correlations of different amounts of use-values.

It seems to me this argument has much more force than most Marxists allow. For at this point we have the *postulate* of identity in essence, and of common measure, only. If the system is to be grounded on itself, rather than being prey to external contingencies, this essence must be actualised. The main point here is that for there to be unity of commodities in a common identity, and determinacy in their relations, they must exist in the same universe and their measure predicated on a common dimension which actualises their commensurability as values.

Although each commodity could be subject to a unique need and a unique supply (e.g. payment for a blackmailer's negatives), for the system of exchanges to be grounded on itself (rather than each transaction registering a specific externally determined conjuncture) the plurality of commodities must be instances of a universal type. There need not be any such identity or resulting immanent determination of exchange ratios. So the further presentation, although it seems to assume that we already know value exists, is really an exploration of its conditions of existence through the development of more concrete concepts which will eventually provide sufficient grounds to set aside any skepticism, and at least validate a research programme based on value.

Before proceeding it would be as well to call attention to the fact that nothing has been said yet about a labour theory of value. People have rightly complained that labour is not common to everything in commodity-form. But in any case it should be noted that – to use an analogy – it is one thing, from having undertaken a number of experiments with a balance, to conclude that material things each have intrinsic to them a definite weight which regularly expresses itself in ratios like 'so much of this balances so much of that', and justifies our speaking of weight as such independent of its expression in such ratios; it is another thing to determine that weight arises from the effect on masses (m) of a gravitational field (g) and that its immanent magnitude is mg.

Before we can even address the Marxian question of 'the source of value' it is necessary to establish what we mean by the value dimension. Can there be such a thing? Its meaning is all the more doubtful when we remember that, unlike weight, value has no connection with anything inherent to the commodity itself as a natural body. It is an alien determination that attaches itself to a good only when the latter is subject to commodity exchange. It does not seem possible to argue that value exists independently of exchange in the same sense as weight exists independently of weighings. It is true that, if the market exists, one can anticipate that a value can be realised on it; but can it make sense to speak of value where there are no markets?

I argue that it is not the case that a pre-existing material content merely takes on the value form; rather, as the form-determined relationships develop, the value content is grasped as result – it is demanded only when the form completes itself in capital. At this stage we have not yet established value – still less an origin in labour. Or rather value has not yet established *itself*. It is not merely that our presentation has not yet reached a proof of value; in so far as it does not pre-exist exchange, value itself only comes to be, and gains any actuality, in the fullest development of the form itself, in money, capital and productive labour, as we shall see. The existence of value is a condition of market exchange being more than an aggregation of accidental transactions, but a systematically unified and ordered process, with some stability, permanence and continuity. But at this stage of the presentation this is by no means secured.

(ii) *Money*

If exchanged commodities are **identified** as substitutable for each other, while yet **different** use-values, this requires a **ground** for its meaningfulness. If such an underlying value **exists** then we can speak of the commodities themselves as 'values' as if value were a **thing**, a **material** that assumed the shape now of corn and now of iron indifferently. But if there is such a **content** hidden away behind the **forms** of exchange, it must prove itself in gaining appropriate expression in the **phenomenal world**.

To speak of a commodity as a thing of value, or simply 'a value', and of things related to one another as values, implies the existence of value in itself as a sort of homogeneous 'matter' underlying the diverse bodily shapes of commodities. According to Hegel, it is an abstraction of the understanding to suppose there is in things 'behind' their phenomenal shape an underlying 'matter'; but here it is not just that the fetishistic consciousness does this; the exchange abstraction itself posits value as this reified essence.

But, as merely implicit, value is a vanishing semblance. To be really of the essence it must become posited for itself; it must gain actuality in its further developed forms of appearance. This is what makes money necessary. Hegel observes that Spirit is 'not an essence that is already finished and complete before its manifestation, keeping itself aloof behind its host of appearances, but an essence which is truly actual only through the specific forms of its necessary self-manifestation'.[13] I would say the same of value. Thus its further concretisations up to market price are not merely more 'finished' forms of value, they are themselves constitutive of its actuality.

In comparison to the brevity with which Marx argues in the first couple of sections of chapter one of *Capital*, most people find the third section over-elaborated. Why these dialectical *minutiae*, when all he is saying is that we need a measure of value, analogous to the standard metre in Paris which gives science a common basis for establishing lengths? Gold serves as a exemplar of value, as the standard metre does of extension. Value, however, unlike extension, is merely a virtual dimension; its actuality is posited only in the *relations* commodities bear to one another. Therefore, Marx is right to show how money, as the value measure of commodities, is evolved in those relations. So how is it to be derived?

Thus far the presentation has argued that the form of exchange posits value in itself. The distinction between use value and exchange value points to the possibility of overcoming the contingency implicit in mere barter; for, if there is a value dimension, order and determinacy will characterise exchange. The difficult thing to grasp here is that, although the possibility of determinate measure is grounded if value is of the essence of the commodity, this essence itself is only actualised in the development of the process of commensuration itself. It is that very process of commensuration which posits commodities as value-masses in the first place. The actuality of value and its expression or measure develop together at the same time. The exchange relation has to be grasped as simultaneously *constitutive* of value and serving as its *expression*. For a commodity cannot express its value in itself, because value gains reality only in the relations of commodities to each other; Marx says value 'can only appear in the social relation between commodity and commodity',[14] that is, as exchange value. The value of linen cannot be expressed in linen; but if another commodity acts as its equivalent, a distinction is drawn in reality between the two aspects of the commodity – its use value immediately present in its own shape, and its value present through the mediation of the equivalent commodity's shape.

In truth the value dimension is constituted at the very same time as its measure. This means that it is even more abstract than space, because extension is perceptible as such prior to the evolution of a unified measuring system. To say that this is equivalent in length to that, through laying them side by side, does not in itself give a measure of either (although it presupposes in its form of expression that such a measure is possible); nevertheless extension is naturally inherent in both, we see. The value dimension, however, has a purely virtual existence in so far as its reality is merely the ideality of the unity of commodities in their abstract identity as exchangeable.

If exchange value is to be real measure, then 'value in itself' must ground the truth of commensuration. As soon as we reach that conclusion, however, through reflecting the commodity into itself, we thereby posit a realm of 'values', wherein is distinguished the essence, value, from its forms of appearance, exchange values. Thus value must now reflect back on exchange value, that is to say, make of it its appearance. In so far as the reality of essence is accomplished only in its appearance the latter is thereby just as much ground as grounded.

As we know already, taken in isolation a commodity exhibits use value merely; it can only double into a use value and a value if the latter determination achieves independent expression. But does it not in every exchange? Certainly, of a single 'accidental' exchange relation, Marx says: 'The simple form of value of a commodity is the simple form of appearance of the opposition between use-value and value which is contained within the commodity.'[15]

The 'insufficiency' (Marx's word) of the simple form to establish this opposition explicitly is that the simple form logically posits symmetry, it can be read in either direction, between measure and measured, between the implicit value and its expression; hence it is difficult to keep hold of the polar relation;[16] the relation collapses to an identity of immanence of value, not an articulated ground for it. Furthermore, while the implicit distinction of use value and value is made manifest in every dyadic relation, an aggregation of barters does not constitute a unified homogeneous value system.[17] Thus we must move to a fuller relative form of value, the expanded form in which the commodity expresses its identity as a value in a whole array of different commodities. This establishes the commodity in that form as something with a value expression confronting it in this totality of relations. The very number of these expressions indicates the indifference of the value expression to any particular equivalent body; hence Marx says we can suppose there is some continuing magnitude present unaltered through the series of exchange values.

The 'defect' (Marx's word) is that there is 'no single, unified form of appearance' of it because each expression excludes the others. Although no unified expression of value is thereby provided, the solution is implicit in this form, for the very same action in which the one commodity sets up its value in expanded form posits it as the single equivalent of the others. In the reversed expression, the general form of value emerges. In this, the universal equivalent functions simply as the incarnation of the abstract identity of all the different commodities as values. As such a unity of the differences it articulates explicitly the value dimension we found necessary to secure the independent status of commodities from the idiosyncrasies of their owners. With this unifying form, value (active as a '**force**') gains consistent **expression**. The point we want to restate yet again is that this is not a superficial development of the essence of value. The actuality of these forms is the very condition of the category of value gaining any real meaning. Marx says: 'By this [universal equivalent] form, commodities are, for the first time [*nota bene*], really brought into relation with each other as values, or permitted to appear to each other as exchange-values.'[18]

The identity of commodities as values is not written on their foreheads, Marx observed. It is true that the simple exchange relation posits the equivalent as the bearer of the value of that in the relative expression, but the symmetry of the relation suggests value is an empty abstraction. In the expanded form of value the very multiplicity of value expressions irresistibly suggests there is an identical content, but only when in the general equivalent form all commodities are unified in the same measure can we speak of a form of value that gives a consistent articulation of the distinction between value in itself as the **inner** content and value for itself as its **outer** expression.

An interesting reversal has in fact taken place in that it seemed originally that the power of exchange possessed by each commodity expressed itself in the equivalent as its passive material, that the commodity actively distinguished its value from itself in positing another simply as its equivalent. But as a consequence of the development of a universal equivalent it is the latter that gains the power of immediate exchangeability insofar as all other commodities value themselves in it. It seems now that the other commodities gain value only when they have it bestowed on them by their recognition in the universal equivalent which solicits them to solicit it. In this **reciprocity of forces**, value and its expression keep changing places.

While a purely formal positing of a universal equivalent would be enough for the function of measure of value, value can gain **actuality** only if such a universal equivalent gains immediate existence, i.e. becomes money. In money, as distinct from commodities, value gains real **substance** and can function as means of payment, medium of exchange, and store of value, powers that will be important in what follows.

To digress: It is important to notice that the presentation of money as a 'substance' is a very different use of the term 'substance' from that of Marx when he derives labour as the substance *of* value in his first chapter; here we are concerned with value *as* substance (corresponding to Marx's use of the term in a later chapter where he speaks of value in motion as 'a self-moving substance').[19] Marx's first use of the term equates with 'stuff' or 'material', with what value is 'made of', so to speak, or – better perhaps – what makes it. Here, in the development of the value form, the dialectic generates categories *of value* that become more concrete and complex. So, as commodity, value seems to 'inhere' so to speak in a use value as a quasi-*property* of it. But, as money, the inverse is true: value is itself a *substance* of which the particular use value (e.g. gold) is merely a transubstantiated outer shell. With capital, we shall argue, value becomes *subject*.[20] (Living labour as the source of value lies *outside* this self-referring system of value forms.)[21]

To resume: Marx's theory of money is very different from both Ricardian and neo-classical conventionalisms. His 'universal equivalent' is no convenient *numéraire*, it is essential that it has actuality. The transition from the implicit immediacy of value in a commodity, and its mediation in the universal equivalent, to the reality of money is necessary because (as we must always remind ourselves) the forms we are concerned with are not pure thoughts but borne by matter, namely commodities. Hence the unity in form of these commodities must be more than thought, it must be practically posited: thus the necessity for a material bearer of the universal equivalent, i.e. the necessity for money.

Money also makes measure explicit. Because, as the universal equivalent, money is posited as value for itself, which is now distinguished from its implicit existence in the integument of the other commodities, it is capable of being applied to them as their measure. To adopt a well-known language, money does not merely solve the *quantitative* problem of providing a measure common to values, it solves the *qualitative* problem of establishing the very commensurability of commodities through relating them to each other as values. Marx argues that goods do not confront one another as commodities (that is, as values) but as use values only, until there exists in *practice* a universal equivalent: it is through 'the social action' of commodities on one another that there is set apart a particular commodity in which they all represent their values. 'Through the agency of the social process it becomes the specific function of the commodity that has been set apart to be the universal equivalent, it thus becomes – money.'[22]

The first function of money as the expression of value, as the existent appearance of the value dimension, is to serve as the measure of value. What exactly is measured? Analogies with other measures such as rulers or weights are very misleading here; for money *constitutes* value in a unity rather than serving as *exemplar* of some property the commodities possessed prior to their commensuration. Money is the 'external' measure of exchangeability of which value is the immanent measure. But in so far as value is – as yet – *determined as pure form*, there is nothing substantial (analogous to mass or extension) to measure. (Commodities are not yet, we stress, determined as products in our presentation; hence we know nothing here of such an immanent determinant as socially necessary labour-time.)

In so far as money unifies the world of commodities, it has the form of *immediate exchangeability*. Although being 'the same value' in the abstract as the commodity it measures, it successfully actualises the posited immanence of value, the essence lying behind the appearance of equivalent exchange, and thereby provides for value to appear in immediate existence, and with determinate measure. Money, Marx says in his *Grundrisse*, is 'value for itself'.[23]

In a peculiar sense, therefore, in the money form value measures itself against itself. Exchangeability is measured by exchangeability. For this self-identity to gain adequate form requires the doubling of the values into commodities and money, into value in itself and value for itself. Thereby, value measures itself *in* itself by itself *for* itself. As immediate equivalent of all commodities money solves the qualitative value problem, through its pure ideality creating a virtual space – the value dimension. Marx speaks of the price form of commodities, as, 'like their form of value generally, quite distinct from their palpable and real bodily form; it is therefore a purely ideal or notional form'.[24]

Both rulers and money allow a unified commensuration. But, in so far as a ruler is itself extended, the relation of equivalence in length follows the logic of transitivity, symmetry, and reflexivity; and it is not too absurd to say the standard metre measures one metre itself. But money cannot measure its own value because money is in effect *measure as such*. Money has no price: money is price.

The value in itself possessed by commodities is now seen to be articulated in a common expression, in money as value for itself. In the case of coined money value is indeed 'written on its forehead'. It is important to recognise the reciprocal determination of these inner and outer moments of value. Our argument went from the phenomenal level down to value as a common ground, and then came up again through the forms of value to demonstrate that value expresses itself in perfected form only as money. This means that money is itself 'of the essence' of the world of value, that it grounds the possibility of such a posited universe of value being actualised as much as it is itself rooted in the simple immediacy of the underlying value substance. It is perfectly useless to discuss here which is **cause** and which **effect**; whether value produces money as its visible form, or whether only money produces the value dimension as a virtual reality in the first place. The dialectical view to take is that each is mediated in the other. For value to be actual requires this doubling and the **reciprocal action** of money and commodities.

(iii) *Capital*

But in such a doubling of the value form there is still an unmediated unity of immediacy and mediation, i.e. of commodities and money. **Universality** (the money form of value) and **particularity** (commodities) have here fallen apart. True they are related: each gains sense only in relation to the other. But if value is to be conceptually coherent it must supersede this doubling of its determinations into separable, if related, manifestations. Its unitary **individuality**, i.e. its true **concept**, is constituted just in so far as it posits itself as being both but neither commodities and money; it is in fact nothing but the **relatedness** of which we have been speaking; the price form posits it in the form of the **judgment**: 'What does this bushel of corn cost? Two pounds' (or 'How much corn can I buy with two pounds? One bushel.'). Value is neither particular (the corn) nor universal (the coin) but the combination of the two definitions is a single **conclusion** (*Schluss*) through the comprehension of these moments as a **totality**.

But this conceptual unity is purely **subjective**, purely formal. We think it when we understand what a price list is, i.e. when we grasp the unity of the two sides. The next step is to elucidate the conditions for this concept of value to be **objectively** determining of itself. This begins with the concluding of bargains, the closing of sales. (Interestingly *Schluss*, the term employed in Hegel's logic for inference or syllogism, is the same as that used in market exchange for closing a sale, just as in English an argument is conclusive and a bargain is concluded.) It is completed in what Marx accomplishes in the section on the metamorphoses of commodity circulation.

In the price of sale the particular and universal determinations of value are *distributed* between the commodity and money; and their identity is merely formal. But in the metamorphoses of commodities both determinations get expressed as moments of a *whole* in so far as the contradiction between the forms of appearance of value (commodities and money) is brought into motion and their unity established in the fluidity of circulation whereby each passes over into the other; the self-same value, doubled into different shapes of existence, appears now as commodity, now as money, now yet again as commodity. But the circulation of commodities through the mediation of money, conceptualised as C-M-C', has no necessity, because the motivation for it is external to the process itself, in that the ends of the chain pass out of circulation. Hence the renewal of circulation depends on the continuance of demand and of supply. The interesting point about the possibility of a temporary hiatus in circulation is that the determination of money as a store of value now emerges; with money in hand the possibility of renewing the circuit when required, or when conditions are favourable, is present. Starting from money gives rise to the movement M-C-M', and therewith a systematic advance is made possible in the interweaving of money and commodities, namely that the M-C-M' circuit has built into it greater possibilities of continuity and self-reproduction than the C-M-C' circuit. Value is now immanent in the activity of exchange; it is itself the object, not the effect and medium of other motives. With the form of capital, value becomes its own end rather than mediator of other relations; that is to say that with capital we have before us an individual '**subject**'.[25]

With M-C-M' the extremes are unified in a spiral of valorisation. Money goes from a passive medium in C-M-C' to a dynamic unifying and initiating role in M-C-M'. Marx says:

> The path C-M-C proceeds from the extreme constituted by one commodity, and ends with the extreme constituted by another, which falls out of circulation and into consumption. Consumption, the satisfaction of needs, in short use-value, is therefore its final goal. The path M-C-M, however, proceeds from the extreme of money and finally returns to that same extreme. Its driving and motivating force, its determining purpose, is therefore exchange-value.[26]

From the circulation of commodities and money emerges capital, we now see. The following passages are reminiscent of Hegel's 'doctrine of the concept':

> The simple circulation of commodities – selling in order to buy – is a means to a final goal which lies outside circulation, namely the appropriation of use-values, the satisfaction of needs. As against this, the circulation of money as capital is an end in itself, for the valorisation of value takes place only within this constantly renewed movement. The movement of capital is therefore limitless.[27]

> It is constantly changing from one form into the other, without becoming lost in this movement; it thus becomes transformed into the subject of a process in which, while constantly assuming the form in turn of money and commodities, it changes its own magnitude, throws off surplus-value from itself considered as original value, and thus valorizes itself independently. For the movement in the course of which it adds surplus-value is its own movement, its valorization is therefore self-valorization.[28]

In investigating the form of capital Marx speaks of M-C-M' as being 'value-in-process'. But this 'self-moving substance' does not merely assume the form of commodities and money, it enters into a 'relationship with itself', as it were, because it 'differentiates itself as original value from itself as surplus-value', only, when both are united in the new capital, to supersede this difference, and 'become one' again.[29] It is, so to speak, 'absolute form' (Hegel).[30]

In *thought* we analyse concepts into moments, e.g. we distinguish within a thing the universal and particular determinations (my humanness on the one hand, and the man before you on the other). Empirically, these are not perceptible distinctions, being mere abstract moments of real being. But the self-development of the value form 'analyses' the concept of value in *reality*; the universal moment is dominant in money and the particular in commodities. If we describe our investigation as value form analysis, we now realise that we just 'look on' while really the restless movement of capital carries out the analysis itself! Capital makes value actual in the sense that it now has a form that posits itself as its own end. That is to say, with the form of capital we have before us an individual 'subject' (Marx's word) that expressly aspires to the totalisation of its determinations and to include within its effectivity all its conditions of existence. The motive of our presentation so far in seeking to elucidate the conditions of existence of value has now become the motive of the form itself!

(iv) *Production*

Hegel concludes the *Logic* by speaking of the Absolute Idea, and its mystifying and mystified transition 'which is not a transition' to the real world through an act of perfect freedom. This idealist distortion of dialectic is firmly rejected here. The logical form of capital is by no means absolute but totally insufficient to maintain itself and it requires a transition to a domain of reality regulated by the form but by no means inessential to it; capital is not free to develop in its concept alone, but must confront the problem of its lack of self-subsistence as mere concept of self-valorisation.

What, then, is the condition next required to grant necessity to the existence of capital as self-valorisation? Capital is defined as 'self-valorising value'; but how can this form maintain itself? The main point here is that while capital has the *form* of self-realisation it still lacks control over its bearers. It is here we remember that at the outset we stated that a primary condition of exchange is the world of use values. With capital we reach a form of circulation of commodities that is its own end, but the self-valorisation process still rests for its possibility on the emergence into being of the goods themselves from some external source. The concept of unconditioned self-development of the value form is undercut by the fact that the appearance of goods in the market place is utterly contingent so far. Clearly, therefore, there is still a large element of conditionedness in the mere possibility of valorisation. It is not *self-grounded*. Circulation in 'its immediacy is therefore pure semblance', a play of forms.[31] Exchange could fade away (as during the decline of the Roman Empire); so capital must take charge of sustaining and developing the value circuit. Hence to make a reality of its concept capital must itself undertake the production of commodities and reduce them to moments in its own circuit. Only on this condition does value in and for itself pass from a mere formal potential to embed itself in a real material process.

To be self-grounded, value must be produced by value. This means that only those goods produced by capital itself count as values, as true commodities both in form and content. Only capitalistically produced commodities have adequacy in both form and content to value in and for itself. The activity of production is an activity of labour. Hence, capital must set itself to make that activity its own activity. Capital makes that activity its own activity insofar as it thoroughly subsumes labour as a content penetrated through and through by the value form. Only now does the presentation find it necessary to address labour. The limitlessness of accumulation inherent in the form of capital is given a solid *ground* in productive labour. Capital can guarantee a surplus only by sinking into production and bringing that activity within its own circuits.

Our presentation has reached the point at which non-produced commodities are now seen to retain the value form but only, as such, the semblance of value; they are lacking in the substance of value because they do not originate within the value circuit itself as it is driven by valorisation. They play no essential role in the dynamic of capitalist development (although two, labour-power and land, as inputs are materially essential, but cannot be treated in this chapter). Products, on the other hand, if capitalistically produced as commodities for sale, gain both determinations of value, being both produced as values and sold as values. In so far as capital conquers the sphere of production it gains reality and permanence instead of being dependent on external conditions to provide the values on which it feeds.

The fact that the presentation only found it necessary to turn to productive labour when the capital form required a ground implies that there are inadequate grounds for positing a labour theory of value at the level of commodity exchange alone. The 'fit' between form and content would be too loose, the relation still too indeterminate. Marx moves so quickly to his 'substance' of value that we lose sight of the fact that value is actual only in the fully developed concept (namely capital). Hence sometimes the impression is given in his discussion that a prior content, labour, reduces the value form to its mere phenomenal expression. The dialectic of commodity production is better presented, I think, as one in which the form sinks into the matter and then develops it as its own content (which, with Marx, we can analyse in terms of such categories as 'labour-power' and 'surplus labour'). Within the value form, instead of the content developing itself through the mediation of its form, the form seeks to secure and stabilise itself through subsuming the matter and turning it into a bearer of self-valorisation. What we are arguing in relation to Hegel's work is that his speculation about an Absolute seeking to actualise and reproduce its entire conditions of existence has reality in capital which has such a drive implicit in its form. Hegel's supposedly universal logic is also the specific logic of capital. At the same time, the logic of the development can issue only in tendencies, which in truth depend on material premises. Unfortunately for capital it cannot actualise itself and conquer all its presuppositions of existence as easily as Hegel's Idea is supposed to. For the true reality is material. As pure form, capital spins in a void. The logic of capital accumulation would run into the buffers pretty quickly were it not for the material fact that workers produce more than they themselves consume. Moreover the labourers are liable to resist their incorporation as internal moments of capital's ideality, i.e. the Idea of capital made real.

Conclusion

In this chapter I developed four main points.

1. The first was presented as an answer to the question how Hegel's logic could be used in Marx's project to do a critique of political economy. I argued that the critical edge of his work does not merely lie in substantive demonstrations of just how exploitation is possible in a system founded on equal exchanges but penetrates to the very structures of the value form, whose logic is a manifestation of the fact that capital is a structure of estrangement founded on the inversion of form and content, universal and particular etc. insofar as exchange value dominates use value. The material abstraction inherent in the system of commodity exchange gives rise to this. The 'autonomization of value' through 'the movement of industrial capital' is 'this abstraction in action' (Marx).[32] The logic of the value forms in their self-relating abstraction is an incarnation in social terms of the self-movement of thought in Hegel's logic. This means that Hegel's logic can be drawn on in our presentation of this ideal character of capital as a value form, and at the same time this demonstration of its ideality means that the system of bourgeois economy is thus presented critically.

2. Secondly, in demonstrating how far capital becomes a real power as self-valorising value we can use the same method of exposition as Hegel did in showing how the Absolute is self-subsistent, namely by starting from an

abstract beginning which gives rise to further categories precisely because of its insufficiency to produce a stable reality. Thus every move in my argument was not one from an established truth to a valid implication but, contrariwise, a movement towards truth away from a hopelessly provisional starting point. Thus the turn made to production in this presentation is a turn to 'the truth of capital', as Hegel might put it.

3. Thirdly, I gave an outline of the dialectic of the value form itself which concluded with an argument that capital lacks assurance of its permanence and growth unless it can control and reproduce all its conditions of existence. The most glaring insufficiency of the definition of capital as self-valorising value is that the bearers of value, namely the commodities as use values, are necessary for capital to feed off but only contingently available to it. Thus to gain control of its conditions of existence capital must produce these commodities. The activity of productive labour as form-determined by capital is thus the next domain to be investigated. It must be established how far capital can make that activity its own activity, both in form, and in the determination of its motive and dynamic.

4. The ontological presupposition of my argument is that commodity exchange creates an 'inverted reality', in which, instead of abstractions being the pale efflorescence of matter, they take possession of it. With the ever-extending commodification of all material things and persons, and the inscribing of all relations within the value form, then mere abstraction is loosed upon the world. Pure forms which develop themselves, and enter into relations with each other, are objectively present in a realm other than thought. But their conditions of existence are material; hence capital drives to shape matter into a content penetrated through and through by the value form.

As we said at the outset, in so far as the presentation traces the imposition of alien forms on the material content of economic life it is itself just on that account immanently critical of the system. However, this is immaterial unless that system is itself immanently unstable and produces the contradiction that will overturn it. The germ of the diagnosis to this effect is seen in our identification of productive labour as a necessary ground for capital. For the further development of this side of the matter can show that confronting the 'subject' capital is another subject, the proletariat, emerging as its contradiction brought forth in the development of capital itself. To this extent it could be shown that, after all, capital cannot reach the infinite self-subsistence of Hegel's Idea, that no genuine unity in difference is achieved, and that the material and ideal sides of the economy remain estranged from one another no matter how much mediating complexes attempt to secure 'room to move' for the contradictions.

APPENDIX

The Categories of Logic and the Forms of Value

Hegel *Encyclopaedia* §18

I	Logic: the science of the Idea in and for itself
II	The Philosophy of Nature: as the science of the Idea in its otherness
III	The Philosophy of Spirit: as the Idea that returns to itself out of its otherness.

Arthur

I	Circulation: the science of Capital in its general formula
II	Production: Capital sunk into its otherness
III	Accumulation: as the unity of Circulation and Production

Hegel *Encyclopaedia* §83

Logic falls into three parts:

I	the Doctrine of Being
II	the Doctrine of Essence
III	the Doctrine of the Concept and Idea

In other words, into the Theory of Thought:

I	In its immediacy: the Concept implicit and in germ.
II	In its reflection and mediation: the being-for-self and show of the Concept.
III	In its return into itself, and its developed abiding-with-itself: the Concept in and for itself.

Arthur

The dialectic of the value form falls into three parts:

I	Commodity
II	Money
III	Capital

In other words, into the theory of exchange

I	In its immediacy: Value implicit and in germ .
II	In its reflection and mediation: 'value for-itself', the showing forth of Value.
III	In its return into itself, and its development of itself: Value in and for itself.

Hegel: *Logic*	Arthur: *Dialectic of Value Form*
I The Doctrine of *Being*	I *Commodity*
A. Quality	A. Exchangeability of commodities
B. Quantity	B. Quantity of commodities exchanged
C. Measure	C. Exchange Value of commodities
II The Doctrine of *Essence*	II *Money*
A. Ground	A. Value in itself
B. Appearance	B. Forms of Value
C. Actuality	C. Money
III The Doctrine of *Concept*	III *Capital* (General Formula)
A. The Subjective Concept	A. Price List
B. The Objective Concept	B. Metamorphoses of money and commodities
C. The Idea	C. Self-Valorisation

[1]   Marx, K. 1975 'Contribution to the Critique of Hegel's Philosophy of Law' p. 91.

[2]   Marx to Engels, 16 January, 1858: Marx, Karl and Frederick Engels, 1983, Letters 1856–59, p. 249.

[3]   Marx, K. 1976 *Capital* Volume I pp. 102–3.

[4]   For a detailed explanation see Alfred Sohn-Rethel 1978 *Intellectual and Manual Labour* (finished by 1951, not published until 1970), esp. pp. 5, 6, 23, 19–20.

[5]   Marx to Lassalle, 22 February, 1858: Marx, Karl and Frederick Engels, 1983, Letters 1856–59, p. 270.

[6]   For a development of this argument see Arthur, C. J. 2000 'From the Critique of Hegel to the Critique of Capital'.

[7]   Hegel, G. W. F. 1975 *Hegel's Logic* §50.

[8]   Marx, K. 1976 *Capital* Volume I p. 125.

[9]   For a critique of such mistakes see Chapter 2.

[10]   More particularly, it is necessary to spell out the *constitutive context* of the value form (corresponding to Hegel's 'Preliminary Notion': Hegel, G. W. F. 1975 *Hegel's Logic* §19–25).

[11]   Reuten, G. and M. Williams 1989 *Value-Form and the State.*

[12]   There is a case for arguing that the category of value springs from that of 'Nothing' rather than 'Being': see Chapter 9.

[13]   Hegel, G. W. F. 1971 *Hegel's Philosophy of Mind* §378 *Zusatz*, p. 3.

[14]   Marx, K. 1976 *Capital* Volume I p. 139.

[15]   Marx, K. 1976 *Capital* Volume I, p. 153.

[16]   Marx, K. 1976 *Capital* Volume I p. 160.

[17]   See Marx, K. 1973 *Grundrisse* pp. 204–05.

[18] Marx, K. 1976 *Capital* Volume I, p. 158.

[19] Marx, K. 1976 *Capital* Volume I, p. 256.

[20] Marx, K. 1976 *Capital* Volume I, p. 255.

[21] This point has been stressed by E. Dussel: *Towards an Unknown Marx* (2001).

[22] Marx, K. 1976 *Capital* Volume I, pp. 180–81.

[23] Marx, K. 1973 *Grundrisse*, p. 459.

[24] Marx, K. 1976 *Capital* Volume I, p. 189.

[25] Patrick Murray has made a similar point: 'In the concept of capital, that *substance* [value] reveals itself as self-activating – as *subject*.': 1988 *Marx's Theory of Scientific Knowledge,* p. 216. Cf. Hegel, G. W. F. 1975 *Hegel's Logic* §213.

[26] Marx, K. 1976 *Capital* Volume I, p. 250.

[27] Marx, K. 1976 *Capital* Volume I, p. 253. For capital as 'limitless' see Chapter 7.

[28] Marx, K. 1976 *Capital* Volume I, p. 255.

[29] Marx, K. 1976 *Capital* Volume I, p. 256.

[30] Hegel, G. W. F. 1975 *Hegel's Logic,* §164.

[31] Marx, K. 1973 *Grundrisse* p. 255.

[32] Marx, K. 1978 *Capital* Volume II, p. 185.

Chapter Six

Negation of the Negation in Marx's 'Capital'

At the end of Volume One of Marx's *Capital* there is
a brief passage on 'the historical tendency of capitalist accumulation'. The passage is remarkable in
several respects. First of all, it is the only – but crucial – place in *Capital* in which the talismanic figure
of 'negation of the negation' is openly employed.
Secondly, one paragraph in it is all he devotes in the
entire three volumes of *Capital* to characterising the
revolution against capital, and the future social order.
Both of these features give rise to conceptual puzzles. This chapter addresses the issues, in part by
bringing to bear evidence from other sources, including earlier chapters in *Capital*, Marx's *Grundrisse*, and
Engels's commentary in his *Anti-Dühring*.

My first topic here is the category of 'negation of the
negation'; this is one of Engels's famous 'three laws'
of dialectic. It is interesting that Stalin omitted it
from his essay on 'Dialectical Materialism' in the
notorious *History of the C.P.S.U (Bolsheviks): Short
Course*. Althusser considered it idealist and for this
reason aligns himself with Stalin, saying that Stalin's
'expulsion of "negation of the negation" from the
domain of Marxist dialectic might be evidence of real
theoretical perspicacity'.[1] M. Rubel, also, claims that
the mobilisation of Hegel's dialectic in *Capital* becomes
'a procedure resembling parody'.[2] Thus both 'anti-
humanist' and 'humanist' wings of French Marxism
are in agreement! Nonetheless I shall endeavour to

vindicate dialectic in general, and this figure of negation of the negation in particular, here.

The solutions offered to the puzzles mentioned above depend on a fundamental distinction between systematic and historical dialectic. Whereas the latter locates the process of double negation in a sequence of historical *stages*, the former – systematic dialectic – addresses itself to the structural relations and contradictory moments of a *given* system – in this case, capitalism.

To begin with, let us remind ourselves of our text:

> [The historical genesis of capital] in so far as it is not the direct transformation of slaves and serfs into wage-labourers, and therefore a mere change of form, . . . only means the expropriation of the immediate producers, i.e. the dissolution of private property based on the labour of its owner.
> The private property of the worker in his means of production is the foundation of small-scale industry [which in turn] is a necessary condition for the development of social production and of the free individuality of the worker himself.
>
> [This mode of production] attains its adequate classical form only where the worker is the free proprietor of the conditions of his labour, and sets them in motion himself: where the peasant owns the land he cultivates, or the artisan owns the tool with which he is an accomplished performer.
>
> [It] presupposes the fragmentation of holdings . . . so it also excludes cooperation, division of labour within each separate process of production, the social control and regulation of the forces of nature, and the free development of the productive forces of society.
>
> At a certain stage of development it brings into the world the material means of its own destruction. . . . Its annihilation, the transformation of the individualized and scattered means of production into socially concentrated means of production, the transformation, therefore, of the pygmy property of the many into the giant property of the few, and the expropriation of the great mass of the people from the soil, from the means of subsistence and from the instruments of labour . . . forms the pre-history of capital.
>
> Private property which is personally earned, i.e. which is based, as it were, on the fusing together of the isolated, independent working individual with

the conditions of his labour, is supplanted by capitalist private property, which rests on the exploitation of alien, but formally free labour.

[But with the further development of the social productive forces] the monopoly of capital becomes a fetter upon the mode of production which has flourished alongside and under it.... The centralisation of the means of production and the socialisation of labour reach a point at which they become incompatible with their capitalist integument.... The knell of capitalist private property sounds. The expropriators are expropriated.

The capitalist mode of appropriation which springs from the capitalist mode of production, produces capitalist private property. This is the first negation of individual private property as it is founded on the labour of its proprietor. But capitalist production begets, with the inexorability of a natural process, its own negation. This is the negation of the negation. It does not re-establish private property [for the producer], but it does indeed establish individual property on the basis of the achievements of the capitalist era: namely co-operation and the possession in common of the land and the means of production produced by labour itself.

The transformation of scattered private property resting on the personal labour of the individuals themselves into capitalist private property is naturally an incomparably more protracted, violent and difficult process than the transformation of capitalist private property, which in fact already rests on the carrying on of production by society, into social property.'[3]

The deployment here of the dialectical figure of 'negation of the negation' has been attacked as a piece of Hegelian nonsense designed to trick us into accepting Marx's anticipated conclusion. This was said in Marx's own day by E. Dühring. Engels defended Marx against Dühring by pointing out that Marx's results were established through impeccable empirical work and scientific theoretical concepts. Only 'after Marx has completed his proof on the basis of historical and economic facts' does he point out that the anticipated movement has the logical form of 'negation of the negation'.[4] The logic is not supposed to guarantee the result in some *a priori* fashion. Althusser holds that, if this is so, the employment of the phrase is 'purely metaphorical'.[5] This would mean that it has no real explanatory function: if the 'proof on the basis of historical and economic facts' fails, a mere logical figure cannot substitute for it; while if the facts do provide the proof then the logical figure is a 'fifth wheel', a decoration doing no work, argues S. H. Rigby.[6]

But if it can be shown that *part* of the explanation of the result is that it links back to an origin through a movement of double negation for well-founded material reasons (not just because of the 'self-movement of the Idea' in Hegel's sense), then this figure is more than metaphor or parody; if it identifies the logical complexity of the structural relations and their transformation, it is literally the *form* of the transition at the most general level, however highly mediated and contingent is the real process.

This aspect of the explanation of a real transition is limited in two ways. First, because the content (the above-mentioned 'historical and economic facts') has to be given due weight; second, because, even granting some priority to the economic in the hierarchy of determinations, there remains the essential part played by other mediations in realising, or frustrating, the immanent tendency identified here, and elucidated below.

I will also deal with another curious feature of the passage in question; namely the characterisation of socialism as restoring to the producer an 'individual property' (*das individuelle Eigentum*) which is not at the same time 'private property' (*das Privateigentum*) because rooted in 'common possession' (*das Gemeinbezitzes*), a process identical with the transformation of 'capitalist private property' into 'social property' (*gesellschaftliches Eigentum*).[7] What on earth does it mean?[8]

Here again Engels endeavoured to come to the rescue. He tried to deal with the mystery of something both individual and social by arguing that Marx 'means that social ownership extends to the land and other means of production, and individual ownership to the products, that is, the articles of consumption'.[9] If it were this simple it is a wonder that Marx failed to state it in that form. I am not content with this solution because it introduces a division between production and appropriation that is rather foreign to the spirit of Marx's thought. I suspect that the object and means of production are indeed referred to under the head of both individual and common property.

I show below that there is a connection between these two puzzles, namely the meaning of 'negation of the negation' and of 'individual property'.

The Emergence of Capitalism

To proceed: it is clear that the meaning of the second negation depends on that of the first. I have a problem with this first.

To begin with then, let us look at the so-called 'first negation'. Marx sets up as the starting point a regime of private property, where 'the worker is the free proprietor of the conditions of his labour, and sets them in motion himself', but since it precludes economic development 'it is compatible only with a system of production and a society moving within narrow limits'.[10]

Then follows a somewhat peculiar sentence in Marx's text: 'At a certain stage of its development, *it* brings into the world the material means of its own destruction' (my emphasis). If we are to believe this statement, the 'first negation' of private property is a self-negation. Marx says that *it* (that is, individual private property based on simple commodity production) destroys itself. This suggests that the original accumulation of capital grew out of the productive effort of some individuals who then persuaded others to work for them; that once we had a mode of simple commodity production, based on 'the fusing together of the isolated, independent working individual with the conditions of his labour', which developed historically into the exploitative system of capitalist commodity production.

This is somewhat inconsistent with the historical account of the emergence of capitalism Marx himself had just given.

In Part Eight on primitive accumulation Marx makes clear that it was not a matter of hard-earned property based on the proprietors' own labour, that it was rather a matter of 'conquest, enslavement, robbery, murder, in short, force' playing the greatest part.[11] The freedom of the new wage-workers to be employed was based at the same time on their deprivation of 'all the guarantees of existence afforded by the old feudal arrangements'. The process of expropriation of the peasants from the land was the main thing. It involved the seizure by proto-capitalist farmers of church lands and commons, plus the 'clearance' of all tenants and labourers. These subsistence peasants, together with ruined artisans were the basis of the new labour force. As Marx summarises the process:

> The spoilation of the Church's property, the fraudulent alienation of the
> state domains, the theft of the common lands, the usurpation of feudal and

clan property and its transformation into modern private property under the circumstances of the most ruthless terrorism, all these things were just so many idyllic methods of primitive accumulation. They conquered the field for capitalist agriculture, incorporated the soil into capital, and created for the urban industries the necessary surplus of unattached proletarians.'[12]

It should be noted that this process included a political moment; it was not merely the automatic effect of economic forces, narrowly construed. This becomes even clearer when Marx outlines 'the genesis of the industrial capitalist'. The necessary conditions for this development come together in England at the end of the seventeenth century. Marx says:

> The combination embraces the colonies, the national debt, the modern tax system, and the system of protection. But they all employ the power of the state, the concentrated and organized force of society, to hasten, as in a hothouse, the process of transformation of the feudal mode of production into the capitalist mode, and to shorten the transition. Force is the midwife of every old society pregnant with a new one. It is itself an economic power.[13]

The main lesson to be drawn from Marx's account is that capitalist agriculture and manufacture arose from the decay of feudalism, not as an outgrowth of a precapitalist mode of simple commodity production.[14] In fact, Marx himself at the start of the first quoted passage allowed that the transition concerned included 'a mere change of form' of exploitation of masses of slaves and serfs. In his *Grundrisse* Marx argues that, since the key resource of capitalism is money, its source should be looked for in merchant's and usurer's wealth.[15]

The First Negation Reconsidered

I would like to suggest at this point an alternative understanding of the dialectic of negation of individual property. This interpretation abandons the historical perspective, with its problematic of causal genesis, in favour of a structural problematic requiring an account of 'genesis' in logical terms, that is, it articulates the ground of the system's *self*-production. To do this, it is illuminating to tie the discussion of negation in the chapter on the historical destiny of capitalism back to the chapter on the transformation of surplus-value into capital.

In investigating the form of capital Marx first defines it solely in terms of the reflux of money in circulation, in which surplus-value emerges, and only later grounds this in the appropriation of surplus labour. He speaks of the circuit M – C – M' as being 'value-in-process', and of capital as an 'automatic subject'. Its identity with itself in the metamorphoses it goes through is asserted in 'the shape of money'. But this 'self-moving substance' does not merely assume the form of commodities and money, it enters into a 'relationship with itself', as it were, because it 'differentiates itself as original value from itself as surplus-value', only, when both are united in the new capital, to supersede this difference, and 'become one' again.[16]

Only after developing this definition of capital as 'self-valorising value' does he ask himself how this form can maintain itself. Then he discovers the substance of surplus-value in surplus labour consequent on the exploitation of wage-labourers. Labour-power is shown to be a peculiar commodity because it possesses the potential to create new wealth in so far as it can create more value than it itself contains. Now Marx has already stressed that commodity owners must face each other in the market place as proprietors of their commodities. Nothing is formally changed when labour-power itself becomes a commodity. The workers treat their own labour as a property alienable at will through a contract. The capitalist purchases this labour-power along with the means of production. From a juridical point of view this is an equal relationship. Buyer and seller 'contract as free persons, who are equal before the law'; 'each disposes only of what is his own'; 'and they exchange equivalent for equivalent'.[17]

However, Marx now goes more closely into the nature of the capital relation thus established, and demonstrates the dialectical inversion inherent in its (logical) development. In the beginning it appears that the capital employed is advanced from funds accumulated in some way independently of the unpaid labour of others, and that likewise the fact that free labourers are available for hire in the labour market is a happy accident. What Marx shows in the chapter on simple reproduction is that the capital relation in its action transforms these conditions of its existence into its consequences. Although the capitalist believes that he lives off profits and retains his original capital, in truth he consumed the original capital after a limited number of cycles of reproduction; the capital he throws afresh into each new cycle soon consists of nothing but the surplus-value extracted from the labourers in previous cycles therefore. Marx summarises the movement as follows:

> A division between the product of labour and labour itself, between the objective conditions of labour and subjective labour-power, was . . . the real foundation and the starting point of the process of capitalist production. But what at first was merely a starting point becomes, by means of nothing but the continuity of the process, by simple reproduction, the characteristic result. . . . Since, before he enters the process, his own labour has already been estranged from him, appropriated by the capitalist, and incorporated with capital, it now, in the course of the process, constantly objectifies itself so that it becomes a product alien to him. . . . Therefore the worker himself constantly produces objective wealth, in the form of capital, an alien power that dominates him and exploits him, and the capitalist just as constantly produces labour-power separated from its own means of realization, in short the worker as a wage-labourer.[18]

It is therefore not an accident that capitalist and worker continue to confront one another in the market as buyer and seller; for 'the process of capitalist production, seen as a total connected process, i.e. as a process of reproduction, produces not only commodities, not only surplus-value, but it also produces and reproduces the capital relation itself, on the one hand the capitalist, on the other the wage-labourer'.[19]

It is clear from this that Marx is interested in demonstrating to us that the question of the origin in time of the capitalist system is less important than the ability of the system to constitute itself as a self-reproducing totality. Capital is *self*-subsistent.

The form of this dialectic was already familiar to Marx from his reading of Hegel (and was probably something he had in mind when he formulated his cryptic remark about a rational kernel in Hegel's work). A totality of this type, organized around two poles, has the following character:

a) both poles are *essential* to each other as a matter of their very definition;
b) each produces its *opposite* through its own movement;
c) each reproduces *itself* through the mediation of its opposite;
d) the totality is constituted out of its moments, but the totality *reproduces* itself in and through its moments even when the material reduced to such

moments existed in some sense prior to the constitution of the totality (i.e. not merely prior to it in the exposition by science of its constitution).

If capitalist production presupposes, in Marx's words, 'a division between the product of labour and labour itself, between the objective conditions of labour and subjective labour-power', then this foundation of the process reproduces itself through the transformation of labour into surplus-value and into capital. Nonetheless, we seem to be committed to the original existence of a capital fund to get the process going. Whence comes this original capital? Does it arise for example, in the hands of the immediate producer as the result of their own labour?

> Where did its owner get it from? "From his own labour and that of his fore-fathers", is the unanimous answer of the spokesmen of political economy. And, in fact, their assumption appears to be the only one consonant with the laws of commodity production. (Marx)[20]

Allowing, for the moment, the truth of this claim, Marx points to consequences of capitalist reproduction that negate its effect. On the basis of the foregoing analysis of reproduction, consequent on the transformation of surplus-value into capital, Marx points to the transformation of the laws of exchange, appropriation, and property, into their opposites. It is worth quoting this remarkable passage:

> It is quite evident from this that the laws of appropriation . . ., based on the production and circulation of commodities, become changed into their direct opposite through their own internal and inexorable dialectic. The exchange of equivalents . . . is now turned round in such a way . . . that the content is the constant appropriation by the capitalist . . . of a portion of the labour of others which has been appropriated without an equivalent. . . . The relation of exchange between capitalist and worker becomes a mere semblance belonging only to the process of circulation, it becomes a mere form, which is alien to the content of the transaction itself, and merely mystifies it.'[21]

> 'To the extent that commodity production, in accordance with its own immanent laws, undergoes a further development into capitalist production, the property laws of commodity production must undergo an inversion so that they become laws of capitalist appropriation.'[22]

It is not necessary that such an 'inversion' in the material content of the relationship of private property be marked by any difference in the legal form of property of course. This continuity of legal form is actually extremely convenient for the bourgeoisie because it allows political economy to confuse 'two different kinds of private property, one of which rests in the labour of the producer himself, and the other on the exploitation of the labour of others'.[23] Hence from Locke to Ricardo the juridical notion 'is always that of petty-bourgeois ownership, while the relations of production they depict belong to the capitalist mode of production'; having justified ideologically property rights founded on labour they then under the cover of such property right 'present the advantages of the expropriation of the masses and the capitalist mode of production', comments Marx.[24]

Returning now to the question whether there is any truth in the claim that the first capital originated in its possessor's own labour, Marx answered this question in a significant fashion, we saw. This *'assumption'*, he said, *'appears [scheint]* to be the only one consonant with the laws of commodity production' (emphases added). Since we are dealing with the logic of commodity production itself the only source of an original store of value which that logic allows is thus labour. Notice that Marx says this *appears to be the case*. In other words, he is indicating that the facts are otherwise. He does not presuppose here a mode of simple commodity production giving rise out of its own development to capitalism, *historically*. The history here is a 'virtual' one. It is history as it must be written from the vantage-point of capitalism as a *given* totality retrojecting its interior moments into the past.[25] That such retrojection is both logically implicit and historically ungrounded is evident from the hypothetical nature of the language Marx uses in discussing it – for example in the following passage.

> Originally the rights of property *seemed* to us to be grounded in a man's own labour. Some such *assumption* was at least necessary, since only commodity-owners with equal rights confronted each other, and the sole means of appropriating the commodities of others was the alienation of a man's own commodities, commodities which, however, could only be produced by labour. Now, however, property turns out to be the right to appropriate the unpaid labour of others or its product, and the impossibility on the part of the worker of appropriating his own product. The separation of

property from labour thus becomes the necessary consequence of a law that *apparently* originated in their identity.'[26]

Notice the words emphasized (by me): 'seemed'; 'assumption'; 'apparently'. Marx characterises this change in the relation of labour to property as a 'dialectical inversion'[27] accomplished 'in the most exact accordance with the economic laws of commodity production and with the rights of property derived from them'.[28]

In other words this is nothing less than a 'logical' version of our 'first negation', where the original unity of labour and property is only a 'seeming' one. Notice that here the property rules are not pre-capitalist ones but those 'derived' from commodity production itself. It is the logic of *this* system that is investigated here in order to show the negation involved. The internal contradiction in the *given* system between the presupposition of equivalent exchange at the surface level of simple circulation and the expropriation of the labour of the workers at the level of production can be construed as the negating of one logic of appropriation by another.

What I am suggesting is that this negation should be understood as a 'virtual' rather than a 'real' process.[29] There is no need to prove the historical existence of a regime of simple commodity production to serve as the thesis producing its own antithesis. What we have is a totality of capitalist commodity production which posits it as an interior moment forever already sublated. That Marx speaks 'virtually' rather than historically in the passages in question refutes any interpretation of *Capital* that equates the systematic presentation of the existing totality with historical stages, as if the first chapter explicated some prior regime of simple commodity production.

If we leave aside the real history and concentrate on the *logic* of the developed relation of private property we see on the one hand a 'subjective labour-power' and on the other hand the 'objective conditions of labour' held by the non-worker. Retrojecting this into a supposed past we can describe it as the negation of an 'original' individual private property, a negation carried through on the same juridical principle of property but with an inverted content such that now wealth is accumulated at the opposite pole to labour.

The material conditions of such a logical opposition have to be brought about historically through processes no longer present (original accumulation). But the reason we have discussed just now the logical contradiction *in* the existing totality is now clear. It allows for the possibility of interpreting the first negation as transformed into an internal presupposition within the existing totality.

This is the same strategy as Marx adopts in the 1844 treatment. Althusser claims that in the shape of the 'negation of the negation' it is Hegelian dialectic which rules Marx's initial synthesis in his *1844 Manuscripts*; that they exemplify a humanist problematic in which man becomes lost to himself and then recovers himself in the reappropriation of his estranged essence; that, in and through the negation of private property, itself a negation of man, he posits himself.[30] However, in no way is this a real history. Marx's theory does not presuppose a Golden Age of unalienated existence subsequently negated. Rather, we see capitalism for the first time develops human potentialities but within a contradictory structure whereby the development of human powers occurs under the form of estrangement. It is not a matter (subsequent to the movement of double negation) of returning to an original Golden Age, but of liberating an interior moment within the capitalist totality. The positing of man for himself is the outcome, but the thesis is developed at the same time as the antithesis. The 'first' is labour; but labour already under the sign of private property, alienable as such; thus its other, private property in the means of production, is the result of alienated labour. In this private property relationship, driving towards dissolution, the proletariat, as the 'negative' party to the contradiction, negates the relationship which makes it a proletariat. The result is to reappropriate (logically), or appropriate (historically), the human powers locked up in capital. In Marx's theory of alienation the communist movement is characterised as the 'negation of the negation' of private property in virtue of the positing by labour of private property as its estranged self and then negating this negation.[31]

In what sense is such a systematic dialectical analysis of the inner contradictions of a whole explanatory of its character and destiny? Obviously if we presuppose capital already exists then we leave aside its historical genesis as a field of inquiry. What we do is to point out that it stands in a logical relation of inversion to its own logical preconditions. As capitalist commodity production it logically presupposes simple commodity circulation, yet 'inverts' 'the law of property' derivable from it, namely that the commodity must have been produced by its owner's own labour. It represents therefore the negation of the unity of the immediate producer with the object of labour. Logically therefore the negation of this negation is implied. To this extent a characterisation of communism as the negation of the negation is helpful in allowing us to conceptualise the structure and its transformation. Yet there are problems in the way Marx presents this overthrow of capitalism.

The Second Negation Reconsidered

Earlier, in our consideration of the chapter on capital's 'historical destiny' we examined the peculiar locution whereby the *first* negation, that of individual property, was presented as a self-negation generating capitalist private property. Now the very same peculiarity also arises with the *second* negation: 'capitalist production begets . . . its own negation'. This is how Marx characterises 'the expropriation of the expropriators'. It is *more* peculiar than the first negation in that the first shift was presented within a broader framework of the development of private property, whereas the second ushers in 'social property' instead, albeit restoring a kind of 'individual property'.

But why should capitalist private property negate itself?

The only gloss on this that is possible is that it does so because it involuntarily promotes 'the revolt of the working class, a class constantly increasing in numbers, and trained, united and organised by the very mechanism of the capitalist process of production'.[32] In a footnote Marx quotes the *Manifesto* on this point: 'What the bourgeoisie produces . . . are its own gravediggers'.[33]

Thus there is a considerable elision in the general dialectic presented. Capitalist property begets its own *negation* only indirectly; immediately, what it begets is its own *negator*, namely the revolutionary proletariat. This executes the sentence capitalism pronounces on itself in so far as it calls forth socially integrated productive forces that require social property for them to flourish, Marx thinks. So capitalism, through its own development, prepares the way for it own supersession in two distinct dimensions: negatively, by forcing the proletariat into revolt against it, and positively, by laying down the basis for a *determinate* negation of itself in a new social order able to benefit from capital's own bequest to it. But it is clear that such an outcome is sure to be

resisted by capital, which will do its utmost to *disorganise* and *atomise* its proletarian nemesis, the growing working class.

This contradiction complements that first one we already examined. Capital
continuously reproduces a form of commodity *circulation* that virtually implies
a certain law of appropriation while at the same time negating it in favour
of an inverted version; in the same manner capital develops a form of social
production that logically implies a new law of appropriation ('social property')
while at the same time blocking it in favour of the existing system in contradiction with it; but, in a sense, it has already *virtually* negated itself ahead
of the *historical* event. Capitalism, therefore, is structurally riven by this system of internal negations. This view of it is much more illuminating than
placing it as the middle phase of a temporal sequence.

The unfortunate thing about setting up the logic of a negation of negation in
this way is that it implies a 'return' in some sense also to individual property. As we saw earlier this is just what Marx said and it demands some discussion of his meaning to make it compatible with common property.

Pre-Capitalist Forms

Some light is shed on the meaning of individual ownership in a socialist
mode of production if we refer to Marx's discussion of pre-capitalist forms
in his *Grundrisse*, because he interprets these forms too as antithetical to private property in the capitalist sense, which dissolves all preexisting communal bonds.

Once, landed property and agriculture were basic and production was mainly
simply of use values. The reproduction of the individuals was guaranteed
(crop failure aside) by the relations of production, even if they were also
exploited. The individual appears from the beginning in unity with the conditions of labour and therefore also can be said to have a property in them.
This is in virtue of another unity, that with the other members of the community. As Marx puts it, there is 'appropriation not through labour but
presupposed to labour', that is, 'the chief objective condition of labour' is
pre-given to individuals in the rules of distribution of the communal organisation. For example, let us take the case of strip farming of common lands.
This system was often used in the feudal village. The relations of production

were governed by a system in which a strip of land was allocated to a family for their use, and these strips were rotated annually. At one level it looks like private production since each family is responsible for its own subsistence; but in fact this individual appropriation is fixed in advance by the rules of allocation of common land. The universal dominates the particular. There is no alienation of land. No accumulation of property is possible. And no one is without work. Marx says: 'The individual can never appear here in the dot-like isolation in which he appears as a mere free worker'; rather, the objective conditions of labour belong to him in so far as he is 'subjectively presupposed as a member of a community through which his relation to the soil is mediated'.[34]

In a very important definition Marx adds: 'Property thus originally means no more than man's relation to his natural conditions of production as belonging to him, as his, as *presupposed* along with his own being ... as his extended body.'[35] Strictly speaking, Marx insists, the worker does not *relate* to his conditions of production at all, as if they were independent; rather there are simply two sides of his being – the subjective, he himself – and the objective, his natural conditions of existence. It is not the unity of labour and its objective conditions which requires explanation but their separation – a separation 'which is completely posited only in the relation of wage labour and capital'.[36] In capitalism the labourer does not exist from the outset in unity with the object of labour but requires to be put in a relation with it through the contingency of 'finding work'. The so-called free worker, Marx says, is 'objectless, purely subjective, labour capacity confronting the objective conditions of production as ... *alien property*.'[37] The process is summarised in the following passage:

> The same process which ... negated their affirmative relations to the objective conditions of labour ... and thereby transformed these individuals into *free workers*, this same process freed these objective conditions of labour (land, raw material, instruments of labour, means of subsistence) from their previous attachment to the individuals. ...

> The same process which placed the mass face to face with the *objective conditions of labour* as free workers also placed these conditions, as *capital*, face to face with free workers.[38]

For individuals to regain through 'association' control over their situation is therefore not just to establish common property but to re-establish individual property in the sense described above, namely that within the framework of community the individual is guaranteed work and subsistence.

This same idea is found in Marx's defence of the Paris Commune; where he says it wanted to make individual property 'a truth':

> The Commune, they exclaim, intends to abolish property, the basis of all civilisation! Yes, gentlemen, the Commune intended to abolish that class-property which makes the labour of the many the wealth of the few. It aimed at the expropriation of the expropriators. It wanted to make individual property a truth by transforming the means of production, land and capital, now chiefly the means of enslaving and exploiting labour, into mere instruments of free and associated labour.[39]

To return to *Capital*, the above passages help clear up the puzzle that Marx chooses to define capital as the 'negation of individual private property', and to describe communism in terms of the restoration of a sort of individual property.

We see now that ownership is no longer a legal relation once private property is abolished, but carries a broader sense of appropriation to the self of the conditions of labour, in a 'real' rather than 'titular' sense, with the emphasis on the unity established between them in the immediacy conveyed by Marx's graphic phrase about nature as 'his extended body'. The appropriation of the object is 'individual' or 'personal' no longer in terms of the exclusive and antagonistic relations of private property. Rather the selfhood of the individual is affirmed socially through the concrete forms of associated production, not through the estranging mediations of private property and exchange.

To realise sociality as the principle of human relations is the only route through which the individuals reappropriate their alienated powers and capacities. This is what Marx argues in a relevant passage from his *Grundrisse*.

> With the positing of activity of individuals as immediately *social*, the objective moments of production are stripped of this form of estrangement; they are thereby posited as property, as the organic social body wherein people reproduce themselves as individuals, but as social individuals.[40]

Notice here again Marx uses 'property' in a pretty broad sense – not as a juridical notion – and that socialism transcends the opposition of individual and social.

In view of the Hegelian antecedents of the figure of 'negation' it is worth contemplating also Hegel's definition of 'individuality' (*Einzelnheit*) as the 'negative unity' of 'universality' (*Allgemeinheit*) and 'particularity' (*Besonderheit*).[41] Hegel therefore stresses that he means by the concept of 'individuality' something quite different from 'its immediacy as a single unit – as in our common idea of individuality'.[42] He means that we need a concept of something which does not result simply from a sundering of the common life of all but which freely affirms, and embodies in its own way, the life of society, complementing, rather than rebuffing, other individualities. There can be no true individuality where universal and particular fall apart and stand abstractly opposed to one another.

Thus 'making individual property a truth' has nothing to do with the exclusive rights of bourgeois legality, the particularism of so-called 'civil society'.

Having begun with 'individual property' the double negation must in some sense return to it. The real point, however, is to re-establish the unity of production and appropriation for the *social individuals*.

The Collective Worker

So far we have concentrated our discussion on the moment of individuality (whether individual property is considered as prior historically or logically), and shown in what sense there might be a 'return' of individual property. To complement this I now consider the dialectic of sociality. Historically, we have already seen, pre-capitalist social formations have a communal organisation that is dissolved in the atomism of modern civil society. The communism of the future could therefore be represented as 'the negation of the negation' in bringing about its return.

For example, Engels argues as follows:

> All civilised peoples begin with the common ownership of the land. With all peoples who have passed a certain primitive stage this common ownership becomes in the course of the development of agriculture a fetter on

production. It is abolished, negated, and after a longer or shorter series of intermediate stages is transformed into private property. But at a higher stage of agricultural development, brought about by private property in land itself, private property conversely becomes a fetter on production. . . . The demand that it too should be negated, that it should once again be transformed into common property, necessarily arises. But this demand does not mean the restoration of the aboriginal common ownership but the institution of a far higher developed form of possession in common which, so far from being a hindrance to production, on the contrary for the first time will free production from all fetters.[43]

Apart from the unjustified teleology of the productive forces implicit in this theory, what is striking is that we are presented with a historical sequence of three stages each of which 'negates' the one before it, and in a formal sense the last returns to the first. What is clear is that there is no real internal relationship between the three stages which would allow us to interpret them as moments of a self-developing totality. Rather the three stages express the linear movement of the productive forces, which happens to end where it started as far as social relations are concerned. The attribution of the dialectical categories is an empty game therefore, 'metaphorical' in Althusser's sense.[44]

However, rather than try to underpin such a perspective with some more or less doubtful teleology, I suggest that once again we should refer to the structural contradictions identified by Marx in the *present* system to ground the genesis of communism. Obviously, if we consider Marx's account of the labour-process there is no intention to return to the scale of operation characteristic of pre-capitalist forms, such things as individual subsistence farming or artisanry. Rather, we take advantage of the principle of the 'collective worker' achieved in the capitalist epoch. If we compare the collective worker of capitalism with the strip farming example, it looks more immediately social with its intricate division of labour, its co-ordination, and almost organic unity of purpose. But because this unity is established by capital, not through the voluntary combination of the workers themselves, the social power appears as the power of capital for which the fate of individuals is a matter of indifference; the individual worker is a mere replaceable part and has no guarantee of existence. 'For capital, the worker is not a condition of production, only work is. If it can make machines do it or even water, or air, so much the better.' (Marx)[45]

Marx says in the *Manifesto* that capital is 'a social power', so to socialise it is not to abolish personal property but to change its social character. It loses its class character. Having purchased labour-powers, capital as the 'subject' (Marx) of the process subsumes these labours under itself and allocates them for the purpose of accumulation. Under communism individual existence is not only mediated by the guarantee of social property but there is a real collective labour process freed from its alienated character.

In Marx's view of communism therefore, individual ownership could not be consummated in the discreteness of pre-capitalist labour processes. This is why he opposes (in his *Critique of the Gotha Programme*) the slogan of the full return to the worker of the fruits of their labour. This makes sense in pre-capitalist societies where exploitation was based on share-cropping or tithing. But it makes no sense now. He points out that with the collective worker there is simply no way of separating the fruits and matching them to contribution. If production is social then the mode of appropriation should be social (the 'social wage' in modern jargon). As Marx said in the passage quoted at the head of this paper, capitalist property 'in fact already rests on the carrying on of production by society', hence it is but a step to transform it into 'social property'.

So, once again, I find it less relevant to refer back to some supposed golden age of communal organisation; I find it more relevant to point to the increasing socialisation of the productive forces, and the increasingly complex and integrated labour processes, as the universal moment which is negated in its subordination to private property and private profit, and which to free itself, and flower for the common benefit, logically requires a second negation.

History and Structure

Let us review the historical stages one last time.

Capitalism negates individual property in that it breaks the essential unity of the producer with the conditions of production, guaranteeing an existence in accordance with the communal order, and replaces it with a contingent relation between individuals and property. The universal side, once dominant over the particulars in explicitly posited rules, is negated with the victory of movable property and the freedom of contract; but, underlying such particularisation, a new universal determinant arises, if negatively, in capital as a social power, that is, in the law of value, market cycles, and above all the restless movement of capital raising up and destroying individuals or whole communities even.

The developing accumulation process leads to concentration and centralisation of capital, and the increasing socialisation of labour. Then 'the expropriators are expropriated', and a new society is brought forth which reunifies the individuals with their means of production, and each other.

Marx's account of pre-capitalist social formations in his *Grundrisse* makes it clear that even if the feudal peasantry are small independent producers their access to their means of production is mediated by their membership of the community, and that *both* of these connections (to their means of production and to the communal guarantees) are dissolved in the process of primitive accumulation of capital. Thus the initial position, or thesis, is itself complex, containing both a particular and a universal moment. These two moments are then reconstituted through the negating movement in new forms whose contradictory unity requires supersession in a synthesis. But this cannot be just a resumption of either moment of the thesis – either a resumption of the universal moment, a restricted immediate community with no technical division of labour, – or a resumption of particularity in the simplicity of an individual labour process.

Hence, it is misleading to see the transcendence of capitalism as related back to that earlier stage. Rather, it is better to see the present articulation of capitalism as involving: a) a conceptually posited origin in the unity of labour with its conditions and product, which is now disrupted, and its poles reconstituted as an opposition between alienated labour and private property; and b) a developing sociality (the collective worker) organised by private capital, hence estranged from the individual, and requiring the individuals to appropriate their collective power so that the limits on its development imposed by the integument of private property may be transcended.

So *both* 'prior' moments (individual property and social unity) are really retrojected ones internally related through a logic of double negation to the transcending movement from capitalism to socialism; the same movement liberates both the individual, and the collective potential of the social individuals. I have given a reading of the return of 'individual property', in which the individual is taken as a 'social individual', that is consistent with the overall character of the final phase as socialist.

Conclusion

The adequacy of Marx's conceptualisation of these transitions remains to be assessed. How helpful is it to call in aid the Hegelian figure of negation of the negation?

It is noteworthy that a teleology is invoked when he says that to perpetuate individual private property – the stipulated first stage – 'would be to decree universal mediocrity';[46] *if* development is to occur, the next stage must come forth. But his appeal to the higher level of development of the next stage is not in itself any explanation of the process of transition. Furthermore, if Hegel's Absolute Spirit does not oversee the whole process, the mere existence in the past of a certain order does not in itself explain its return at the third stage of negation of the negation.

It is true to say that a birds-eye view of historical stages of development in terms of dialectical concepts does illuminate their specificities. For example, compared with pre-capitalist society, and socialism, the capitalist stage can be understood as being dominated by the moment of difference (rather than unity), or as being more contradictory.[47]

But such a comparison does not seem to be *explanatory* of the transitions.

Whatever historical perspective we use to base the movement of double negation, whether we emphasize simple commodity production or communal organisation, or some combination, the problem arises as to why this linear sequence should be more than metaphorical. What present influence on the expropriation of the expropriators can the alleged 'original condition' have? Better, then, is a reconstruction of the dialectic of individual and social within capitalism itself. Marx's dialectic refers us to a dialectic of unity and difference in which there is real dynamic potential. The 'virtual' unity at the origin, displaced by the moment of difference (with the alienation of labour from its object), is 'virtually' restored as a unity-in-difference (with the socialisation of the productive forces and the large scale organization of the immediate producers).

I believe the figure of 'negation of the negation' is explanatory insofar as it *conceptualises* both the original negative relation of a moment to itself and the other it has 'produced' (e.g. the above mentioned contradiction in a law of property based on a law of value), and the pressure for change arising out of such a contradiction as a tendency to transcend it. It might be thought that truth depends on the content, and the form in which it is conceptualised is a matter of indifference. But not all descriptions (or metaphors for that matter) are equally illuminating. Furthermore, objects differing in complexity require appropriating conceptually in logical forms of differing complexity. The movement of negation of the negation grasps a process of immanent development, *inneraction* – a more complex process than an external interaction.

None the less, what the analysis does not achieve, contrary to any self-sufficient idealist dialectic, is a complete account of this transition in actuality. For that requires more than the identification of the virtual first negation and the potential negation of this negation. It requires reference to the specificity of more concrete mediations. Especially important here is observation of the situation and character of the proletariat and its class-consciousness.

But I cannot enter now on a theory of the social formation in its complexity. The double point I want to make is that the revolution against capital *must* be understood as arising out of the contradictions in the existing property relationships without being metaphysically *guaranteed* simply by the logic of these forms. A materialist dialectic does more than notice that capital and labour are in conflict, it grounds the necessity of this struggle in a structural contradiction, but unlike idealist dialectic it does not hypostatize logic and thereby interpret a logical form as an empirical necessity.[48]

Labour and private property do not run up against one another in an external fashion: grasping them as moments of a dialectical totality, in the capital relation, Marx remarks that the destiny of the proletariat is foreshadowed in the most fundamental structure of its being – its position as 'dissolved and self-dissolving private property'[49] – and that grounds its 'expropriation of the expropriators'. If this dialectic, in itself, is underdetermining as far as the real process of transition is concerned; yet it is the fundamental to its explication.

1   Althusser, L. 1969 *For Marx*, p. 200n.
2   Rubel, M. 1981 'Plan and Method of the "Economics"' pp. 221–2.
3   Marx, K. 1976 *Capital* Volume I, pp. 927–29.
4   Engels, F. 1962 *Anti-Dühring*, p. 184.
5   Althusser, L. 1969 *For Marx*, p. 200n.
6   Rigby S. H. 1992 *Engels and the Formation of Marxism*, pp. 128–32. Engels defended dialectic also as a 'means of discovering new results' (Engels, F. 1962 *Anti-Dühring*, p. 171). Rigby attacks this as *a priori* deduction of reality; but this is unfair to the heuristic role of Engels's idea.
7   Marx, K. 1976 *Capital* Volume I, p. 929. In the first edition of *Capital* the paragraph on 'negation of the negation' (Marx, K. 1983 *Das Kapital Erster Band 1867*, pp. 609–10) does not contain the phrase 'It does not re-establish private property . . .'; thus the conclusion appears even more paradoxical. This phrase originates from the French translation (of 1872–75), and came into subsequent editions on Engels's editorial initiative (Marx, K. 1989 *Das Kapital I 1883* p. 713). In French it reads: '*Elle rétablit non la propriété privée du travailleur*' (Marx, K. 1989 *Le Capital 1872–75*, p. 679). In the English edition of Engels it reads: 'This does not re-establish private property for the producer.' (Marx, K. 1990 *Capital 1887*: p. 662)
8   It is worth drawing attention to the fact that the passage in question is little changed from original formulations of 1844. In the *Economic and Philosophic Manuscripts*, at the end of a discussion of land rent, there is a parallel ambiguity on socialism: he speaks of 'association' preserving the advantages of scale, yet at the same time it is said to realise the tendency of 'division' of the land, namely equality, and to bring forth 'personal property' (*das persönliches Eigentum*) for the producer. (Marx, K. 1975 '*Economic and Philosophic Manuscripts of 1844*', p. 268.)
9   Engels, F. 1962 *Anti-Dühring*, p. 180.
10 Marx, K. 1976 *Capital* Volume I, pp. 927–28.
11 Marx, K. 1976 *Capital* Volume I, p. 874.
12 Marx, K. 1976 *Capital* Volume I, p. 895.
13 Marx, K. 1976 *Capital* Volume I, p. 916.
14 The whole question of whether there ever existed a regime of simple commodity production, and if there was whether it obeyed any law of value, and if it did whether it originated capitalism out of itself, is controversial. I doubt all these propositions myself; see chapter 2.
15 Marx, K. 1973 *Grundrisse*, pp. 505ff.
16 Marx, K. 1976 *Capital* Volume I, pp. 255–56.
17 Marx, K. 1976 *Capital* Volume I, p. 280.
18 Marx, K. 1976 *Capital* Volume I, p. 716. Note that the language here is reminiscent of a parallel passage in his *1844 Mss*: 'The worker produces capital, capital

produces him – hence he produces himself, and man as worker, as a commodity, is the product of this entire cycle.' (Marx, K. 1975 *Economic and Philosophic Manuscripts of 1844*, p. 283.)

[19]   Marx, K. 1976 *Capital* Volume I, p. 724.

[20]   Marx, K. 1976 *Capital* Volume I, p. 728.

[21]   Marx, K. 1976 *Capital* Volume I, p. 729.

[22]   Marx, K. 1976 *Capital* Volume I, pp. 733–34. The Fowkes translation is modified here because in an excess of enthusiasm for dialectics he puts 'dialectical inversion', which is not in the German source (Marx, K. 1983 *Das Kapital Erster Band*, p. 613). Still more accurate is simply 'change into' (Marx, K. 1983 *Capital Volume One*, p. 551) following the original in the French edition (Marx, K. 1989 *Le Capital 1872–75*, p. 508; cf. also Marx, K. 1983 *Das Kapital Erster Band* 1867, p. 472 n. 23), whence this passage came into the fourth German edition (1890) on Engels's editorial initiative; oddly, it is missing from *Capital Vol. I, Marx-Engels Collected Works* Vol. 35, (see Marx, K. 1996 *Capital* Volume I, p. 583).

[23]   Marx, K. 1976 *Capital* Volume I, p. 931.

[24]   Marx, K. 1976 *Capital* Volume I, Appendix p. 1083.

[25]   'That is why all modern economists have proclaimed . . . *property in ones own labour* [to be] *the basic premiss of bourgeois society*. This premiss itself rests on the *premiss of exchange value as an economic relationship dominating the whole aggregation of relationships of production and commerce*, and so is itself a historical *product* of bourgeois society, the society of developed exchange value. On the other hand, since examination of more concrete economic relationships than those represented by simple commodity circulation seems to bring out laws contradicting [the said law of appropriation], all the classical economists . . . allow this *view, springing as it does from bourgeois society itself,* the right to be called a universal law, but banish its strict reality to the golden age when *no property* existed as yet. . . . *That would produce the strange result that the truth about bourgeois society's law of appropriation would have to be transferred to a time when this society itself did not as yet exist*, and the basic law of property to the time of propertylessness. . . . However that may be, the process of circulation, as it *appears on the surface* of society, knows no other way of appropriation, and if contradictions should arise in the progress of the examination, they must, like *this law of the original appropriation through labour, be derived from the development of exchange value itself.*' (Marx, K. 1987 'Original text of *A Contribution to a Critique . . .*' p. 463.)

[26]   Marx, K. 1976 *Capital* Volume I p. 730. Engels cites this passage against Dühring but totally misreads it as a historical transition explained by 'purely economic causes': Engels, F. 1962 *Anti-Dühring,* pp. 225–26. Moreover he does not observe the significance of Marx's hypothetical language.

27　Marx, K. 1976 *Capital* Volume I, p. 730 n. 6 (*'dialektische Umschlag'*: Marx, K. 1983 Das Kapital *Erster Band* p. 610 n. 23). Compare Marx, K. 1973 *Grundrisse* p. 458.

28　Marx, K. 1976 *Capital* Volume I, p. 731.

29　Marx himself uses the term 'virtual' in a cognate connection: 'In the United States of America the workers are as yet only virtually replaced by agricultural machinery, i.e. the machines allow the producer to cultivate a larger area, but do not actually expel any agricultural labourers employed.' Marx, K. 1976 *Capital* Volume I, p. 637.

30　Althusser, L. 1969 *For Marx*, p. 198.

31　See Arthur, C. J. 1986 *Dialectics of Labour.*

32　Marx, K. 1976 *Capital* Volume I, p. 929.

33　Marx, K. 1976 *Capital* Volume I, p. 930.

34　Marx, K. 1973 *Grundrisse*, pp. 485–86.

35　Marx, K. 1973 *Grundrisse* p. 491. Marx, K. 1981 *Ökonomische Manuskripte 1857/58*, p. 395.

36　Marx, K. 1973 *Grundrisse*, p. 489.

37　Marx, K. 1973 *Grundrisse*, p. 498. Marx, K. 1981 *Ökonomische Manuskripte 1857/58*, p. 401.

38　Marx, K. 1973 *Grundrisse*, p. 503. Marx, K. 1981 *Ökonomische Manuskripte 1857/58* p. 406.

39　*The Civil War in France*, sec. III: Marx, K. 1986 'The Civil War in France', p. 335.

40　Marx, K. 1973 *Grundrisse* p. 832; Marx, K. 1981 *Ökonomische Manuskripte 1857/58* p. 698. Marx, K. 1987 'Economic Manuscripts of 1857–58', pp. 209–10, mistranslates 'objective' (*Vergegenständlich*) as 'reified' throughout this section.

41　Hegel, G. W. F. 1991 *The Encyclopaedia Logic* §163–§165. In relation to the topic of this section we may share Marx's pleasure when he discovers the origins of these logical categories in the forms of property:

'But what would old Hegel say if he had heard in the next world that *das Allgemeine* in German and Norse [originally] means nothing but the common land, and *das Sundre, Besondre* – nothing but the separate property divided off from the common land? So the logical categories are coming damn well out of "our intercourse" after all.' (to Engels, 25 March, 1868, Marx, K. and F. Engels 1965 *Selected Correspondence*, p. 202)

42　Hegel, G. W. F. 1991 *Elements of the Philosophy of Right*, §7.

43　Engels, F. 1962 *Anti-Dühring*, p. 190.

44　A still more absurd example is given by Ben Brewster in the *Glossary* attached to the English translation of Althusser's book *For Marx*, with the latter's *imprimatur*. In the definition of 'negation of the negation' it is said: 'For Marx, it describes the fact that capitalism, having come into being by the destruction of feudalism, is itself destined to be destroyed by the rise of socialism and communism.' Certainly, just as they stand, this sequence of modes of production hardly even qualifies as 'metaphorical' double negation. Incidentally no reference to Marx is supplied.

[45]   Marx, K. 1973 *Grundrisse* p. 498.

[46]   Marx, K. 1976 *Capital* Volume I, p. 928.

[47]   For a discussion see Smith, T. 1990 *The Logic of Marx's 'Capital'*, pp. 62–64.

[48]   Still less does it, 'like Hegel', find the negation of the negation 'everywhere' (Marx, K. and F. Engels 1976 *The German Ideology,* p. 305).

[49]   Marx, K. and F. Engels 1975 'The Holy Family', p. 36.

Chapter Seven

The Infinity of Capital

It is a running theme of this book that interesting, and illuminating, connections may be drawn between Marx's *Capital* and aspects of Hegel's idealist philosophy, because capital itself is a very peculiar object, requiring conceptualisation in forms analogous to those of Hegel's 'Idea'. In this chapter I shall address the concept of capital mainly in so far as Hegel's two concepts of the infinite throw light on it. Hegel distinguished between 'the spurious infinite' and 'the true infinite'. Only the 'true' infinite secures for beings their autonomy; conversely, concepts of the infinite that fail to comprehend it adequately cannot grasp reality.

The Movement of Capital

The key passage from Marx's chapter on 'The General Formula for Capital' on which I wish to comment is the following:

> The repetition or renewal of the act of selling in order to buy finds its measure [*Mass*] and its goal in a final purpose which lies outside it, namely consumption, the satisfaction of definite needs. But in buying in order to sell, on the contrary, the end and the beginning are the same, money or exchange-value, and this very fact makes the movement an endless one. Certainly

100 pounds sterling become 110. But, considered qualitatively, the 100 is the same as the 110, namely money; while from the quantitative point of view, the 110 is, like the 100, a sum of definite and limited [*beschraenkte*] value. . . . The value of the 110 has the same need for valorization as the value of the 100, for they are both limited expressions of exchange-value, and therefore both have the same vocation, to approach as near as possible to absolute wealth. . . . The simple circulation of commodities – selling in order to buy – is a means to a final goal which lies outside circulation, namely the appropriation of use-values, the satisfaction of needs. As against this, the circulation of money as capital is an end in itself, for the valorization of value takes place only within this constantly renewed movement. The movement of capital is therefore limitless [*masslos*].'[1]

In this passage quoted from Marx several terms reminiscent of Hegelian categories are employed.[2] Of great importance is Marx's statement that 'the movement of capital is limitless'. The term here translated 'limitless' (*masslos*) is a category of Hegel's logic, usually translated 'measureless'.[3] Hence the reference back in the Marx quotation above is not to 'limited' but to 'measure' in the first sentence.[4] The 'measureless' is linked to the notion of 'infinite progression',[5] treated earlier in the *Logic* under the head of 'spurious [*schlechte*] infinity'.[6] Hegel there says that 'this infinite progression is not the genuine infinite, which consists rather in remaining at home with itself in its other, or (when it is expressed as a progress) in coming to itself in its other.'[7]

Hegel introduces first the incontestable notion that 'something only is what it is *within* its limit and by *virtue* of its limit', by which he explains he means qualitative limit.[8] The argument proceeds by developing the 'dialectical' consequence that there is 'something else' beyond the limit, and that 'everything finite is subject to alteration'. It is here that the infinite is evolved as a category: 'Something becomes an other, but the other is itself a something, so it likewise becomes an other, and so on *ad infinitum*.' This is, of course, the 'bad infinite', which needs to be superseded. This occurs when something and other are grasped as phases of the same thing 'and this relation to itself . . . in the other is *genuine infinity*', says Hegel. Thereby the category of *Being-for-Itself* is developed.[9]

When Marx stresses that accumulation is achieved 'by means of throwing money again and again into circulation'[10] he appends an interesting quotation from Galiani's book on money: 'Things possess an infinite quality when moving in a circle which they lack when advancing in a straight line.'[11] While from a mathematical point of view a straight line may be infinitely long, Galiani intends us to note that at any given moment in the advance the line has a definite start and finish: the circular path by contrast, once having been established (like a planetary orbit), has no beginning and no end, even though it *has* a length.

While Marx deliberately chose another economist to lend authority to his argument that the movement of capital accumulation is circular and infinite, he would have done equally well here to have cited Hegel; for as we have seen the latter has very interesting things to say about 'infinity', which apply very well to capital. Hegel also uses the metaphor we have just come across: 'Infinity has rightly been represented by the image of the circle, because a straight line runs on indefinitely and denotes that merely negative and false infinity which, unlike true infinity, does not return to itself.'[12] Hegel's analysis of unilinear progress is quite subtle; it is both finite (at any given time) and infinite (in tendency) for there is always something beyond the finite. Hence in this alternation it never attains completion. But the circle has no beyond because the movement stays within a set of points defined by it. It is complete in itself. So the movement always returns to itself and abides with itself.[13]

It hardly needs pointing out that in the circuit M – C – M (M = money; C = commodities) money *does* relate itself to itself. But Marx also pointed out here that the movement of capital is constantly renewed because the aim in question, namely valorisation, is open-ended; there is no possibility of reaching a conclusion, for at every stage there remains the possibility – indeed the necessity – to go further, while at every stage there is an infinite distance still to travel.

So both Hegelian concepts of infinity are relevant to Marx's discussion. Let us explore them in turn.

The True Infinite

Capital, as self-related, appears in one way under the head of the genuine infinite. We saw in the passage quoted from 'The General Formula for Capital' chapter of Volume One that the renewal of investment on the basis of the return achieved in the previous cycle presented us with a circular development. At that stage of Marx's exposition this was *purely formular* and the possibility of accumulation likewise merely a formal potential. However by the end of the first volume Marx has grounded this movement of accumulation in production, and the exploitation of labour; thus by the start of the second volume we have a concept of capital that does not merely cover its form but which grasps a wealth of content and founds itself on the permanent movement of valorisation.

The circular quality of this process is beautifully developed by Marx in *Capital* Volume Two under the head of 'The Metamorphoses of Capital and their Circuit'. Capital in its own process achieves the positing of such elements as money and commodities as abstract moments of itself and produces itself by supervening upon them in its circuit through them. With regard to the total process of the capital circuit (wherein money capital purchases factors of production which, used as productive capital, give rise to saleable commodities and thus restore the money form again) Marx gives the following summary: 'Money capital, commodity capital and productive capital . . . are simply particular functional forms of industrial capital, different forms with which capital clothes itself in its different stages, alternately assuming them and casting them aside'.[14] Notice the importance of the metaphor of 'clothing' here. It indicates the conceptual character of capital as something that cannot be immediately identified with *any* of its forms of appearance. It is rather their unity, a process going on through their connection in a circuit of *transformation* of capital.

Marx sums up the nature of the circuit thus: 'All premises of the process appear as its result, as premises produced by the process itself. Each moment appears as a point of departure, of transit, and of return.'[15] All moments are purely internally related figures of a given whole of self-positing capital which unifies its own phases and exists in their unity.[16] Hence capital 'can only be grasped as a movement and not as a static thing'.[17] At each stage of the process, in going beyond itself, a given shape of capital is only returning to another of its shapes, and since the whole movement forms a circuit it remains always itself as it traverses every stage in its round; thus capital in its movement attains genuine infinity; its circuit allows it to remain always within its own terms of existence, its divisions are internal moments, its relations are only to other parts of itself, hence its advance is not to something beyond itself but only into itself, bringing forth from itself all its potentialities and displaying them to itself. Capital thus develops a wealth of content for itself, new products, new productive forces, and so forth. Marx even speaks in this context of capital's 'civilising mission'.[18]

Capital may be seen as the avatar of Hegel's absolute concept, described in the *Phenomenology of Spirit* as follows: the absolute concept as infinity is the 'absolute unrest of pure self-movement';[19] as such it is 'the soul of the world, the universal life-blood which courses everywhere, neither disturbed nor checked by any distinction that presents itself, but itself every distinction that arises as also their supersession'.[20]

The False Infinite

Let us now turn to the relevance of Hegel's 'false infinite'. All this wealth of content just mentioned is incidental to the only purpose capital is capable of recognising according to its concept of itself, namely the accumulation of value, a one-dimensional purely quantitative measure of its achievement which negates all content. If capital is to actualise itself as Being-for-Itself in the M – C – M circuit then, in furthering itself through these phases, it must become different from itself in this its own otherness as well as identifying itself in it. In the case of money as a pure quantity the only possible difference between two instantiations of this universal is in amount. (Conversely there would be no purpose in capital risking itself in circulation in order to return to itself unchanged.) Alteration is the superseding of limit, which here must mean a limited amount. Thus, simply to be itself capital must become ever larger.[21]

In every measure of itself it finds only its existing limit, which, under the imperative of valorisation, is a restriction to be superseded. Marx argued in his *Grundrisse* as follows: hooked on the general form of wealth (money), capital has an unrestrained and limitless urge ('*schranken- und masslose Trieb*') to go beyond its bounds ('*Schranke*'); every limit ('*Grenze*') necessarily appears as a barrier ('*Schranke*') for it to pass.[22] Capital is so structured that its truth lies not within itself but always beyond itself – a case of Hegel's bad infinite.

Locked into this treadmill of accumulation, capital does not value its activity and its product in any other terms than those of convertible currency.[23] Since what it creates is qualitatively identical with the original investment, the difference, Marx argued, 'counts for nothing', the surplus-value coalesces with the original investment into a 'simple presupposition' of a repetition of the same movement.[24] From this point of view capital must embark on an infinite progression of reinvestment of its earnings. 'In M – C – M the very form of the movement implies that . . . the end of the movement already contains the principle of its resumption. For . . . since the result and the starting-point are qualitatively the same, being a sum of money, self-valorisation remains as much a necessary activity for the money which emerges from the process as for the money which started it off.'[25] What was a good reason for the original investment of £100 is a good reason for reinvesting the valorised capital of £110.[26] It is reminiscent of compulsive neurotic behaviour, for example of repeated washing of hands.

The Measurelessness of Money

Thus far the discussion has assumed a definition of capital as self-valorising value. However I would like now to address the claim (implicit in the passages from *Capital* and *Grundrisse* discussed) that there is something about the concept of money that ineluctably leads to the 'vocation' of capital to embark on infinite expansion. This issue is addressed in Marx's *Grundrisse*; we shall come to it shortly. It is worth noting at the outset that the money spoken of in the *Grundrisse* passage is 'money as capital' or money in 'motion'.[27] However, it is useful to return to the origin of money as measure of the value of commodities and to dispose of the idea that money is merely a *numéraire*, no different in essence from a commodity. Close attention to what Marx says about the form of value shows that such an interpretation is quite wrong, for the *practical* effectivity of money as the representation of value is what grants commodities a value form in the first place. It is indeed precisely this idea of the *constitution* of value in money, which is thereby granted 'immediate exchangeability', that sets off Marx's theory of money from both classical and neo-classical theories, for which money merely 'veils' the 'true' relations, whether of utilities or labours.

A *numéraire* is merely a typical *example* of a range of objects with a *given* quality selected to serve as a standard of comparison. Thus all objects possessing the quality of length may be compared with the standard metre kept in Paris or with copies thereof. Those who think of gold as a *numéraire* assume that commodities are given as values and that one of them, a pound of gold, is taken as such an exemplar of value to serve as a common standard of worth. However, Marx's derivation of money in chapter one of *Capital* is not of this kind; he argues that since value is *constituted* only in the relations of commodities (they are not values, merely use values, in isolation) only with money as their universal equivalent is an adequate expression of value given; in other words a commodity does not 'have' value as a *given* property as it might have a given length. Any analogy between value and length is thus illegitimate.[28]

According to Marx's theory of value form it is not the case that all commodities including the money commodity adequately instantiate the concept of value. It is a peculiarity of the value form that, since value is not inherent in an isolated commodity but is constituted only in exchange relations, the moments of its concept are, as it were, 'distributed': Marx notes that money is its universality and the commodities its particularity.[29] Notice that 'money' is necessarily *singular* (indicating that it is an undifferentiated mass of *value*) and appears only as amount, thus giving sense to the circuit M – C – M', if M' is a larger amount of money than M; on the other hand 'commodities' are necessarily *plural* (hence being different *values*); and also qualitatively different goods, thus giving sense to the circuit C – M – C', where C and C' are different commodities.

The moment of measure is also distributed. The worth of commodities is measured in money but money itself has no price, it *is* price. One can ask how much money a thing is worth but one cannot ask how much £3 is worth. The last is not meaningful in a much more radical sense than the judgment that a metre rule is one metre long. For money is not a *numéraire*, a commodity selected from others to serve as their *representative*. Rather it is only insofar as money is *the representation of value* that commodities become posited as values in their relationship to it. This relative priority of money over commodities obtains even if money is a commodity evolved from others to serve this special function (as gold was for example). Established as the universal moment of the concept of value money has a quality (immediate exchange-ability) denied to the commodities as particular manifestations of value. This is why – even if it is 'commodity-money' – it is not really 'representative' of them, any more than a monarch is representative of his subjects, albeit 'only human'.

Money as value for itself has a quality that makes it distinct from commodities; it is their general equivalent, but a finite amount of money would itself be merely a particularisation of the general concept, whereas the purely general cannot be further determined, not even by a magnitude. The purely general is then a 'measurelessness'.[30] Hegel pointed out that everything is defined by its limit; but money has no quantitative limit in its character as the value 'substance'. In it quality and quantity are indifferent to one another. Thus it is exempt from the general principle that quantity turns into quality.[31] There is no transition from quantity to quality since money is formed in opposition to the qualitative heterogeneity of commodities to function *purely quantitatively*. Metal is thus its appropriate incarnation: 'A peculiar feature of metals is that in them alone all relations are reduced to a single one, namely their quantity, for they have not been endowed by nature with any difference of quality either in their internal composition or in their external form and structure.'[32]

In examining the merits of Marx's argument in the *Grundrisse* it is also necessary to look carefully at the different functions money performs. We have discussed the function of money as constituting a value dimension inhabited by commodities; we have shown that money is their measure just in so far as it constitutes their value form. Now this very opposition between money and commodities is further developed when Marx introduces 'money as such', as the *general* form of wealth, which it is only by a thoroughgoing abstraction from any *particular* form of wealth, notably that of commodities. Money as such Marx explains in the *Grundrisse* as follows: 'With money, general wealth is not only a form, but at the same time the content itself. The concept of wealth, so to speak, is realised, individualised in a particular object.'[33] In other places similar formulations occur as follows. In *Capital* he characterises money as 'the only adequate *form of existence*' of value, for commodities exist primarily as use values.[34] It is 'the universal representative of material wealth',[35] 'the independent presence of exchange value, the universal commodity'.[36] In its bodily presence, e.g. gold, money's 'mode of existence becomes adequate to its concept';[37] it is 'value for itself';[38] 'gold is the material existence [*Dasein*] of abstract wealth in contradistinction to commodities which represent only . . . separate facets of wealth'; 'it is universal wealth in an individual form'.[39]

The notion of money as 'measurelessness' arises only then, but *not* when it functions in other ways which can easily be seen to require only finite amounts. Thus when money functions as the circulating medium in C – M – C the amount required is set by the needs of circulation and is thereby limited. However, a contradiction emerges in that to function as measure of value of commodities it must descend from the 'measurelessness' of the general concept of wealth to measure particular amounts of it, namely commodities. Yet *as* a particular amount it becomes reduced to an instance of itself and hardly distinguishable from a *numéraire*, being now simply the determinate equivalent of a definite value body. As Marx says, money is distinguished from commodities in expressing value 'more perfectly'; but when serving as a medium of their circulation it sinks to their level, as it were, its 'intrinsic quality' of value is obscured and it 'becomes mere use value, although admittedly use value for determining the prices etc. of commodities'.[40] Only in the form of capital accumulation does it escape the circumscription of this finitude. But thereby, as was argued above, capital tumbles into the free fall of the 'bad' infinity.

Marx argues that, in the sense of *money as such*, a limited amount of it contradicts its essential character of generality. He says that the fact that in reality money always appears in definite amounts 'contradicts' its essence as 'measurelessness'.[41] Now this is a purely conceptual point about its form. This essence does not in itself ground the drive of accumulation; but it prefigures the form this will take. For it prepares the way, so to speak, for a further more complex form, namely capital, in which there is an inherent drive for expansion. As the 'general concept' of wealth, money as capital 'preserves itself only by constantly driving beyond its quantitative barrier, which contradicts its . . . form'.[42] Money is not by definition expansionary, but its characterisation as limitless means that when, with capital, it is set as the aim of circulation then the 'vocation' of money as capital can only be to accumulate more.

It is only when money is set as the aim of the capital circuit that we see that the necessity arises for an endless drive to accumulate 'wealth'. But there is an instance of such an aim being set at a less developed level in the case of the miser. Although under no *objective* compulsion to hoard the miser is so enamoured of the concept of money as the general form of wealth that he makes it his subjective aim. In *Capital* Marx introduces this theme in the last part of his chapter on money:

> The hoarding drive is boundless in its nature. Qualitatively or formally considered, money is independent of all limits, that is it is the universal representative of material wealth because it is directly convertible into any other commodity. But at the same time every actual sum of money is limited in amount, and therefore has only a limited efficacy as a means of purchase. This contradiction between the quantitative limitation and the qualitative lack of limitation of money keeps driving the hoarder back to his Sisyphean task: accumulation. He is in the same situation as a world conqueror, who discovers a new boundary with each country he annexes.[43]

One way of looking at the problem of the 'bad' infinity is to bring to bear again the dialectic of quality and quantity. When Marx says of capital that it attempts to approach 'absolute wealth' by incremental addition, it seems 'wealth' is a qualitative concept and the question is at what point does the capitalist form of wealth emerge from less adequate resources. Normally quantity turns into quality as when we gain a full glass of water drop by drop (and it makes sense in the process to speak of getting closer to the goal). But capital is a bottomless sink of value and always demands more. There is no realisation of absolute wealth no matter how much capital is accumulated. No actual amount is any closer to it than any other, lesser, amount. No accumulation of money is ever 'wealth as such' even though that is the very concept of money. Its everyday existence contradicts its essence; and the resolution, such as it is, can only be an endless striving to actualise its concept. Money is really value for itself only when functioning as the aim of the capital circuit. A fixed sum is always a collapse to use value, as indeed is the miser's hoard of gold; apart from circulation it is just a metal dump. As Marx observed, the superiority of the capitalist over the miser is that he accumulates by throwing his money again and again into circulation.[44] This iteration is absolutely necessary if the movement of M – C – M' is to actualise value-for-itself, the truly infinite, as against the finitude of the world of commodities.[45] Capital, in a word, is money in motion; and only thereby is money preserved *as value* distinct from its bodily form as a use value.

Capital's measure of success cannot be a fixed amount, no matter how large. To freeze its motion, to fix it, is to render it lifeless. Does this mean capital as a spiral of accumulation has no measure of itself at all? By no means. Hegel makes clear that something which is measureless from one point of view can yet have a new kind of measure;[46] thus when water becomes steam it is not measurable as a saucepan-full but it may now have a new dimension such as the pressure in a boiler. Money appears in a new form when *referred to itself* in the capital circuit, and this gives a clue to its appropriate measure; in the circuit $M - C - M'$ capital measures itself against itself through the moment at which its abstract identity with itself is explicitly posited, namely money; but it is inherent to the concept of capital that the increase there registered serves only as a presupposition of further expansion; mere increase is therefore sublated, the true measure is the *rate* of accumulation. That is the measure that is appropriate to the quality of quantitative expansion.

While the concept of money as measureless means no amount of incremental increase gets any nearer to absolute wealth, one can yet look at the *rate* of increase, just as velocity (length traversed every minute) is different from length itself. The true measure of success of the valorisation process is not the absolute amount of surplus gained in a circuit[47] nor even the ratio of gain to investment, the true measure of money in motion is the gain *per annum*. If one draws a graph with time as the horizontal axis and accumulation as the vertical axis it only takes a moment's inspection to see that initial amounts of capital have no bearing on success because the capital with the highest rate of return *per annum* (graphically the one with the steepest slope) will eventually overtake all others. Furthermore, mathematically, while it it perfectly true that no capital is getting any closer to infinity it makes sense to say that one is getting there *faster* and is hence most in conformity with the concept of capital as the drive for absolute wealth.

In the real world the rate of profit is always so specified, namely as an annual rate such as ten per cent per year (or with loans a rate per month or per day). Capital is the movement between two instances of itself, M and M'; the *relation* of these is an immanent measure of growth; this is its own proper measure which allows different capitals to be meaningfully compared, whereas to compare externally one capital sum with another is to reduce wealth to the level of use value, *stocks* of gold. Money as capital *flows* and the rate of return is what expresses its success.

But the conceptual space for this self-expansion won here requires the presence of further conditions of existence to allow the material possibility of accumulation: the forms cannot realise their logical potential unless materially supported (there is no surplus-value without the exploitation of labour). However, the form-determination of capital as inherently self-expanding makes capitalism utterly different from any other mode of production. This drive is the infinitising of capital.

Conclusion

The truly infinite character of capital is that it returns to itself in its circuit, and the spurious infinity of capital is that it is embarked on the escalator of accumulation and cannot get off. These two aspects combine in the image of a 'spiral': this is how Marx characterises the movement of capital in the *Grundrisse*.[48] Mathematically a spiral is indeed simply the synthesis of a circular movement in the horizontal plane and a straight line in the vertical plane. In the M – C – M' movement capital returns to itself in money form but of course as *more* money; the second M incorporates an increment. Without such an increment capital would be 'going round in circles' as it were; and even if in its productive phase it effected some useful transformation of materials into goods the point of this could only be the augmentation of material wealth not of *values*. As Marx puts it: 'If it ever perceived a certain boundary not as a barrier, but becomes comfortable within it as a boundary, it would have declined from exchange value to use value, from the general form of wealth to a specific, substantial mode of the same.'[49] This would therefore be completely contrary to the concept of capital as self-valorising value; it would be a kind of running on the spot, not *getting* anywhere. So in the value form the good and bad infinities get all mixed up; because here we have a Being-for-Itself furthering itself through its own otherness; but whose peculiar essence is to be pure abstraction of quality (use value), namely quantity (value); hence the movement is limitless, it must always go on, for its return to itself always fails to close with itself because its very essence is boundlessness. Marx says: 'Capital as such creates a specific surplus-value because it cannot create an infinite one all at once; but it is the constant movement to create more of the same.'[50] So a particular capital never measures up to its concept and is compelled to throw itself into ever more twists of the spiral of accumulation.[51]

Apologists for capitalism argue that just as Greek culture was built on slavery so Western civilisation was only possible under the spur of the drive for valorisation. Marx agrees here with regard to the past, granting that the improvements in productivity, and the creation of an 'industrious' spirit,[52] were premised on the compulsive quest for accumulation. But he argues that with regard to the future the acquisitions of the past may be freed from capital's one-dimensional criterion. Now the social synthesis provided by the alien mediator (money) can be superseded, and 'socialised humanity' develop itself in freedom, knowing itself to be an end-in-itself, not content to remain what it already is, but being always 'in the absolute movement of becoming', as Marx puts it in his *Grundrisse*.[53] And what is this but the genuine infinity?

The lesson of this study is that to understand the concept of capital both of Hegel's concepts of the infinite (the true and the spurious) need to be drawn upon. Capital in its circuit is self-referring and relates itself to itself – the true infinite – but at the same time its spiral of development is in the service of purely incremental advances in amount. It can only develop as more of the same. In coming to itself as valorised value it achieves only an abstract identity with itself as a form, the developed wealth of content being degraded to its mere bearer. The liberation of the content may be achieved for us by throwing off this its bourgeois form.

It is probably true to say that Marx's arguments are not as clear as they might be. But, in the view of this writer, the solution is not to de-Hegelianize Marx, but to take seriously Marx's hint in the second edition of *Capital*, and to refer on all points of form to Hegel's logic.

---

[1] Marx, K. 1976 *Capital* Volume I, p. 252, p. 253.

[2] E.g. measure, limit, limitless, and infinite: Hegel uses two terms: '*Grenze*', which may be translated 'limit', and the stronger '*Schranke*', which Miller – in the *Science of Logic* – translates as 'limitation', and Garaets et al. – in the new translation of *The Encyclopaedia Logic* – as 'restriction'.

³ Hegel, G. W. F. 1991 *The Encyclopaedia Logic*, §109.

⁴ If one followed Engels' English edition and said the first process 'is kept within bounds by the very object it aims at' (Marx, K. 1996 *Capital* Vol. I p. 162), then the contrast could be put by saying the second movement is boundless.

⁵ Hegel, G. W. F. 1991 *The Encyclopaedia Logic*, §109.

⁶ Hegel, G. W. F. 1991 *The Encyclopaedia Logic*, §94 & §95; see also Hegel, G. W. F. 1969 *The Science of Logic*, pp. 139ff.

⁷ Hegel, G. W. F. 1991 *The Encyclopaedia Logic*, §94 Addition. This distinction between the bad and the true infinite is widely deployed by Hegel in more concrete contexts. It turns up in his political philosophy in which genuine infinity is said to characterise the free will (Hegel, G. W. F. 1991 *Elements of the Philosophy of Right*, §22). Gary K. Browning has covered much of the relevant material in his *Hegel and the History of Political Philosophy*, 1999.

⁸ Hegel, G. W. F. 1991 *The Encyclopaedia Logic*, §92 Addition.

⁹ Hegel, G. W. F. 1991 *The Encyclopaedia Logic*, §95.

¹⁰ Marx, K. 1976 *Capital* Volume I, p. 255.

¹¹ *'Questo infinito che le cose non hanno in progresso, hanna in giro.'* When Marx first came across it he referred to it as 'a beautiful statement by Galiani': Marx, K. 1973 *Grundrisse*, p. 847.

¹² Hegel, G. W. F. 1991 *Elements of the Philosophy of Right* Addition to paragraph 22.

¹³ The image of the 'spurious infinite' (*Schlecht-Unendliche*) is 'the *straight* line; the image of true infinity, bent back into itself, becomes the *circle*, the line which has reached itself, which is closed and wholly present.' (Hegel, G. W. F. 1969 *Science of Logic* p. 149). Note that '*schlecht*' can also mean in dialect 'straight'; so there may be a pun here.

¹⁴ Marx, K. 1978 *Capital* Volume II, p. 109.

¹⁵ Marx, K. 1978 *Capital* Volume II, p. 180.

¹⁶ Marx, K. 1978 *Capital* Volume II, p. 161. For more on this see my 1998 'The Fluidity of Capital and the Logic of the Concept'.

¹⁷ Marx, K. 1978 *Capital* Volume II, p. 185.

¹⁸ Marx, K. 1978 *Capital* Volume II, p. 958; Marx, K. 1973 *Grundrisse*, pp. 408–10.

¹⁹ Hegel, G. W. F. 1949 *Phenomenology of Mind*, p. 209; Hegel, G. W. F. 1977 *Phenomenology of Spirit*, p. 101.

²⁰ Hegel, G. W. F. 1949 *Phenomenology of Mind*, p. 208; Hegel, G. W. F. 1977 *Phenomenology of Spirit*, p. 100.

²¹ Marx, K. 1973 *Grundrisse*, p. 270.

²² Marx, K. 1976 *Ökonomische Manuskripte 1857/58*, p. 249; Marx, K. 1973 *Grundrisse*, p. 334. Compare Hegel's categories of '*Die Schranke und das Sollen*' in Hegel, G. W. F. 1969 *Science of Logic* pp. 131–33.

23 Interest in the boundlessness of money-making goes back to the Greeks of course, as Marx acknowledges, quoting Aristotle on the subject (Marx, K. 1976 *Capital* Volume I, pp. 253–54). Aristotle thought that C-M-C was inherently limited but that the M-C-M circuit, being limitless, was an unnatural perversion of it. Fowkes (Marx, K. 1976 *Capital* Volume I, p. 254n.) queries Marx's translation of Aristotle basing himself on the absurd supposition that the standard English translation of the *Politics* by Jowett is more exact than Marx. Contrary to Fowkes's insinuation, Marx did not impose such terms as 'economics' (*Oekonomie*) and 'chrematistics' on the Greek, for these terms are simply transliterations of Greek words; Jowett (who believed in free translation) resorted to paraphrase of them in order to bring out their supposed sense. In any case '*Oekonomie*' in German (as in Greek) covers also domestic economy so Marx's rendering is in fact not far from Jowett's (while 'economics' in the modern English sense would in German be '*Nationaloekonomie*'). But it *is* interesting that Marx gave these renderings – and the purely English 'circulation' – in opposition to the standard German translation of the day, which was Jowett-like; see the comparative passages in Marx, K. 1990 *Capital 1887*, pp. 817–19.

24 Marx, K. 1973 *Grundrisse* p. 335.

25 Marx, K. 1988 'Economic Manuscript of 1861–63', p. 19.

26 Marx, K. 1976 *Capital* Volume I, pp. 252–53.

27 Marx, K. 1973 *Grundrisse*, pp. 269–70.

28 The analogy is deployed in criticism of Marx by John Mepham in 'From the Grundrisse to Capital' 1979: p. 166. An interesting disanalogy is that if we are talking of a material object then it could not grow forever without passing beyond its proper limits; for example, because the bulk of the body expands at the power of the cube, and the cross-section of the leg to the power of the square, there is a limit to human giantism beyond which the weight is not self-supporting. But, as we already observed, amounts of money are limitless.

29 Marx, K. 1976 *Capital* Volume I, p. 255.

30 Marx, K. 1973 *Grundrisse*, p. 271.

31 But to be a capitalist distinct from a small investor requires a minimum sum (Marx, K. 1976 *Capital* Volume I, pp. 422–23).

32 Galiani, *Della Moneta*, quoted by Marx: 1987 'Original text of *A Contribution to a Critique . . .*' p. 456.

33 Marx, K. 1973 *Grundrisse*, p. 218.

34 Marx, K. 1976 *Capital* Volume I, p. 227.

35 Marx, K. 1976 *Capital* Volume I, p. 230.

36 Marx, K. 1976 *Capital* Volume I, p. 235.

37 Marx, K. 1976 *Capital* Volume I, p. 241.

[38] Marx, K. 1987 'Original text of *A Contribution to a Critique . . .* ' p. 441.

[39] Marx, K. 1987 *A Contribution to the Critique of Political Economy*, p. 359.

[40] Marx, K. 1973 *Grundrisse*, p. 268.

[41] Marx, K. 1973 *Grundrisse*, p. 270.

[42] Marx, K. 1973 *Grundrisse*, pp. 270–71.

[43] Marx, K. 1976 *Capital* Volume I, pp. 230–31.

[44] Marx, K. 1976 *Capital* Volume I, pp. 254–55.

[45] For example, a single circuit, M – C – M', could only be undertaken as a purely speculative exploit, in which a particular conjuncture makes contingently possible a large profit on which the speculator could retire. (See Veblen's *Theory of the Leisure Class* on the distinction between an exploit and regular work.) The object of his endeavour is in effect still C not M, the latter functioning merely as an intermediary agent. However, 'capital personified' seeks to secure a regular predictable return, and in principle would abhor wasting its substance on riotous living or embarking on incalculable risks. (Weber's *The Protestant Ethic and the Spirit of Capitalism* treated at length the distinction between 'the spirit of capitalism' and pre-capitalist forms of wealth getting and spending.)

[46] Hegel, G. W. F. 1969 *Science of Logic*, p. 371.

[47] This is only relevant if one is thinking of 'cashing in' one's gains in order to purchase use values.

[48] Marx, K. 1973 *Grundrisse*, p. 266; p. 620.

[49] Marx, K. 1973 *Grundrisse*, p. 334.

[50] Marx, K. 1973 *Grundrisse*, p. 334.

[51] Incidentally, this means that for Marx accumulation is not explained primarily by the pressure of competition; this merely ensures individual capitalists are forced to conform to the concept of capital, in effect to be capital personified. (Marx, K. 1976 *Capital* Volume I, p. 433; Marx, K. 1973 *Grundrisse*, p. 335; pp. 649–52.)

[52] Marx, K. 1973 *Grundrisse*, p. 325.

[53] Marx, K. 1986 'Economic Manuscripts of 1857–58', p. 412.

Chapter Eight

The Spectre of Capital

This chapter is rooted in Marx's insight into the 'meta-physical' character of capitalist commodity production. Throughout the first chapter of *Capital* there are references to 'ghostly objectivity'; 'sensuous super-sensuousness'; 'mysteriousness'; 'turns into its opposite'; 'stands on its head'; 'metaphysical subtleties and theological niceties'; 'fantastic'; 'absurd'; and so on. This language I take to be much more than rhetoric. Many have complained that Marx's concept of 'value' is metaphysical. They have not seen that Marx himself said this, but saw it as a feature of reality. Such a 'metaphysical theory of value' is what I aim to vindicate. Capitalism is marked by the subjection of the material process of production and circulation to the ghostly objectivity of value. Our title, and text, flirt with the language of Jacques Derrida's commentary on this aspect of Marx's work.[1]

We will argue that there is a void at the heart of capitalism. It arises because of the nature of commodity exchange, which abstracts from, or absents, the entire substance of use value. What is constituted therewith is a form of unity of commodities that does not rest on any pre-given common content – which does not exist, it will be argued. The historical specificity of capitalism is that an 'ontological inversion' occurs whereby (exchange) 'value', immediately just the negation of use value, gains self-presence, real 'Being', albeit that of an empty 'Presence'. Thus value emerges from the void as a 'spectre' that *haunts* the 'real world' of capitalist commodity production. This original *displacement* of the material process of production and circulation by the ghostly objectivity of value, is supplemented when the spectre (in the shape of self-positing capital) takes *possession* of it.

In a short essay such as this, such large claims necessarily take on a programmatic character. Only the barest indications of the argument are given. First a form-theoretical account of commodity exchange is given; then the fundamental ontology of value is outlined, founded in a dialectic of 'Nothing' and 'Being'; finally the spectre of this 'Nothingness' is claimed to be hegemonic.

Commodity Exchange

In this first section the nature of commodity exchange is analysed, using the categories of 'use value' and 'exchange value'. I follow here Marx's terminology so it should be explained that in his usage 'use value' is identified with the natural body of the good concerned. It is the various properties inherent in it that allow it to have various uses, but rather than focussing on such *relations* Marx employs the term *substantively*, such that it is possible to speak of a commodity as 'a' use value. Putting the point this way heightens the sense of paradox when it is contrasted with its 'value', because, again, Marx takes this too not in a relational sense in which it stands for an exchange ratio, but substantively again, such that the commodity is 'a' value. There is thus consubstantiation here. Every commodity 'contains', as it were, two substances in its body, its use value and its value; the former is specific to each type of commodity, but the latter is a (capitalistically produced) universal substance of which each commodity is an instance or certain amount.

Now, while speaking of a commodity as 'a use value' might be deemed a somewhat peculiar locution, there can be little objection, in that the natural body of the commodity taken under this description is clearly a substance present to inspection. To speak of 'value' as a substance, by contrast, could be taken as highly objectionable. From the time of Samuel Bailey's attack on Ricardo, such a view has been rejected (other than by Marx) in favour of an account in which there is no value substance, and insofar as it appears as a property of commodities, something they 'have', this has been analysed as a purely relational property identical with 'value in exchange', and accordingly labile. Thus it is problematic simply to assert that value is a substance inherent to the commodity. The argument below represents the first steps in a chain designed to *ground* such a presupposition through a dialectical development of the form of exchange.

It will be argued that (monetary) exchange gives rise *immediately* to a world of pure form empty of content. The two major schools that claim to be able peremptorily to reduce 'value' to a definite content are those adhering to the labour theory of value and to the marginal utility theory. These will be briefly considered, and rejected for failing to grasp the objective validity of the 'real abstraction' predicated on exchange relations.

Whatever may be true before and after exchange, in the sphere of exchange itself the commodity is entirely abstracted from its character as a use value. It is of great importance here that this abstraction, and the 'nominalist' (i.e. empty) universal it yields, are not effects of consciousness but objectively constituted in the real process of exchange. This is a *material* abstraction from the character of the commodities as use values, which is 'absented' for the period of exchange; the commodities acquire as a new determination the character of values; and the natural bodies of the commodities concerned play the role of bearers of this determination imposed on them while passing through this phase of their life-cycle. They become subject to the *value form*.

What is at issue in the value form abstraction is by no means the same sort of abstraction as natural science employs when it studies mass, for example, and treats bodies under this description regardless of their other properties. For mass is indeed a given property of the bodies concerned, inhering in each. But value is a socially imputed property; as Marx says, not 'an atom of matter' enters into it.[2] There seems no natural limit in the *form* of exchange itself to *what* people might take to exchanging. At first sight, therefore, it seems an empty mediator, tailor-made to registering various heterogeneous relations. The key advance of value form theory is the insight that the value form develops to the point at which, with self-valorising value, it is constituted as a *self-relation*, and 'takes over' the world of production and consumption given to it.

The exchange determinations are dimensionally incommensurable with use. Notice that to say 'we *abstract* from use' is very different from generating the abstraction 'utility' from heterogeneous use values, by disregarding the *particularity* of use. Böhm-Bawerk was correct to notice, although wrong to complain, that Marx abstracts even from the genus itself, when he abstracts from the use value of commodities.[3] Exchange is certainly not an *actualising* of the 'common property' of utility. As Marx rightly pointed out, the thing must be realised as an exchange value *before* it can be as a use value. It might be said that exchange is underpinned by the comparative preferences for A and B by the parties, but in this case what is actualised is some weight of such preferences in the minds of the exchangers rather than an identity *in the commodities* A and B. The latter identity, i.e. of A and B, is the *value* in exchange of *them*, whatever external conditions shape the ratio of exchange. Moreover, exchange could not be based on *their* identity as use values, or it would have no point; rather they must be different, so that one person's preference may be for A and one for B. The non-identity of the commodities as use values is set aside then in their identity as Beings of Exchange (as we shall call them later).

If use value is 'suspended' for the duration of exchange this 'absenting' is equivalent not to destruction but to 'distantiation', so that use value remains potent at a level removed from exchange determinations; the natural body of the commodity appears in exchange, but merely as a 'bearer' of value, its use value having been substantively displaced. As Roy Bhaskar says, what is absent at one level, region or perspective may be present at another; this is 'the duality of absence'.[4] Value and use value are not two polar properties of a commodity like North and South. They are immediately contraries. Where value *is*, use value *is not*: if use value *is*, value is nothing: – two different regions of being in which what is present in the one region is absent in the other. It is a feature of the structure of commodity relations that use value and value exhibit such duality (yet eventually interpenetrate).

Labour

Having rejected the relevance of 'utility' to exchange value let us turn to 'labour'. It should be remembered that Marx does not succeed in *Capital* chapter one in *demonstrating* the labour theory of value. He simply stipulates that value relations pertain to exchange of products of labour, and that other exchangeable things have price but not value. Nor is it just a problem that the deduction (if it is one) given in chapter one is insufficient, it is that the nature of exchange is such that at this level of abstraction *nothing* determinate can be posited without arbitrary foreclosure of the dialectic of the value form. Those who do insist on the labour content cannot explain why this form should be so void of determinacy that anything and everything can be inscribed in it.

It is certainly justifiable to claim that an accidental universal (in this case exchangeability) must be disaggregated so as to focus on a real universal (in this case labour products) but this must be justified explicitly, and, moreover, it is still necessary then to explain how other things can appear as identical in form to the chosen class. If this can only be done by granting that the commodity form is not peculiar to products, and that its abstractly general character allows it to cover other content, that answer shows this form can be analysed on its own account. So the argument that there is indeed a content to the value form in labour cannot be correct as far as the pure form of exchange is concerned because many non-products are coherently inscribed within the form. It requires an additional argument to secure a version of the labour theory of value (such as I have provided earlier),[5] and so far from value being treated simply as the social form of appearance of labour, it will be shown here that value is an unnatural form that clings, vampire-like, to labour and feeds off it.

As Marx rightly said in his *Grundrisse,* it is impossible to start with labour and show the commodity is a form it takes on. Because this form is an alien *imposition* on labour, one has to start from circulation in its developed form, he says.[6] It is *through* exchange that abstraction imparts itself to labour, making it abstract human labour, because it is the form of exchange that establishes the necessary social synthesis in the first place before labours expended may be commensurated in it.

But Marx failed to grasp that this implies a method of exposition which engages the value form first, and then provides reasons to narrow the focus of the enquiry to products, rather than one that starts from production, i.e. 'value', and then inexplicably allows the scope of the commodity form to include non-values. In dialectical terms, Marx has a dogmatic beginning insofar as he initially presupposes the items exchanged are labour products. This could be justified externally by appeal to the broader concerns of historical materialism with modes of production. But for any attempt to follow the model of Hegel's dialectic an absolute beginning without imposed conditions is needed. Only after developing the forms of circulation can one give grounds for picking out as systematically important those commodities which are products of labour.

To sum up: exchange brings about a *sui generis* form without any given content, because *all* use value is absented, not merely all *determinate* utility but the *category* itself. It is presupposed *to* exchange and actualised *after* exchange but simply not present *in* exchange.

Money

When exchange 'absents' the use value inherent in the natural body of the commodity it does so by asserting that all commodities are identical as exchangeables, but, since this last is *not* a property inherent as such to commodities, rather one which is imposed on them, to hypostatise it, as if it were, is to posit some *imputed* universal – whether property or substance. Thus, if exchange declares all commodities identical as 'values', it cannot do so on the basis of abstracting a common property already present within the realm of use value because there is no such commonality. *Only the very fact of being exchanged unites the commodities generically.* Since the range of exchangeables is unlimited, to characterise anything thus is not to pick out something belonging to the nature of the object but a reference to the operation on it. In fine, exchange does not flow from an *inherent* power of exchange *in the commodities*. Rather, the operation of gathering them into the class of exchangeables reflects itself into them, imputing value as the substance of them, which then appears fetishistically as an inherent power. More precisely it is money that is socially imputed with the power of immediate exchangeability, and commodities are classed as exchangeable in virtue of the worth imputed to them in their price.

Money, as a medium of circulation, seems simply to 'stand for', stand in the place of, commodities, for reasons of convenience. On such a view theory would give this metal mediator short shrift, treating it as a veil behind which lies the 'real economy', whose laws are investigated in abstraction from their current forms of appearance. Such an approach would be mistaken for failing to grasp the nature of money, and its central place in a capitalist economy.

Let us borrow an example from Marx to illustrate the peculiarity of money. Whereas 'animal' 'stands for' cats and dogs etc., it is merely our concept of them, but when money 'stands for' commodity value it is objectively present, and enters into objective relations with the said commodities; it is 'as if' 'the animal' existed *beside* the cats and dogs, and entered into relations with them.[7] What is absurd when we hypostatise 'animal' is nonetheless objectively valid when money 'stands for' commodities. Their concept is incarnate in coin. Moreover, this 'convenience' of the exchange system takes over from what it is supposed to mediate, reducing the extremes to *its* supports in *its* activity, namely the *making* of money.

Since money represents the emptiness of commodities as value-bodies, it need share no common property with them, and, indeed, need have hardly any 'natural body' at all, an electronic charge will do. It is true that money is supposed to represent in external form the essence of commodities but since there *is no* common essence (other than their relation to money) money represents the presence of this absence! Albeit some use value (e.g. gold) may be selected to play the role of its visible body, this clothing is contingent. But since it is the function that counts, not the particular body of money, it can be replaced by a symbol of itself.

To sum up, money 'stands for' commodities not because it represents some common property in them (which in some theories of money must also be shared by it), but rather contrariwise, money takes it upon itself to stand in place of them, therewith *imposing* this common relation on them, putting as their essence this ideal signification, of being worth so much money. The common content is therefore not a pre-given one but a dialectically developed one, introjecting the *form* of value.

The Ontology of Value

We have explicated the doubleness of the commodity (as use value and value) and described monetary exchange so as to situate the dialectic of capital, to be discussed shortly. This takes absolutely seriously the consequences of what we have said about the constitution of exchange value coinciding with the 'absenting' of use value.

Roy Bhaskar has argued that ontological monovalence, a purely positive account of reality, cannot account for *real* negation or absence. It must be admitted that absence is a reality as much as presence.[8] Moreover, since 'absenting' is certainly a real process, what has become absent through such a process leaves not simply 'nothing', but a 'determinate nothing' structured by the specific process that brought it about. Now we will situate value theory in this context through establishing that value is constituted in the exchange process by a determinate negation of use value. Although it is the thesis of this paper that exchange and circulation set up an 'ideal world' of pure forms, empty of content, which then take hold of production, this is consistent with, indeed depends upon, an *emergent powers materialism*.[9] The focus is on the emergent properties of the determinate absence of use value. In virtue of the mechanism of emergent powers it is possible to suppose that, if there is at the base level real determinate non-being, then a more complex practice might *redetermine* this as a pseudo-positive *presence*. Value will be shown to mark an 'empty presence', and yet, it will be argued, this spectral objectivity prevails over the material of economic life.

Now the exposition of the argument proper begins by first presenting a Table of categories and then a commentary upon the dialectic of these shapes of value. This dialectic will be modelled on that of Hegel, with the most important categories being those of 'Nothing' and 'Being'.

	'production' ⇨	exchange ⇨	'consumption'
A. 'value' as absence:	real being	Nothing	real being
B. 'value' as presence:	non-being	Being	non-being

The focus here is on exchange; terms in quotation marks are overly concrete for this level of the exposition, but used to help give a more accessible 'picture' of what is going on; the capitals head the key categories the scheme is intended to explicate; line A is understood as originating the dialectic, through absenting real being (use value) during exchange, and line B is derived from

A as a quasi-inversion of it. At A, then, 'production' and 'consumption' (or, more abstractly, the presenting of goods for exchange and their removal) are presupposed to exchange as realities, and a wealth of use values gets transferred through exchange from one hand to another. While use value is here presented *to* exchange it is suspended for the period *of* exchange; this absenting of use value while commodities cross the the space of exchange constitutes their 'value' as all that is not use value, sheer nothingness. This line, therefore, is characterised by 'the positing of value as absence (of use value)'. Immediately, the exchanging commodity is simply predicated as 'not use value' but this absence 'makes space' so to speak for the emergence of 'Nothing' into positive self-presence (as illustrated in the middle column above).

The movement from A to B is a switch to an inverted world in so far as line B is itself a determinate negation of the whole of line A. Whereas at A 'value' is nothing but absence of use value, in accordance with Bhaskar's opposition to ontological monovalence it is here taken as a reality axed around the *presence* of absence grasped as resulting from *the negation* of use value. The 'ontological inversion'[10] is the moment of 'negation of negation', but whereas the first negation is brought about *by* exchange, the second negation is effected *in the space of exchange*, a space predicated on absence of the 'real being' of commodities as use value. So, instead of returning to the starting point, and recollecting that the commodity is, after all, use value, 'absenting the absence' results in the (abstract) 'Nothing' becoming its opposite, (abstract) 'Being'. At B therefore the space is filled by . . . what? Sheer 'Being': the Being of exchange. At B, 'value' makes itself *present* to us through *displacing*[11] the real being of commodities, which are hence posited prior to exchange as the 'non-being' of 'value', before they are present *in* exchange *as* 'value', only to be 'devalorised' as they pass beyond it. So this inverted world of 'value' transforms real being (use value) into 'non-being', and 'Nothing' into 'Being' ('value'). Hence Line B is characterised by 'the positing of value as presence'.

Notice that the movement *across each line* is characterised by ontological reversal but that *from line to line* by ontological inversion. The difference is that the reversal maintains the original presupposition, and posits in the same 'universe', so to speak, the opposite. But the ontological inversion supplants the entire 'universe' together with its existing regional presences and absences such that *all* is represented as other than it is, as standing on its head.

In explicating 'the presence of value', I draw attention to two different distinctions: first, between the sheer 'Nothing' of line A and the sheer 'Being' of line B indicative of a transition from one world to another, and, second, between the 'Being' and the 'non-being' of line B where the latter has no capital letters, indicating that 'non-being' is here a correlative moment of 'Being' and hence implicated in the world of exchange even if only in the mode of being denied, of absence. Thus, following Hegel,[12] I shall distinguish between a structure characterised by the *correlative* moments 'Being' and 'non-being', and the unstructured immediacy of 'Being' and 'Nothing', where 'Nothing' does not refer to the absence of some related term but a sheer void, an immediacy, unrelated to anything outside itself; 'Being' likewise in Hegel is such an immediacy, sheer indeterminacy, and as such indistinguishable from 'Nothing'. (In a moment I shall explain why such immediacies are justified.)

It follows that I distinguish value *as* Nothing from the non-being *of* value. The former lies always at the heart of the dialectic of value, even where 'value as presence' veils this emptiness. The latter refers to value's determinate negation, namely use value, a sphere where considerations *other* than value are in play (see line B): 'non-being' might be thought a strange way to refer to the visible reality, use value;[13] but what is meant is that there is *nothing of value* in it as such a visible reality, that 'turn and twist it as we may' we can never find 'value' there. (Considered as something destined *for exchange* its 'Being' in exchange may be ideally anticipated, but here is only a potential.)

Now why should there be any inversion of line A into line B in the first place? It must be emphasised that this 'perspectival switch'[14] from A to B is as such only a presentiment of the reality of the inverted world of capitalism (where, as Marx said, everything is 'topsy-turvy'); as such it is merely a shadow cast by exchange. To give the shadow substance would involve a long development, in which new, more concrete, categories are brought to birth, precisely through the consideration, at each stage, of the *insufficiency* of the shape of value under consideration to prove that it has *made itself present*. Thus this argument can follow somewhat the same lines as that of Hegel's onto-logic, his attempt to constitute the universe out of the self-movement of thought; however in this case it is the self-movement of capital that has to be shown to constitute the universe of value.

So I stress there is no 'proof', here at the start, of value as a positive presence; it is rather the completely ungrounded indeterminate beginning of the 'spirit world of capital' (as I shall develop it); it stands in need of grounds and it must be legitimated *retrospectively* when the 'Being' of value borne by commodities is conceived as a moment of the capitalist totality.[15]

An Absence in Hegel's Dialectic

Since the categories 'Nothing' and 'Being' are reminiscent of Hegel let us turn aside to consider this. One significant disanalogy is in the *starting point*. Hegel starts by reducing real being to (abstract) 'Being', passes to 'Nothing' and back again, resolving this instability in 'Becoming' and collapsing this to '*Dasein*' (usually translated as 'determinate Being', or, literally, Being-There).

On the basis of the absenting of use value we start from sheer 'Nothing', but then make a transition, through the consideration that this is a determinate nothingness, to its possible inversion as 'Being'. What corresponds to the Hegelian instability of 'Being' and 'Nothing' is the wavering of value between absence and presence. This might be called the 'transitoriness' of value, which has the advantage of connoting both the shifting of 'value' from 'Nothing' to 'Being' and back *and* the predication of 'value' on the *transit* of commodities across exchange. Let us examine more closely the movement of exchange. Although commodities pass *across* this space, nonetheless something is posited *in* this sphere. When a commodity is exchanged its duality as a 'Being' *of* exchange, value, and a 'non-being' of exchange, use value, bifurcates. One use value is replaced by another use value, but the very same value persists *in* exchange. It is the 'Being Present' of value, the equivalent of Hegel's *Dasein*, mentioned above.

However, we must explain that this '*Dasein*' is not the same as Hegel's, and redeem our earlier pledge to justify our originating category, 'Nothing'. It is worth pondering why Hegel, whose dialectic is pervaded by determinate negation, starts from terms (namely 'Being' and 'Nothing') lacking any determinacy. This is bound up with his methodological principle that in philosophy nothing at all may be presupposed, for that would amount to dogmatism. So the beginning should not commit him to anything, and as a true beginning must not refer back beyond itself, it must not itself be mediated. An obvious objection is that his beginning is indeed a mediated result, for Hegel arrived at it through a complete abstraction from all determinate principles. Hegel himself, however, insists that this fact lies 'outside the science'.[16] He brackets the abstract negativity of the thought process that produced it, and takes as absolute beginning the immediacy of 'Being', leaving until the result of its dialectical development the mediations grounding this beginning. If it is accepted that such 'clearing of the ground' may be left aside so that 'science' itself begins with pure immediacy, and develops immanently, there remains a tricky problem. For Hegel does not clearly distinguish between a beginning that strips away all determinacy from being leaving the indeterminate immediate 'Being', and a more radical abstraction from being itself, as a genus, to leave nothing at all. While admitting this, namely 'Nothing', could have been the beginning and end of the dialectic, he dismisses it by saying that the 'Nothing' would itself have being and so this beginning would join with his in an unstable identity of 'Being' and 'Nothing'.[17] But Hegel dissimulates, because within a couple of moves he has definitely prioritised 'Being' over 'Nothing', so his starting point was not innocent after all. Let us see how this happens.

It seems to happen immediately with the transition to 'Becoming', but Hegel again argues this category is understood by him to comprehend a movement of both coming to be and ceasing to be, indifferently. Cynthia Willett has used the image of a circle to illustrate this; one can move round in either direction even though the same thing is the ground of the movement. Hegel's 'option for the positive' comes out only with the next category, '*Dasein*', referring to Being-There or determinate Being in general. This, he admits blandly, resolves the opposed moments of 'Becoming' in a stable result that is a 'one-sided unity' favouring 'Being'.[18] What is lost here is the logical alternative 'one-sided unity': 'determinate Nothing', or the self-presence of Nothing. While Hegel gives no reason for his choice, it is in fact legitimate insofar as he takes for granted that his project is a reconstruction of reality, assumed of course to embody the truth of Being. But, as Willett argues in her brilliant paper on the subject, if Hegel resolves the circle of coming and going into an upward pointed spiral, its shadow side, logically equally possible, is a downward pointed spiral.[19]

The circle needs a shove to get it moving orthogonally. The shove 'upwards' is justified only because of Hegel's reconstructive method. His concern is with *truth* (the usual philosophical topic) and since truth is the whole, only the *whole truth* retrospectively explains the transition. But if we deconstruct Hegel's dialectic, a certain 'prejudice-for-truth' is revealed. Occluded is another possibility: a world of falsity, where everything is inverted. This would be a 'downward' spiral, the concretisation of nothingness, the apotheosis of the false, insofar as 'Being' is denied, and demoted to the other of 'Nothing'. No doubt such a hellish dialectic, in which, contrary to the vision of 'the whole as the true', the whole is the false, could not occur to Hegel. But it is precisely the case in capitalism, we argue. Living as we do in the belly of the 'rough beast' born in Manchester, this possibility must be taken seriously.

Since the downward spiral, concretising 'Nothing', reflects the upward spiral, concretising 'Being', all the more determinate categories of the downward spiral may be expected to develop in parallel to the upper, with the understanding that they qualify the 'Nothing'. It is rather like the physicists' hypothesis of a world of 'anti-matter'. It is important to Hegel's ontologic that the stages gone through, in developing the Absolute Idea, are *constitutive of it*, not abandoned husks of its immature shapes. They are *preserved*, albeit as sublated moments of the self-comprehending Absolute. This is why even the most primitive, 'Being', is itself a way of referring to the Absolute, albeit very abstractly; for the Absolute certainly *has* being; indeed, in a way, it is nothing other than the fullest expression of 'Being'. As a *dialectical* development, this concretisation of 'Being' is equally always constituted at each stage with reference to its opposite, at the start sheer 'Nothing'; but in Hegel's dialectic 'Being' encloses this 'Nothing', albeit Nothing is carried along 'within' *Dasein*.

In the dialectic of capital are shapes of its 'Idea' homomorphic with those of Hegel, as I have argued earlier,[20] but with an inverted meaning. 'Nothing' is at the origin, and encloses 'Being'. The more concrete and complex shapes of the onto-logic are likewise posited as the building-up of the shadow world of nothingness.

This 'negative teleology'[21] must be distinguished from simple inadequacy, lack, or conflict, characterising pre-capitalist formations. What is historically specific to capitalism is that 'Nothing' perfects itself when it develops its

'Presence', whereas generally Hegel would be right to give a positive exposition merely marred by the negative as when he notes the unassimilability of mass poverty to his positive dialectic of the modern state.

Let us return to the status of our own founding category 'Nothing'. In accordance with the above exegesis of Hegel in which attention was drawn to the fact that Hegel set aside the activity of abstraction giving rise to his originating category 'Being', our category 'Nothing' is not to be understood merely as the non-being of use value, but in its own terms as an immediacy. What lies 'outside the science' for the project of reconstructing the inner dialectic of the 'Substance-Subject' capital, is the external force (exchange) that took hold of goods – against their will so to speak – and transformed them into commodities, comprehensively negating their use value.[22] *Within* the space of exchange, then, this leaves us with this immediacy, namely 'Nothing', as the point of origin of the dialectic of capital. But if this 'Nothing' is not able to affirm itself as a 'Being' of exchange, it loses any ontological standing. To put it another way, without Line B as its concretisation, line A would refer solely to use value and would read; real being – non-being – real being; 'value' would be meaningless.

For Hegel 'Nothing' is reduced , in effect, to the lack of determinacy of his 'Being', and a signal that the latter requires concretising until it has achieved plenitude in the Absolute. For us, 'Nothing' is the more abstract category; hence it is logically prior to its immediate 'Being' as such a beginning. (It will be recalled that I drew attention to Marx's abstracting from the genus 'use value' altogether.) This 'value as absence', then, is what is concretised in the dialectic of capital. When it becomes absolute it becomes its opposite 'value as presence' (but an *empty* presence because it is the fullest expression of its *origin*). However 'full of itself' it is, it must yet *prove* itself as *present to* its world, through inverting its constitutive context, i.e. *effecting* line B, as opposed to line A.

The Spectre

The remainder of this paper sketches the way this 'Nothing' claims to make itself present to itself, and its others, rather than stay as the mere absence of use value. It must be capable of determining itself to be-ing there, a negative form of the *Da-Sein* of Hegel's onto-logic, an *empty presence*. In further determining itself to concrete actuality and power the same stages would have to be traced as those of Hegel's logic, up to the Absolute Idea. Only at that point is 'value as presence' conceivable as *making itself present*, rather than merely haunting a fetish form of consciousness.

It follows from the argument thus far that there is a void at the heart of capitalism, that the circulation of commodities and money as seemingly material objects supports a world of pure form. In proportion as the Being of Exchange develops (see line B in the table above) the 'real being' of commodities itself becomes merely the shadow of value, its other being, its *non-being*. – At best the material bearer of value; but the common *substance* of every commodity would be its value, which displaces its natural substance; the commodity is a 'sensuous-supersensuous thing' ('*ein sinnlich übersinnliches Ding*': Marx).[23] This 'presence' at their heart is *there* in the value form taken by commodities. Yet it *is not*. It is a spectre. Derrida rightly distinguishes between the ideality of spirit and its embodiment as a spectre.[24] If we treat value as the spiritual essence of the capitalist economy, its range of incarnations all centre on a single origin, namely money, the transubstantiated Eucharist of value; 'the spectre' is this hollow armour, at once mute metal and possessor of the magical power to make extremes embrace. The spirit is made metal and stalks among us. The spectre interpellates all commodities as its avatars, an uncanny identity of discernibles, a spectral phenomenology. This negative presence, posited thus, fills itself out through emptying them of all natural being, and forming for itself a spectral body, a body of spectres. In capitalism all is *always* 'another thing' than what it is.

So far, then, from 'value' being some mundane material property or stuff, it is a shape opposed to all materiality, a form without content, which yet takes possession of our world in the only way it can, through draining it of reality, an ontological vampire that bloats its hollow frame at our expense.

'Value as presence' *contrasts* immediately with the spheres where it is not, positing them as its non-being. But the result of the systematic development of the value form is to *subsume* them under it. The name of this active negativity is ultimately 'capital'. Only the emergent powers characteristic of this form of value can *effect* the inversion and reduce use value to a moment of valorisation. Value is a *sui generis* form arising from capitalist commodity exchange, sinking into production, and then reflecting back on exchange so as to accomplish its *self-production*. This movement 'Being – non-being – Being' is parallel to that of Hegel's absolute negativity; value negates itself, in taking the shape of a material production process, but then recovers itself in fuller form. So, even when the value form grounds itself on production, the former is not reduced to the mere appearance form of the latter, a previously empty form seized by this content; rather, the form of self-determination achieved by this ideality maintains itself, takes production *within* its power, thereby *form-determining* production so as to shape it into its own content (real subsumption of labour for example).

The empty presence of value gains a content when it produces itself – but this is a strange sort of content we shall see.

The value form, following its development to the general formula of capital, gives itself reality through sinking into production and *making* products the incarnation of value. But, whereas Hegel has the Absolute Idea itself originate the reality its categories inform, capital confronts production and consumption as alien domains that it must subdue and actively seek to *inform* with its shapes. It must *take charge* of presenting commodities to exchange through shaping industry as capitalist industry so as to guarantee that there *be* commodities for exchange, that there be *new value*. So the forming of existent commodities as values in exchange is not enough; there must be real *positing* of value, occurring in real time and space 'prior' to exchange. Then value as *presence* overlaps (*übergreifen*: an important term in Marx) constellationally (Bhaskar's term)[25] what is outside exchange, subsuming it, 'formally' and then 'really', to the self-production of value. If this form has sufficient determinacy to be a power in the world then an ontological *inversion* obtains.

But it is important to realise the domain that objectively predicates itself on this inversion is the pure form of exchange. Such ontological inversion does not, and could not, abolish the reality outside exchange, which still stands (on its own feet, so to speak); but it is *haunted* by it; still worse, at the emergent level of ontological complexity achieved by capital (self-valorising value) the spirit of capitalism *takes possession* of the real world of production and consumption. When capital attempts to ground itself *on* production, it runs into economic determinations springing from use value. This should have dethroned value; but instead the opposite happens; the spectre prevails. The spectre 'takes possession' of use value, estranges its meaning, drains away its truth, and substitutes a new one. Just as those 'possessed' by spirits use their own larynx and tongue but speak in another's voice, so use values are 'possessed' by capital, in the spiritual as well as the legal sense. Capital speaks through them only of its own concerns, profit and accumulation.

The Positing of Value

This raises the question of how exactly to connect categorially the value endorsed in exchange with the positing of value as result of the activity of production.

A clue is given in the *language* of Marx's *Capital* when he first introduces the topic of the labour process. Here he gives an 'idealist' reading even of concrete labour, as a 'form-giving fire'[26] that freezes into fixity: 'What on the side of the worker appeared in the form of unrest [*Unruhe*] now appears, on the side of the product, in the form of being, as a fixed, immobile [*ruhende*] characteristic. The worker has spun and the product is a spinning.'[27]

The proper place for such metaphysical considerations is really the other section (on the valorisation process) of that chapter, where the idea of an activity passing into fixity makes good sense of the relation between the activity of value-positing and the resulting value. This result must have a material product to inhabit but what counts is its conceptual form as value, hence absenting its determinate material features and reducing it to nothing more than the *abstract result* of activity. Thus the value 'substance' is nothing other than the *condensation of the activity* that posited the commodity as a value; the *act* of positing value results in its own fixity.

In the passage earlier quoted there is an unmistakable reminiscence of Hegel's language of 'Becoming' determining itself to 'Being'. Hegel writes: 'Becoming is an unstable unrest [*Unruhe*] which settles into a stable [*ruhiges*] result.'[28] So Marx deliberately identifies the process of production with Hegel's restless 'Becoming'. However, there is an inflexion of this category to be noted; originally when discussing the 'Becoming' of value in the space of exchange, its inner moments were identified as 'Being' and 'Nothing'. Now, as already something, value is grappling with the sphere of its *non-being*, the domain of production as a real process of determinate transformation of use values.

What was an inner relation is here external, such that 'Being' *faces* its non-being and must internalise it. This more concrete level of 'Becoming' is an unstable unity of 'Being' and 'non-being'.[29]

When 'Becoming' *comes to rest* in a result, namely a marketable commodity, value is *posited*. The result value, abstracted from its contingent use value support, has to be considered simply as *what has become* from the unrest of its becoming, simply as its conclusion in finite determination.

The difficult problem is to understand production as at one and the same time a labour process and the bearer of value in motion. At the level of the production of real being, use value undergoes a determinate transformation from raw material to goods, mediated by labour. Now the absolute negativity of capital takes this within its grasp such that concrete labour is reduced to the bearer of the abstract activity of transformation, namely negating of use value. Capital is not interested in the particularities of the determinate transformation of material, only in the reproduction of value. In accord with the earlier mentioned structure of inversion this negating of use value simply *is* the positing of value. If value abstracts from the genus use value, then value positing abstracts from the genus 'labour', not merely from the concrete forms of labour. The use value positing of labour is abstracted from so that now it counts merely as the bearer of value positing insofar as all concrete determinacy involved in use value positing is absented leaving the logical category of positing *per se*.

Self-valorising value posits itself in comprehending within itself production, through negating *dialectically* (i.e. *preserving* the material side within it) the realm of the real labour of production. So far from labour embodying itself in commodities and thereby constituting them as values, the value form embodies itself in production, subordinates its purposes to value creation, and realises itself in the product, posited as nothing but its own othering, when it successfully gains control of the labour process.

With this sinking of the value form into production, such that production is formed as production *for exchange*, the empty presence of value appears to gain a material filling. But this is not quite so; for the manner in which the spectre (capital) takes possession of the labour crystallised in products is such that this too becomes, as the stuff of an ideal objectivity (value), itself constituted as a 'spectral objectivity' (Marx: *'gespenstige Gegenständlichkeit'*), reduced to 'pure jelly' (Marx: *'eine blosse Gallerte'*), ectoplasm.[30] Marx picks out the implications of this transition from labour into value when he writes in the 1861–63 manuscript: 'This process of the realisation of labour is at the same time the process of its de-realisation. It posits itself objectively, but it posits its objectivity as its own non-being [*Nichtsein*], or as the being of its non-being [*das Sein ihres Nichtseins*] – the being of capital.'[31]

The abstract objectivity of value mediates itself in the abstract activity of value positing. Conversely what abstract labour 'produces' can be only an abstract product such as value, 'the being of its non-being', whose magnitude is a function of the amount of spectralised labour absorbed.

This raises the issue of determining the magnitude of value. Money is its measure, but what is the immanent determinant of the magnitude measured in money terms? We have defined value as an empty presence; but how can there be 'plenty of nothing'? The answer is that this is a determinate nothing resulting from the passing into fixity of the restless process of its becoming, a cessation that sublates its origin, i.e. preserves the process in the product as a definite magnitude. Value posits itself as a quantity of negating activity fixed as what *is posited*. The only possible measure of such negating activity is the time it goes on for.

When we examine a product we may judge that 'a lot of work has gone into it' but such work is generalised concrete labour evident in the carving, polishing, etc. However if we have as product only a *spectral* 'body of work', how can that be represented as 'six hours worth'? It can – simply *as* mediated result: mediated in *what*? It does not matter! as long as the result of six hours can be represented as twice that of three hours: hence the peculiar immaterial dimensionality of money. The dimensionality of the source (time) is simply given a different categorial status in the product as finite result of so much time that *has* passed. (Hegel points out that the 'Essence' is a past tense of Be-ing: 'The truth of *being* is *essence* [*Wesen*]. . . . The [German] language has preserved essence in the past participle [*gewesen*] of the verb *to be*; for essence is past – but timelessly past – being.')[32] A crystal of accumulated time, the fixing of time that passed, is the magnitude represented in money.

'Nothing' nothings

The commodity understood as the *result* of capitalist production is not merely the visible immediacy of use value, but a truly metaphysical entity, as Marx promised. The void at the heart of bourgeois life results in the most accomplished irony: accumulation as an infinite increase in emptiness is mistaken for a plenitude of wealth. What capitalist accumulation is (un)really about is the sublimation of material wealth into a ghost of itself. Capital is a spectre in that through it the originally posited 'Nothing' gains *its determinacy*, subsuming, transforming and negating the 'real being' of the capitalist economy. But is it really *present*? Is it not rather a halo, a mirage, a semblance of actuality? To those who doubt that 'Nothing' can have agency and power I reply: 'It acts therefore it exists.' That it acts is demonstrated by the impossibility of trying to say what is going on in a factory without referring to valorisation; and what is that but increase in money? And what is money but the empty universal that not only 'stands for' real wealth but elbows it aside and takes precedence? In money making the spirit of capitalism is able to enter into commerce with the earthly reality of production and consumption.

This 'Spirit' inhabits such material as a secret subject, animating it, and, vampire-like, communicating spectrality to all with which it has intercourse. Under the hegemony of the spirit world of capital, the phenomenal subject is itself a spectre. Or – better – we exist for each other only as capital's zombies, its 'personifications', 'masks', 'supports', to use Marx's terms. A world of spirits is therewith incarnated in us, 'our' activity, and 'our' products. 'Now nothing but Spirit rules in the world' said the post-Hegelian Max Stirner.[33] He knew this, but he could not elucidate it. Instead he blamed our 'fixed ideas', as if the fault were in us. But the fault is in reality; hence the needed critique is not critique of a false view of the world, but one that moves within the object itself, granting its objective validity, epochally speaking: in the society of the spectre the false is *out there*.

[1] Derrida, J. 1994 *Specters of Marx*, Chapter 5. But it has to be said that Derrida vastly overgeneralises the purchase of his 'hauntology'. Here we take 'hauntology' to be a specific region within ontology, characterised by inversion.

[2] Marx, K. 1976 *Capital* Volume I, p. 138.

[3] Böhm-Bawerk, E. V. 1975 *Karl Marx and the Close of his System*, p. 74.

[4] Bhaskar, R. 1993 *Dialectic*, p. 60, p. 346.

5   See Chapter 3.

6   Marx, K. 1973 *Grundrisse*, p. 259.

7   Marx, K. 1976 *Value*, p. 32. The example may have been drawn from Hegel: Hegel, G. W. F. 1991 *The Encyclopaedia Logic* §24 Addition, p. 56.

8   See Bhaskar, R. 1993 *Dialectic,* Chapter 2.

9   '*Emergence*: A relationship between two terms such that one term . . . arises out of the other, but is capable of reacting back on the first and is in any event causally and taxonomically irreducible to it.' Bhaskar, R. 1993 *Dialectic,* p. 397.

10 The Marxian notion of ontological inversion presupposes a stratified ontology obtains, rather then the 'flat' ontology of empiricism. See Bhaskar, R. 1991 'Dialectics' p. 147.

11 *Verrückung* (= displacement; derangement) is an important term in Marx, as Backhaus has pointed out: Backhaus, H.-G. 1992 'Between Philosophy and Science', pp. 61–2. In his usage of *Verrücktheit* Marx draws on its double meaning as 'dis-placement' and 'madness'. For example, he says that in the value form the relation between private labour and the collective labour of society appears '*in dieser verrückten Form*', translated by B. Fowkes as 'this absurd form' (Marx, K. 1976 *Capital* Volume I, p. 169).

12 Hegel, G. W. F. 1969 *The Science of Logic*, p. 83.

13 I distinguish value's origin in 'Nothing' from the 'non-being' of value. The latter is how the dialectic of capital posits the realm of use value. R. Albritton, following Sekine, grasps this but, from my standpoint, confuses this *non-being* of value with the *Nothing* of the dialectic of value itself. (Albritton, R. 1999 *Dialectic and Deconstruction* p. 70). I take the dialectic to begin from the value form; if so, then *both* the initial moments (Being and Nothing) must be moments of value. Incidentally, Sekine and Albritton see 'reification' (rather than 'inversion') as the crucial critical category; value is taken as a positive social reality, albeit reified.

14 '*Perspectival switch*. The switch from one transcendentally or dialectically necessary condition or aspect of a phenomenon, thing or totality to another which is also transcendentally or dialectically necessary for it.' Bhaskar, R. 1993 *Dialectic,* p. 401.

15 The method of systematic dialectic depends in my view on the possibility of such retrospective validation: see Chapter 4.

16 Hegel, G. W. F. 1969 *The Science of Logic*, p. 99.

17 Hegel, G. W. F. 1969 *The Science of Logic*, p. 99–100.

18 Hegel, G. W. F. 1969 *The Science of Logic*, pp. 106; 110.

19 Willett, C. 1990 'The Shadow of Hegel's *Science of Logic*', p. 92.

20 See Chapter 5; although I now contextualise the dialectic of capital differently, this demonstration of the homology between Hegel's categories and those of

Marx may still be affirmed, in virtue of the aforementioned reflection of their 'spirals'.

21 Backhaus, H.-G. 1992 'Between Philosophy and Science', p. 85.
22 Notice that, just as Hegel's Logic ends with Absolute Method, which in effect reinstates the mediating activity bracketed at the absolute beginning, so the perfected value form, capital, realises itself in a *circuit of exchanges*, so this (seemingly external) condition of existence of value is then *internal* to its completed concept.
23 Marx, K. 1962 *Das Kapital: Erster Band,* p. 85.
24 Derrida, J. 1994 *Specters of Marx,* p. 126, p. 136.
25 '*Constellationality*: A figure of containment within an over-reaching term . . . from which the over-reached term may be diachronically or synchronically emergent. It may take the form of identity, unity, fluidity etc.' Bhaskar, R. 1993 *Dialectic,* p. 395.
26 This particular phrase is taken from Marx, K. 1973 *Grundrisse,* p. 361.
27 Marx, K. 1976 *Capital* Volume I, p. 287.
28 Hegel, G. W. F. 1969 *The Science of Logic,* p. 106.
29 For Hegel's anticipation of such more concrete 'becomings' see *The Encyclopaedia Logic,* §88 Addition, p. 145.
30 Marx, K. 1962 *Das Kapital: Erster Band* p. 52 (Marx, K. 1976 *Capital* Volume I, p. 128). Re: '*gespenstige*'. This has the same root as the 'spectre' of communism announced in the first sentence of the *Communist Manifesto*. Notice that, for Marx, communism is not of course a 'spectre' but 'the *real* movement which abolishes the present state of things' (Marx, K. and F. Engels 1976 *The German Ideology,* p. 49). However, the beginning of the *Manifesto* reports the experience of the bourgeoisie. For them, who take the spectrality of capital *for reality,* everything must be inverted and the truth of communism seen as an unnatural abomination.
31 Marx, K. 1994 'Economic Manuscript of 1861–63', p. 202. E. Dussel quotes this appropriately on p. 176 of his 2001 *Towards an Unknown Marx.*
32 Hegel, G. W. F. 1969 *The Science of Logic,* p. 389.
33 Stirner, M. 1995 *The Ego and Its Own,* p. 88; this English translation puts 'mind' for '*Geist*' here.

Chapter Nine

Hegel's Theory of the Value Form

In situating Hegel's understanding of economic relationships it is useful to outline three broad approaches to the subject. First there is *naturalism*: the assumption is that the science concerns relationships between humanity and nature, and, more particularly, imperatives flowing from the scarcity of resources relative to need. All the economic categories are mapped onto natural categories such as labour, land, machinery, productivity, fertility, location in space and time, and so forth. As Marx observed sarcastically, these people seem to think that rents grow out of the soil along with the crops. Second, there is the attempt to explain economic phenomena in terms of the interplay of subjective choices. The important thing about this is that what is presupposed is a *monological subject*; that is to say, whether it involves utility maximisation, preference schedules, cost-benefit analysis, or whatever, it assumes the agency of a self treating its conditions of existence, including the presence of other agents, as given, and external to it. Third, there is the recognition of economics as a properly *social* science. It attempts to discern objective laws; these are not natural laws, however, but necessities inherent to specific social forms of organisation of the economic metabolism. It is also historical in that it seeks to understand the genesis, development and decay of such social forms. This third approach is capable of absorbing elements of truth in the previous two views, it should be noted.

Karl Marx is the greatest representative of this understanding of economic activity. As early as 1847, he writes: 'Economic categories are only the theoretical expressions, the abstractions, of the social relations of production.'[1] At the same time, he acknowledges the paradox of bourgeois relationships, namely, that the economists' model of a rational economic agent has a certain validity, precisely because this social form dissociates individuals from each other. But he points out against Smith and Ricardo that this 'individual' is not an original presupposition of all economies but a historic result: 'Only in the eighteenth century, in "civil society", do the various forms of social connection first confront the individual as a mere means for his private purposes, as external necessity. But the epoch which produces this standpoint, that of the singular individual, is also precisely that of the hitherto most developed social relations.'[2]

Marx's predecessor, G. W. F. Hegel, also firmly locates economic activity within the social and historical domains. His work stands in sharp contrast to the empiricism, naturalism, and individualism of the bulk of economic thought today. Many trends in recent Marxist theory ignore Marx's Hegelian heritage and assimilate his work to alien methodological paradigms. A prime example of this is John Elster's work. In order further to illuminate these methodological remarks let us consider a passage from his book: *An Introduction To Karl Marx*. There is an interesting contradiction in his chapter on methodology, in which he proclaims himself a methodological individualist. Methodological individualism suggests that ultimately all explanations in social science should reduce to facts about individuals; instituted social relations are merely their expression. Thus Adam Smith explains commodity-capitalist production relations in terms of a 'natural propensity' for individuals 'to truck, barter and exchange'. As Steven Lukes,[3] in a well-known paper, has shown, this method has no serious prospects of success, yet it continues to exercise its fascination. Elster repeats Hobbes's error of supposing such reductionist strategies to be typical of natural science, and hence of science as such. Whatever may be the case with certain natural sciences, it is clear that social science cannot eliminate explanatory concepts such as social structure, social norms, relations of production, and so forth. Nor does Elster! In flat contradiction to the thesis of methodological individualism he casually concedes that 'relations between individuals must be let in on the ground floor of social explanation'.[4] To admit this is to admit that he is thoroughly muddled.

Let us elucidate the contradiction further. The features of this standpoint map remarkably well on to those of the 'abstract understanding' described by Hegel in his *Logic*. In the section on 'Essence' Hegel describes the explanatory terms used in this kind of thinking as correlative pairs whose inner unity is not explicitly actualised; rather their connection is simply posited unreflectively. Given this approach, an object of study – society in our case – will be seen to involve two aspects – in our case the individuals and their relations – but whichever is taken as essential the other will be left over as inessential, unincorporated in the explanation. That turns out to be a mistake, continues Hegel, because the very distinction between the essential and the inessential at the same time affirms their unity in that each can be identified only through the mediation of its opposite, which must hence *also* be affirmed. However, if the thinker lacks any grasp of the true mediatedness of the whole then they can only treat the two aspects of the object in a contradictory way: the allegedly self-subsistent differences must yet be connected in the whole. The abstract understanding 'combines the two statements . . . by an "also", without bringing these thoughts into one' in a unified account, says Hegel.[5] This applies marvellously to the contradiction in Elster: essentially we are dealing only with 'individuals', but their 'relations' *also* are admitted to be necessary to social explanation.

It should be noted that Hegel thinks that valuable, if limited, results may be obtained with this method. This will be so wherever the relations concerned may be treated for certain purposes as purely external relations. But if, in fact, the nature of the social totality (family, production, symbolic order, etc.) *constitutes* individuals as they appear and act socially, while at the same time the social relations are nothing but their relations and alterable by them according to determinable possibilities, then to understand how this can be requires a more sophisticated logic. It is not a matter of establishing the social relations appropriate to a plurality of already formed individuals (Hobbes), nor of inserting the individuals into transcendent social structures (Althusser) or 'discourses' (post-structuralism), but of seeing self-development as a process of social mediation.

However, what if the dominant structure of social relations should in fact be so constituted as to actualise its 'Idea' merely as 'a structure of essence' in Hegel's terms? This is precisely the case with modern bourgeois society. As we shall see, what Hegel characterises as the sphere of 'civil society' exhibits just such falling apart of univeral and particular, form and content, which are related without being unified. It is not surprising then that ideologists generalise a methodological principle for social theory on this basis; that is to say, they express the ideology of the 'man' of civil society, namely the pre-given individual taken as a self-grounded point of reference for monological calculation in their relations with other such people. (That so-called 'strategic action' is still monological is pointed out by Habermas.[6]) Social structures then become *invisible* and all attention is directed to the individuals whose choices are perceived as the dynamic factor and as having explanatory primacy.

Another instance where Hegel's comments are of relevance today is his verdict on mathematisation. He warns us against being impressed by mathematical formulae. There is a real danger, he says, in uncritically exaggerating the range of validity of quantification and 'in considering as exact sciences only those the objects of which can be submitted to mathematical calculation'.[7] Certainly, in modern economics a mass of equations correlating all factors serves only to flatten the hierarchy of structures and to blend away the determinate form of the relationships concerned. The question of where the primacy of determination lies gets lost, as does that of the form of relationship in virtue of which this determinacy exists.

The purpose of this chapter is to see what Hegel has to say about economic issues (citations in *Capital* show that Marx was aware of relevant passages in Hegel's *Philosophy of Right*).

Hegel's Jena System

Hegel was familiar with political economy, and he credits it with great achievements in his last important work, *The Philosophy of Right*. But, much before that, it is drawn on in unpublished manuscripts[8] written in the early years of the nineteenth century in Jena (but predating his 1807 *Phenomenology of Spirit*); these show his thinking on economics to be dominated by Adam Smith's *Wealth of Nations*; he cites continually the pin-factory case from it.[9]

The importance of the Jena fragments goes beyond that of early anticipations of the later system, or the evidence they give of the impact of Smith on the young Hegel. They have an independent status as efforts to comprehend the dialectic of the social totality. Lukács and Habermas are right when they bring out the qualitative difference of the Jena efforts at a systematisation and the mature system.[10] This early work is somewhat more critical and materialist in its dialectical development of the determinations of the social structure than is the later. In particular, 'the system of needs and labour' is given a fundamentally constitutive role that it lacks in the *Philosophy of Right*. For this reason it is illuminating to treat first the Jena attempt at coming to terms with the economy.[11]

Hegel's philosophy is concerned with the development of *Geist* (spirit). 'Spirit' is Hegel's label for a form of consciousness that overcomes the dualities of subjectivity and objectivity, and which Hegel believed is being realised here and now in the world itself, in social life and definite forms of social consciousness instantiated in it. His aim was to demonstrate that social life may be experienced as whole and undivided through all the multifarious roles and activities people undertake, because the totality is constructed as a unity-in-difference. This consciousness is grounded in certain key mediations.

In Hegel's first effort to construct a system of philosophy, one of these key mediations is productive activity. According to Lukács what was decisive here 'was the possibility of exploiting the conception of labour derived from Adam Smith'.[12] It will be seen also that, like Smith, he does not distinguish systematically between two different senses of the division of labour. Marx, criticising Smith, distinguishes clearly the division of labour *within* manufacture from the social division of labour *between* manufactures mediated by trade.[13] But Hegel conflates them in his discussion.

Labour, Hegel points out, is not an instinct, but embodies a rational appreciation of the end-means relation. Its dialectic tends to evolve more and more universal forms: e.g. the tool which can be used not just once but many times, and not just by one worker, but by anyone. Labour itself also tends towards a form of self-expression rather than mechanical toil. It becomes a skill to be learnt and passed on; new techniques are discovered; nature is understood and conquered.[14]

The subject-object dialectic here takes the following form: the object, originally raw material, absorbs the activity of the producer and comes out with a new form; the subject, as the active principle, finds its activity incorporated in the object, but comes out of the process with a heightened sense of its universal power as a reflective consciousness. Such a dialectic cannot get under way if people merely appropriates nature's gifts *as such*.[15] Lukács sums up: 'Only if man places labour between his desire and its fulfilment, only if he breaks with the instinctual immediacy of natural man, will he become fully human.'[16]

Here Hegel introduces a favourite motif: that of the cunning of reason. The producer is cunning enough to know how to appropriate natural forces and set them to work on his behalf, 'and with only a slight effort controls the whole process'.[17] 'But this deceit which he practices against nature', Hegel says, 'does not go unavenged.' For: 'the more he subjugates nature, the lower he sinks himself'; labour may be saved for society as a whole but for the individual it increases, he observes, 'since the more mechanical it becomes, the less it is worth, and the more must one labour in this way'.[18]

How exactly does Hegel explain this? The starting point of the analysis is that there is an indefinite number of needs and wants, and the things that serve to satisfy them have to be worked up into the appropriate form. Therefore labour itself is directed towards a multitude of activities and itself becomes universal, but *abstractly* universal labour, because the labour and its product are not in concrete unity with the needs of the labourer but apportioned through the division of labour in the light of the general pattern of demand. It is for 'need' in general, not for 'his need'. Here Hegel is speaking of the social division of labour *between* manufactures and the labour is abstract because, although undertaken as an independent enterprise, it has meaning only as a particular *part* of universal social provision. Hegel's discussion then slides seamlessly to its division *within* the production process:

> Since his labour is abstract in this way, he behaves as an abstract I – according to the mode of thinghood – not as an all-encompassing spirit, rich in content, ruling a broad range and being master of it; but rather, having no concrete labour, his power consists in analysing, in abstracting, dissecting the concrete world into its many abstract aspects.

> Man's labour itself becomes entirely mechanical, belonging to a many-sided determinacy. But the more abstract [his labour] becomes, the more he himself is mere abstract activity. And consequently he is in a position to withdraw himself from labour and to substitute for his own activity that of

> external nature. He needs mere motion, and this he finds in external nature.
> In other words, pure motion is precisely the relation of the abstract forms
> of space and time – abstract external activity, the *machine*.[19]

Here the labour is abstract in the sense that it has no specific quality because
it is mere mechanical motion. Such a division of labour may increase wealth,
but because man subjects nature to himself 'in this formal, and false way, the
individual only increases his dependence on it . . ., the skill of the single
labourer is infinitely limited, and his consciousness impoverished.'[20]

Thus the significance of labour undergoes a reversal. The artisan who is master of his craft, and skilled in the use of his tools, serves as a model for the
emergence of humankind out of nature, the formation of culture, and the
development of self-awareness. But when Hegel found himself faced with
the reality of the modern labour-process he saw that the labourer falls back
into bondage to nature and need. The emergence of social life out of nature
has not freed people from dependence on external conditions because, although
primitive need and instinct have been superseded by cultivated need and the
exercise of reflective understanding, the existing structure of social life forms
a 'second nature' in the sense of an external sphere constraining the individual; no true self-determination has been achieved. The consequences of
this for the worker are spelt out as follows:

> His possibility of preserving his existence . . . is subject to the web of chance
> enmeshing the whole. Thus a vast number of people are condemned to
> utterly brutalising, unhealthy, and unreliable labour in workshops, facto-
> ries and mines, labour which narrows and reduces their skill. Whole branches
> of industry which support a large class of people suddenly fold up because
> of a change in fashion, or a fall in prices due to inventions in other coun-
> tries; and whole masses are abandoned to a poverty which cannot help
> itself.[21]

Hegel demonstrates that for such abstract labours to become universal labour
for society requires the *form of value*. As a case of this universal labour for the
needs of all, each labour is socially specified as being of value. This is the
form in which it becomes recognised. Hegel stresses that this universality
established across individual needs and labours remains merely formal,
in that the supersession of the isolation of the labourers is accomplished
in a 'formally universal abstract simplicity', because the concrete order of

material production exists only as an indefinite number of singularities dissociated from one another ('*Auseinanderlegen*').[22]

Conceptually they are connected as labours of an abstractly similar kind, namely directed at the production of goods, but how is this *conceptual* connection realised? How are they *really* connected? Hegel's argument is that it is money that does this. In his words: 'their universal concept must become a thing like them, but one which as a universal represents all; *money* is this materially existing concept, the form of unity or the possibility of all things needed.'[23]

In mediating use values money likewise mediates the labour that produced them. Hegel says: 'The universality of labour or the indifference [identity] of all labour is posited as a middle term with which all labour is compared and into which each single piece of labour can be directly converted; this middle term, posited as something real, is *money*.'[24] (This remarkable derivation clearly anticipates Marx's treatment of abstract labour and money.)

If goods are not produced within a communal framework, if they persist thus as bare singulars, they can be brought into relation only with other singular items. Money is peculiar in that it has absolute singularity; it is both the abstract universal and a particular; thus it can bring about the 'relative identity' of all values, and establish a universal intercourse between them, a 'relative totality'.[25]

Value as such is an abstract concept, it has no existence outside the connection between goods generated by human practice. To be more than an empty notion, to really mediate the particulars, it must become something real, paradoxically precisely as an object like them, a singular, money. Hegel has grasped the necessity for value-relations to attain objective form. He speaks of 'the identity of the *essence* [value] and the *thing* [money]', and says 'the essence of the matter is the matter itself: value is hard cash'.[26]

Hegel is aware of the problem of alienation here: 'In my labour I make myself into . . . *something alien*,' he says.[27] Conversely, hidden within this lifeless matter is 'spirit', a social substance: because of man's fall from grace, the spirit must be made metal and circulate among us, so to speak. 'A man is as real as the money he has.'[28] Because people relate to others in these reified terms, the underlying social substance cannot be explicitly actualised. Thus in commodity production the agents are estranged from their own system of relatedness. Hegel paints the picture for us: 'Need and labour, elevated into this universality, thus form a monstrous system of . . . interdependence . . . a self-propelling life of the dead, which moves hither and yon, blind and elemental.'[29]

It is interesting to see that Hegel treats the quantitative as well as the qualitative side of value. From the point of view of the subject, he argues, everything that is 'surplus' to his own particular requirements (and *a fortiori* anything produced for the market) has value only in the abstractly universal sense; hence 'it is pure quantity as far as the subject is concerned'. Since he is not interested in making use of it himself he is not interested in its specificity. The same disjunction between quantity and quality applies to the subject's labour: 'A relation is established between the subject and his surplus labour; the bearing of this labour for him is ideal, i.e., it has no real bearing on [his own] enjoyment.'[30]

But the product does have a bearing on other commodities equally specified as pure quantities in this way. 'The abstraction of this equality of one thing with another,' says Hegel, 'is value; or rather value is itself equality as abstraction, the ideal measure; whereas the actually found and empirical measure is the price.'[31] Notice here that Hegel makes a clear distinction between the external measure established empirically (hence open to contingency) through the mediation of money, and the immanent measure rooted in the pure concept of value equivalence itself. The temptation for economists is always to drop one of these or subsume it somehow into the other – 'if we have price why do we need value?' or 'if we have value-relations money is a mere numéraire for standardising relative magnitudes'. Hegel knows very well that both are required for a complete understanding of commodity exchange.

Hegel argues that, because in money productive activity appears in reified form, the social relations of producers must appear as those of owners of commodities. He derives *private property* as 'the resting side' of labour, 'parcelled out' as it is in autonomous enterprises.[32] My product gains an ideal bearing on my person when it is recognised as my property. 'All that I have, I have through work and exchange. . . . The source, the origin of property here is labour.'[33] The 'contradiction' is that, as we observed above, as 'surplus', as a value, the product has no *real* bearing on my individual needs and labour but is actualised *ideally* in exchange as an abstract universal quantity. It is true that I am therewith recognised through my ownership as a (legal) person,[34] but Hegel emphasises that this form of social recognition is precisely formal, that is, abstracted from the concrete content of need, labour, and possession. He speaks of 'that harshness of spirit, wherein the individual, altogether alienated, no longer counts'.[35] Thus the unity of the individual's life falls apart into the public and the private spheres.[36]

Although in these early manuscripts we find that Hegel frequently goes over the same material at higher levels of mediation, the general thrust is clear: that *juridical categories are conceptually derived from economic ones*. This fact has been noticed by Lukács and by Habermas, who also emphasise the importance of the later reversal of this conceptual ordering found in Hegel's main work of social philosophy, *The Philosophy of Right*.[37]

It is not hard to see why Hegel is driven to this reversal when we observe the contradictions in his treatment of labour. Like Smith, he has conflated the category of productive activity with that of (abstract, dissociated) labour as it is determined within the prevailing social relationships.[38] The constitutive role of labour, in the self-formation of the individual, and in social being, is compromised by the social division of labour. In particular, true reciprocal recognition of economic agents cannot occur at this level because their intercourse condenses into the reified sphere of value. At the economic level it is *commodities* that recognise each other's worth. Only at the juridical level do the subjects effect such recognition in so far as their products become socially recognised as possessions of their owners who alienate them through contracts.

To sum up, we can see that in his first attempt at a systematic theory of social consciousness Hegel intended to include in its foundations forms closely identified with the system of needs and labour. But in so far as he perceives that in the bourgeois world the dialectic of this sphere does not escape from reified forms of intercourse it seems that spirit must be actualised on a different ground. Thus, even in the Jena system he is concerned 'to justify the juridical duplication of economic life' (Lukács[39]). This implicit preference for juridical forms over economic forms results in the displacement of the importance of labour by the time of his *Philosophy of Right*, in which 'the system of needs and labour' is not treated until half way through, now as a material content of a civil society *already* constituted by ethical and juridical forms, independently of the dialectic of labour. The ordering of the economic and juridical determinations gets reversed. The tension between an incipient materialism and the limitation of his bourgeois standpoint results in an idealist reconciliation of spirit with the substantial forms of bourgeois life, in which he founds social activity on subjects recognising each other as property owners.

Value in Hegel's Philosophy of Right

Hegel's main work of social theory, *The Philosophy of Right*, is structured in three parts. First, under 'Abstract Right' Hegel introduces the concepts of 'person' and (private) 'property'; then, under 'Morality', this 'person' becomes further developed as a moral agent concerned not only with rights but with 'good'; finally, in 'Ethical Life' Hegel shows how both right and good must be grounded in social practices and institutions such as 'the family', 'civil society', and 'the state'.[40] It is within civil society that 'the system of needs and labour' takes its place, because in the modern world economic activity has largely separated itself from both family provision and political privilege. As a separate sphere it has become the object of a special science. Political economy, Hegel says, 'is one of the sciences which have arisen out of the conditions of the modern world' (para. 189). It is a social science for Hegel because 'the system of needs' is structured from the outset through forms of social relationship; it is not reducible either to the expression of a natural process, or to an aggregate of individual calculations. Political economy is not only a social science but the science of a specific social structure, which Hegel calls 'civil society' and which he also explicitly recognises is *modern bourgeois society* (para. 190).

In the Jena system, Hegel had attempted to thematise value in the context of economic relationships directly, as the form necessarily taken on by the product when it is produced on the basis of contradictory conditions, namely by labours that are simultaneously *universal* labours of society and yet *dissociated* from one another. But in his book, *The Philosophy of Right*, Hegel does not thematise value in the section on needs and labour but much earlier, at the start of the whole development. This first part, 'Abstract Right', corresponds to the traditional concerns of 'natural law' theory, specifically the justification of an institution of property right. Property itself is treated here not as the expression of relations of production, but in more idealist fashion as appropriation through an exercise of will; and even 'forming' the object is understood as having the significance merely of a 'mark' by which others may recognise a claim to ownership.

The right to property is introduced by virtue of the necessity for the will to exhibit its essential freedom in 'an external sphere' (paras 41–4). Of course, one way of doing this is to 'form and shape' things (para. 56), and another is to use them (paras 59–64), and yet another is to trade them (paras 65 and 71), but none of this has any economic significance at the level of abstraction Hegel is concerned with here. All these determinations of possession are employed by Hegel to articulate the abstract concept of *right*. This, therefore, when actualised in a concrete order of right, socially constituted, namely the 'system of ethical life', is already given as the form within which economic life must be expressed and regulated. Since Hegel has already derived the category of value in his consideration of 'abstract right', it has no essential connection with 'the system of needs and labour' as the concrete order of social reproduction of the material basis of bourgeois society. If, as Hegel concedes (para. 196), the objects meeting needs are largely the products of human labour, none the less value is to be thematised within the *juridical forms presupposed* by that activity rather than at the level of the *economic content* (needs and labour) *regulated* by it.

Let us then turn to look in detail at his derivation of value. It occurs in the context of a discussion of the use to which a thing may be put according to the will of its owner:

> A thing in use is a single thing determined quantitatively and qualitatively and related to a specific need. But its specific utility, being *quantitatively* determinate, is at the same time comparable with other things of like utility. Similarly, the specific need which it satisfies is at the same time *need in general* and thus is comparable on its particular side with other needs, while the thing in virtue of the same considerations is comparable with things meeting other needs. This, the thing's *universality*, whose simple determinate character arises from the particularity of the thing, so that it is thereby abstracted from the thing's specific quality, is the thing's *value*, wherein its genuine substantiality becomes determinate and an object of consciousness. (para. 63.)

First of all, the approach strictly distinguishes quantity and quality. (This may well have influenced Marx, whose discussion of the commodity relies on a similar disjunction.) Then we see that Hegel is interested in the fact that the category of quantity implies the possibility of some commensuration. Furthermore he recognises that bringing the objects within the same universal framework involves abstracting from the specific quality each has such that each counts merely as a particularisation of the universal: value.

In his lectures addressed to this material Hegel goes to some trouble to sharpen further the distinction between quality and quantity. In this quantitative form (value) the qualitative (use) 'disappears'. Value as a quantitative relation is 'indifferent to quality'. He gives a mathematical analogy to illustrate his point. A circle, an ellipse and a parabola are very different curves but, in spite of this, the distinction between them can be erased in their algebraic expressions, in so far as it reduces to a question of the magnitudes of coefficients. At the same time a pure quantity cannot be a measure. We cannot say of something that it is worth, say, 'six'. It has to be six of something: for example, 6 oz of gold, or £6. So Hegel observes that 'the qualitative provides the quantity with its quantum and in consequence is as much preserved in the quantity as superseded in it'. Hegel, however, recognises that the specific quality of such a universal equivalent is irrelevant: 'it counts not as itself but as what it is worth'. In particular, money 'is only a symbol of another universal – value'. (para. 63 Addition.)

In his marginal notes to his own copy of *The Philosophy of Right*,[41] Hegel again remarks that what makes up the value of the one commodity is a determinate amount of *another*; that value when expressed in money terms is thereby presented '*fur sich*' (by, or for, itself), as he puts it;[42] and, conversely, money cannot be of utility *immediately* but must therefore first be transformed into specific use values. For values to be separated from use in this way and commensurated with each other only acquires meaning with exchange. In line with this, Hegel's next reference to value occurs in the treatment of contract:

> Since in real contract each party retains the *same* property with which he enters the contract and which at the same time he surrenders, what thus remains *identical* throughout as the property implicit in the contract is distinct from the external things whose owners alter when the exchange is made. What remains identical is the *value*, in respect of which the objects

of the contract are *equal* to one another whatever the qualitative external differences of the things exchanged; it is their *universal* aspect. (para. 77.)

Here Hegel, like Marx, distinguishes sharply between the 'external things' with their 'qualitative external differences' and the 'identical' value positing equivalence in the exchange. This distinction becomes explicit when money is involved. For Hegel, money as 'the really existent and universal value of things and services' is thus 'not one particular type of wealth among others, but the universal form of all types', expressed in an external embodiment, and it is thus able to serve as a vehicle of social commensuration (para. 299).[43]

Hegel therefore distinguishes between two kinds of commodity exchange:

(1) Exchange of . . . one specific thing for another that is likewise of a specific nature.[44]

(2) Exchange of a *specific* thing for one characterised as *universal*, one which counts only as value, without the other specific character, utility – i.e. for *money*. (para. 80.)

Hegel is arguing that value is a form imposed on the specific use values as their universal mediator, and that this involves a violent abstraction from their specificities. He is arguing that there is nothing in the natural substance of goods that demands recognition in value. It is rather the other way round: this form is imposed on the objects concerned, and posits value as their *inner* substance so that, in spite of their visible heterogeneity, as *values* they are of identical substance and thereby commensurable. It might be said that in spite of their heterogeneity as specific use values they are all nevertheless 'of utility' in the abstract, so there is some sort of prior basis to this 'value'. But, although Hegel speaks of 'need in general', he makes no attempt to derive a measure of value from some utility inherent in these goods, and neither does he derive any rules of proportionality in exchange from this characteristic. Notice also that when Hegel sees money as 'value for itself', he does not say it measures utility but that it *lacks* utility.

If value has any reality at all, it is a social reality, and the bearers of value acquire it only in this framework. Things are not commensurable because they already have value inherent in them. Rather they gain value when they are posited as equivalents of one another in the form of value. Value is an abstract universal arising from the activity of social subjects. This abstract universal, although it necessarily gains reality as a measure, namely in money, does not simply represent a quantity of something else inherent to goods. Value is a purely social form, it seems.

At this level of abstraction the question of what conditions, if any, might determine exchange values is therefore left open; it might well be an arbitrary matter on what specific terms a contract of exchange is made. That Hegel believes it not to be arbitrary becomes apparent only when *The Philosophy of Right* reaches the more concrete level of 'civil society'.

But in the lecture courses he gave while writing the book he is already more explicit about the underlying determination of value in the section on 'Contract'. He there expands on the topic as follows:

> With contracts of exchange one has to envisage comparing things in their diversity; they may be dissimilar, but what makes them similar, their value, is an abstraction. I merely posit an identity between two things according to their externality. It is I who, in comparing them, bring them into relation. This likeness between them is their value, an abstract way of viewing them, according to which they can be assimilated to one another despite being qualitatively diverse. Now the value depends on the labour needed to produce the thing, value being determined by the art and effort involved, the rarity of the object etc. The comparison is made on the basis of this value, which is a quantitative determination, a measure. Price is the value in an empirical case.[45]

At first sight this passage seems contradictory. First there is a strong statement of the value form as external to things, an 'abstraction' which 'I' *impose* on them. But then it seems in ascertaining the *magnitude* of their value I am constrained by the dependence of value on 'the labour needed to produce the things' and so on. The apparent contradiction is resolved if it is recognised that the social agents, who create a unified form (value) within which to regulate exchange of heterogeneous commodities, do not behave in an arbitrary manner; their will is naturally informed by rational considerations. Of course any 'empirical price' may be contingently determined, but one is entitled to expect some pattern to emerge in the valuation of goods where exchange is systematic and regular. Certainly, at the level of abstraction of contract, this would not necessarily follow. One agent may succeed in imposing their own conception of the value of thing on the other. Indeed where exchange is not mediated by money, allowing comparison on the same scale of price, such contingency is highly likely. Only with the universal dimension of money-price would exchange-ratios be set by intersubjective comparison and social determination. It is at the global level, where exchange is a systematic and regular social mediation, that socially necessary labour times impose themselves on exchange. To return to *The Philosophy of Right*: it is in the discussion of civil society that Hegel considers 'the mediation of *need* and the satisfaction of the *individual* through his work and through the work and satisfaction of the needs of *all the others*' (para. 188). In this context the formal relation of contract serves to bear such more concrete determinations. Here 'mass relationships and mass movements' give rise to law-like phenomena in which it is possible to recognise a certain 'rationality' (para. 189). This is what Hegel finds in the discoveries of political economy (which we shall consider below).

Let us now assess Hegel's trajectory. It is clear that there is a certain loss of concreteness in The *Philosophy of Right* as compared with the derivation in the Jena system. Instead of deriving the form of value from dissociated production, and exchange, Hegel presents value as arising first on the side of use (para. 63) in so far as consciousness (rather than material practice) effects this abstraction from the particulars. Furthermore this universal, when concretised as an equivalent, or as money, is presented as a 'symbol', that is to say a conventional measure, not the concrete mediation it was in the Jena system. At this level of abstraction the (apparently subjective) commensuration seems rather pointless. Only through the form of identity posited in contracts of exchange, does a more objective determination of value emerge (para. 77). Money is introduced a little later in this section (para. 80) in a contrasting form of exchange to simple commodity exchange: still there is nothing here on its necessity, for example, as the concretisation of value, or even as a medium of circulation. That idea finally turns up in the discussion of 'the business class': 'the universal medium of exchange, money, which actualises the abstract value of all commodities'. (para. 204).

The bearers of the value form have subtly changed. Here in *The Philosophy of Right* the form of value links together independent owners of use values and generates an abstraction from the specific quality of their goods. In the Jena system, while Hegel is certainly concerned with the mutual recognition effected by property owners, he underpins this juridical form with a form of value borne by 'needs and labours', generating an abstraction also of labour. As we have said, in *Philosophy of Right* the social synthesis of needs and labours in the material reproduction of society is treated after the form of value has already been thematised. Although at this level Hegel again analyses the abstractness of needs and labours (paras 190–2), one must conclude that the derivation of value is subject to an idealist shift.

What we have seen so far shows that Hegel is not guilty of the commodity fetishism criticised by Marx in the first chapter of *Capital*, which concerned the appearance of value as a quality inherent in the *body* of the commodity. Hegel insists, no less strongly than Marx, that value is a form imposed on goods in the relations established by social activity. But for Marx this form is the object of criticism: commodity fetishism is a sign that the 'process of production has mastery over man, instead of the opposite'.[46] Yet Hegel interprets the same situation as one in which by imposing this social form on things 'man exhibits his mastery over them' (para. 58 Addition). In accordance with this principle Hegel advances the claim that it 'is the thing's *value* wherein its genuine substantiality becomes determinate and an object of consciousness' (para. 63). In asserting that the thing has 'genuine substantiality' for us only in value Hegel has thus ended by fetishising the commodity *form*.

The Logic of Civil Society

As has already been said, because 'the system of needs' is taken up by Hegel only in the context of bourgeois society, it is thematised on the ground of structures already presupposed to it, namely the network of relationships established by private persons holding various products as private property and contracting with one another to exchange them. What is the nature of this system, according to Hegel?

While social life as a whole is presented as a concrete totality centred on the state, Hegel argues that, as a dialectically articulated self-reproducing whole, its interior moments make possible particular types of relationships and behaviour, with associated forms of consciousness. One behaves differently as a family-member, a competitor, or a colleague.

> In right, what we had before us was the *person*; at the level of morality, the *subject*; in the family, the *family-member*; in civil society [*bürgerlichen Gesellschaft*] as a whole, the *burgher* (or bourgeois). Here at the standpoint of needs (compare Remark to Paragraph 123) it is the concretisation [*Koncretum*] of the [abstract] conception [*Vorstellung*] that is termed man [*Mensch*]; here is also the first, and indeed properly the only place, to speak of *man* in this sense of the word. (para. 190.)[47]

The clue to the meaning of Hegel's reference to 'man' here is that, while people always exist concretely in definite social roles which relate them to others, if we consider *who* it is we are concerned with in the system of needs, then the answer is that the determination involved is that of neediness, and this is something characterising people *independently* of any particular social relation; thus as human beings simply.

The reference back to paragraph 123 is illuminating; for there Hegel speaks of the way subjects characterised as particular people may generalise across their given needs a concept of happiness, or welfare, to be pursued, but where 'this happens at the level of thinking which does not yet apprehend the will in its freedom but reflects on its content as on one natural and given' (para. 123).

Now, at the more unified level of 'ethical life', Hegel is showing us that this subject, and hence its will and the content it addresses, are socially constituted. None the less, at the moment of civil society, we are concerned with the differentiation of this whole into particulars, a differentiation also of form and content. This means that the socialised character of this 'man' is here unrecognised; although we know his needs and interests are socially developed ones, and although his very individuatedness is grounded in social forms, he *takes himself* to be self-subsistent and takes his needs as *given*; if not natural they are at least 'second nature' to him.

The ambiguity in Hegel's treatment arises from the fact that this standpoint of so-called 'man' is in truth, because of the position of the system of needs as an interior moment of 'civil society', really that of *bourgeois man*. As the discussion of the process of meeting needs shows, it is presupposed that this needy 'man' is dissociated from others and that the social synthesis is achieved through an abstract set of relations between self-seeking individuals (paras 190–92). Hegel describes it in terms reminiscent of Smith:

'subjective self-seeking turns into a contribution to the satisfaction of the needs of everyone else' (para. 199).

It is in the context of the discussion of 'the system of needs' that Hegel mentions with approval the achievements of political economy, citing Smith, Say and Ricardo. He says: '*Political economy* is the science that starts from this view of needs and labour but then has the task of explaining mass-relationships and mass-movements in their complexity and qualitative and quantitative character' (para. 189). It demonstrates that a universal law is at work even in the contingencies of individual transactions guided only by the perception of private interest on the part of those involved. Hegel comments that it seems incredible that there are such necessities 'because at first sight everything seems to be given over to the arbitrariness of the individual.' (para. 189 Addition.) He says: 'To discover this necessary element here is the object of political economy, a science which is a credit to thought because it finds laws for a mass of accidents.' (para. 189 Addition.) It shows that underlying connections exist, that apparently arbitrary events in its domain are linked together systematically.

This 'understanding' has been achieved by the specifically 'modern' science of political economy (para. 189). Nevertheless there are, and must be, limits to its totalisation in so far as it is a form of the system's own self-presentation, uncritical of it. For, within the tripartite structure of social life which Hegel establishes – family, civil society, state – civil society exhibits the logic of *difference* (whereas in the other two aspects unity is more to the fore). Of course, it is Hegel's view that in so far as the individuals' existence in civil society is underpinned by the whole state they are concretely bound together. But the point is, he holds, that at *this* level, and considered only as members of civil society, they are to be taken as self-sufficient individuals considering only their own interests; as *bourgeois* individuals, in fact. The primary focus of their activity at this level is that of securing the satisfaction of their individual needs. Yet they are not Crusoes: their activities are systematically interrelated (para. 182).

The problem is to identify the logic operative in this system. It is germane here to notice that Hegel relates it to the analytic faculty of the 'understanding' (as opposed to the synthetic grasp of 'reason'). Here it is useful to appeal to Hegel's *Logic*, because the logic of social life as a self-determining whole is that of its final category: the 'idea'. In the 'idea', categories such as universal and particular, form and content, necessity and freedom, are unified; but the abstractness of non-philosophical 'understanding' persists in handling them as dualities rather than in a unified conceptual scheme.[48] However, in like manner, in civil society itself these aspects are not experienced in *unity* but merely in *relation*, because the whole is determinate only implicitly in the domain of civil society, dominated as it is by difference, rather than identity, by dissociation rather than community. Problems arise with political economy not only because the 'understanding' is inherently a dualistic mode of thought, but also because civil society itself, the object of study, is characterised as the stage of *division* in the articulation of the social order.

Hegel says of civil society: 'The idea in this its stage of division imparts to each of its moments a characteristic embodiment; to *particularity* it gives the right to develop and launch forth in all directions; and to *universality* the right to prove itself . . . the power standing over it and its final end. It is the system of ethical life split into its extremes and lost . . . Here the Idea is present only as a *relative totality* and as the *inner necessity* behind this outward appearance.' (para. 184.)

In his *Encyclopaedia* Hegel actually defines civil society in this way: as 'the relative totality of the ties relating independent persons to one another in a formal universality.'[49] In a relative totality the sides of the whole, e.g. form and content, are merely related to one another, not mediated with each other in an organic whole. That Hegel can compare this social structure with that of the planetary system (para. 189 Addition) shows that the nature of the object itself has a merely mechanical order of regulation, not a self-determining one. Indeed Hegel here calls civil society an 'atomistic' system.[50] As Marx will later note, 'the egoistic individual in civil society may inflate himself into an *atom*', but nevertheless need directs these egoistic individuals into material intercourse with one another.[51] The deficiency of political economy is that it absolutises the standpoint of the individual of civil society, without grasping the fact that it is the *social* relations that create such forms of individuality rather than the other way round. In spite of its atomistic character, civil society forms a unity, but it is not consciously organised as such; it arises from the relationships of individuals within a formal universality. Because of this, Hegel explains:

> This unity is not the identity which the ethical order requires, because at this level, that of division . . . both principles are self-subsistent. It follows that this unity is established here not as freedom but as the necessity whereby the particular must rise to the form of universality and . . . find stability in this form. (para. 186.)

But dull economic compulsion does not enable the individuals concerned to recognise each other as more than individual centres of rights. Thus no genuine community of citizenship is present here. The state enforcing right appears in civil society as 'the external state, the state based on need, the state as the understanding envisages it' (para. 183). Hegel is saying that, although political economy rightly draws attention to the objective synthesis achieved through 'an invisible hand' (Smith), 'civil society' cannot fully actualise the unity in freedom of its elements because the falling apart of universal and particular here means that the freedom of each seems to conflict with that of others and the universal order appears as external necessity; hence civil society must be complemented and contained by the more comprehensive free sovereign activity of the state.

Hegel does not explicitly criticise political economy for abstracting from the determinations of the social order as a whole, presumably because the system of needs and labour *is*, really, partly thus abstracted. But Hegel understands the limits of political economy very well. Thus his appreciation of it cannot stretch to the derivation from it of an ethical theory (utilitarianism) or a political theory (liberalism).

Conclusion

From the purity of the form of contract derived in the first part of Hegel's *The Philosophy of Right* it might be thought that there is no material determination of the exchange-ratios arrived at, that values are established in the free choices of the agents themselves, choices unconstrained by conditions such as socially necessary labour times, and not conforming to prescriptions of economic rationality. But it is clear that Hegel does not hold such a position because, at the same time as he stresses the free character of contract, he returns several times in his discussion of the system of needs to the compulsion exercised on individuals by the objective system standing over against them, which results in everyone contributing to everyone else's welfare (paras 184, 186, 199). In truth there are complementary mistakes: (a) getting confused by the self-grounded *form* of exchange into a belief in the unconditioned freedom of the agents participating in it; (b) reducing the form to the natural expression of a determining *content*, which negates the role of social agency entirely. Hegel avoids both.

It is strange, however, that Hegel nowhere makes the obvious criticism of political economy, later to be developed by Marx; namely that it does not address the question of the form of value with the result that its labour theory of value tends towards a naturalism and subjectivism. This may be because Hegel has already theorised the social forms *within which* the dynamic of the system of needs and labour develops along the lines mapped out by political economy. Having established through philosophical argumentation the nature and necessity of these presupposed forms, he is content to give credit to political economy for its scientific discoveries in relation to the content of the system. Smith tends to naturalise the form of value and to subjectivise the content. The kind of labour theory of value Hegel found in Smith is constituted on the basis of the postulated universal subjective preference to avoid 'toil and trouble'; hence closely tied to economies possible through the division of labour; and, finally, socially satisfying needs through the operation of the invisible hand. This does not offer any alternative to Hegel at the level of *form-determination*; rather, it presupposes the social objectivity of the value form of the product of labour; hence Hegel would not find it competitive with his own account in the way he might have found a Marxian derivation.

The young Hegel not only draws on the work of Adam Smith but goes *beyond* it in that he asks the question why the products of labour take the form of value and begins to investigate the dialectic of this form and the reification and fetishism involved. But then in the later work he falls *behind* Smith in so far as social form is articulated primarily in ethico-juridical terms, instead of through economic categories as in Smith. At the same time, in view of Marx's criticisms of Smith and Ricardo for failing to analyse the *form* of value, Hegel's discussion is of great interest.

Finally it must be said that Hegel's intentions are manifestly apologetic. While in the early work Hegel gives a terrifying picture of market movements as 'a self-propelling life of the dead',[52] in *The Philosophy of Right* the market is presented as a fundamentally rational structure, albeit prey to contradictions that cannot be resolved within it. In spite of his awareness of these grave problems arising from the private property system, he endorses its forms as moments in the realisation of the idea of freedom. In line with this, when he shows that value is a social form acquired by the product of labour, he declares this form itself to be the 'substantial actuality' of the thing, thereby *fetishising* the form of value.

1 Marx, K. 1976 *Poverty of Philosophy*, p. 165.

2 Marx, K. 1973 *Grundrisse*, p. 84.

3 Lukes, S. 1977 'Methodological Individualism Reconsidered'.

4 Elster, J. 1986 *An Introduction to Karl Marx*, p. 23.

5 Hegel, G. W. F. 1975 *Hegel's Logic*, p. 166.

6 Habermas, J. 1974 *Theory and Practice*, pp. 150–1.

7 Hegel, G. W. F. 1975 *Hegel's Logic*, p. 146.

8 These are: '*System der Sittlichkeit*' (1802/3); '*Fragmente aus Vorleslungsmanuskripte zur Philosophie der Natur und des Geistes*' (1803/4): '*Vorlesungsmanuskript zur Realphilosophie*' (1805/6). The first is available in a Hegel collection edited by G. Lasson (1923); the other two are both in the *Gesammelte Werke*, the first in *Band 6, Jenaer Systementwürfe* I, the second in *Band 8, Jenaer Systementwürfe* III. I take the liberty of referring in the text to these three generically as 'the Jena system', and I quote from them without further specification there. In the notes below the three are abbreviated respectively as SS, JS 1, and JS 3. The English translations used (but sometimes varied from) are: for the first two, by H. S. Harris and T. M. Knox, 1979, *Hegel, System of Ethical Life and First Philosophy of Spirit*; the last, by Leo Rauch, 1983, *Hegel and the Human Spirit*. In the notes the German page ('xx') is given first and then the English equivalent ('yy'), thus: 'xx = yy'.

9 JS 1, 323 = 248; JS 3, 224 = 121. It has been shown that Hegel cites the English text of the Basle edition of *Wealth* published in 1791, not the German translation. He had such a copy in his library, presumably acquired when he was a tutor in Berne. See Waszek, N. 1983 'The origins of Hegel's knowledge of English'. However, it is not accurate to imply, as does Lukács, that in economics he was nothing but a disciple of Smith: he took a more cautious view of the free-enterprise system, and his remarks on the need for government intervention point to the influence of Steuart, on whom Hegel wrote an early paper, now lost.

10 'Hegel's economics during the Jena period', Ch. 5 in Lukács, G. 1975 *The Young Hegel*; 'Labour and Interaction: remarks on Hegel's Jena Philosophy of Mind', Ch. 4 in Habermas, J. 1974 *Theory and Practice*.

[11] It should be noted that Hegel's pre-Phenomenology Jena system was unavailable to Marx; so nothing that follows in this section should be counted an influence. S. Benhabib refers inappropriately to this material in order to show Marx's 'indebtedness to Hegel as regards the structure of modern exchange relations'; see Benhabib, S. 1984 'Obligation, contract and exchange' p. 300 (but cf. p. 176).

[12] Lukács, G. 1975 *The Young Hegel*, p. 322.

[13] Marx, K. 1976 *Capital* Volume I, p. 470. In *The German Ideology* Marx is still somewhat influenced by Smith's conflation; see Arthur, C. J. 1986 'Marx and Engels: *The German Ideology*'.

[14] JS 1, 320 and 300 = 246 and 231.

[15] JS 3, 205 and 224 = 103 and 120.

[16] Lukács, G. 1975 *The Young Hegel*, p. 325.

[17] JS 3, 207 = 104.

[18] JS 1, 321 = 247.

[19] JS 3, 224–5 = 121; see also JS 1, 321–2 = 247, SS, 433–4 = 117–18.

[20] JS 1, 323 = 248.

[21] JS 3, 243–4 = 138–9.

[22] JS 1, 322–3 = 247–8.

[23] JS 1, 324 = 249.

[24] SS, 474 = 154.

[25] SS, 440 = 124.

[26] JS 3, 269–70 = 166.

[27] JS 3, 227 = 123.

[28] JS 3, 269–70 = 166.

[29] JS 1, 324 = 249.

[30] SS, 434–6 = 118–19.

[31] SS, 437 = 121.

[32] JS 1, 324–5 = 249.

[33] JS 3, 227 = 123.

[34] SS, 437 = 121.

[35] JS 3, 270 = 166.

[36] JS 1, 325–6 = 249–50.

[37] 'The limitations of Hegel's economic thought', Ch. 7 in Lukács, G. 1975 *The Young Hegel*; 'Labour and Interaction: remarks on Hegel's Jena Philosophy of Mind', Ch. 4 in Habermas, J. 1974 *Theory and Practice*.

[38] Marx, in his 1844 manuscripts, points this out with reference to Hegel's *Phenomenology*; see Arthur, C. J. 1986 *Dialectics of Labour*.

[39] Lukács, G. 1975 *The Young Hegel*, p. 383.

[40] Hegel, G. W. F. 1967 *Grundlinien der Philosophie des Rechts*, [1821]. Hegel's text uses

paragraph numbers so we cite these in the text. English translations consulted were those by T. M. Knox, 1967, *Hegel's Philosophy of Right*, and by H. B. Nisbet, 1991, *Elements of the Philosophy of Right*; these English editions were also sources of the lecture 'Additions' cited.

41 The following passage is based on the *Randbemerkungen* in Hegel, G. W. F. 1967 *Grundlinien der Philosophie des Rechts*, p. 344.

42 And as Marx also puts it (Marx, K. 1973 *Grundrisse*, pp. 456 and 459).

43 Compare Marx, K. 1973 *Grundrisse*, p. 218.

44 For this first case I have replaced the text of the cited paragraph from *The Philosophy of Right* with that from a lecture, which is less obscure: Hegel, G. W. F. 1995 *Lectures on Natural Right and Political Science*, p. 87.

45 Hegel, G. W. F. 1995 *Lectures on Natural Right and Political Science*, p. 87. Compare also: 'Manual labour in general, a day's wages, these are the final elements of the price of things in relation to each other.' (Lecture cited in Hegel, G. W. F. 1991 *Elements of the Philosophy of Right*, p. 411.)

46 Marx, K. 1976 *Capital* Volume I, p. 175.

47 Marx, in discussing the concept of a simple labour-power, says: 'in civil society, a general or a banker plays a great part but man as such plays a very mean part' (Marx, K. 1976 *Capital* Volume I, p. 135), and gives a reference to this passage of Hegel. Unfortunately, this Penguin translation of *Capital*, in supplying the passage itself, garbles it.

48 Hegel, G. W. F. 1975 *Hegel's Logic*, pp. 277–8.

49 Hegel, G. W. F. 1971 *Hegel's Philosophy of Mind,* para. 517.

50 Hegel, G. W. F. 1971 *Hegel's Philosophy of Mind,* para. 523.

51 Marx, K. and F. Engels 1975 'The Holy Family', p. 120.

52 JS 1, p. 324 = 249.

Chapter Ten

A Clock without a Spring: Epitaph for the USSR

It is important following the 'fall' to point out that the debate over the nature of the Soviet Union is still germane to socialist theory and practice. Analysis of no-longer-existing socialism is significant more generally, for it is clear that the lessons are not specific to the extremes of the Russian situation but are relevant to the theory and practice of transition in general. Indeed it makes more pressing the question of what a *real* and *permanent* supersession of capitalism requires. Anyone interested in such a question must draw the lessons of this failed attempt; and anyone who is a Marxist must give an account of 'what went wrong' consonant with Marxist theory itself.[1] In the second part of this chapter I sketch some views on these questions. In the third part I consider the views of István Mészáros, embedded in his larger work *Beyond Capital*. But first let us set the scene for our analysis of the transition from capitalism to the USSR by addressing the question of the dialectic of form and content.

Form and Content

It is necessary first to distinguish between matter and form on the one hand, and content and form on the other. If I cut a gingerbread man out of dough, the dough is the matter out of which the form is made but it is not a content; the same form could be made out of any work-able material; and the matter is indifferent to the form externally imposed on it. (A more interesting case is the logical form of a proposition being inde-pendent of the variables in it.) We speak here then of the two sides indiffer-ently united.[2] When we have a case of form and content the two sides penetrate one another such that just this form fits just this content. We require this of a book in which the contents should take the form of an orderly arrangement but in which what counts as orderly is not determined solely by formal con-siderations but is itself a function of the content, for example certain state-ments function as beginnings ('once upon a time') and certain statements as endings ('they lived happily ever after').

Let us now apply these categories to the history of capitalism. Capital is in form self-valorising value; but for the purposes of this discussion the process of valorisation may be taken as embodied in the material process of pro-duction and the latter treated as a content taking the shape of capital's pro-duction of itself through appropriating surplus labour. It is often said that capital precedes capitalism, by which is meant that other forms of capital preceded industrial capital. Although Marx himself said this, in one place at least he recognised that strictly speaking this is false because sheer form with-out adequate content is not capital.

> Money can be lent out to productive purposes, hence formally as *capital*, although capital has not yet taken control of production, there is no capi-talist production yet, hence no capital exists yet in the strict sense of the word. . . . Like merchant's wealth it only needs to be formally capital, cap-ital in a function in which it can exist before it has taken control of pro-duction; the latter capital alone is the basis of an historical mode of social production of its own.[3]

Only in this latter form does capital gain an adequate content. Merchant and money-lending capital have the form of self-valorising value but lack an ade-quate content. The merchant certainly profits from circulating commodities but since he does not produce these commodities himself the 'matter' of his valorising process is externally given.[4] Marx shows that capital (in the hands of usurers and merchants) may exploit the direct producer, through the exer-cise of market power, even when the latter is not formally subsumed under capital.[5] Then he distinguishes within capitalism two different stages of development of the capital relation, the formal subsumption of the pre-capitalist labour process, which remains materially the same in this first stage, and the real subsumption of labour as capital transforms the labour process into an adequate content for capital. The *'formal subsumption of labour under capital'* obtains simply when 'the labour process is subsumed under capital (it is capital's *own* process) and the capitalist enters the process as its conductor, its director. . . .'[6] But this 'subsumption under capital of a mode of labour already developed before the emergence of the capital relation' forms a great contrast 'to the *specifically capitalist mode of production* (labour on a large scale etc.) . . . which *revolutionises* the kind of labour done and the real mode of the entire labour process.'[7] 'The capital-relation as a relation of compulsion is common to both modes of production, but the specifically capitalist mode of production also possesses other ways of extracting surplus-value.'[8] With industrial capital the unity of form and matter is at first still somewhat external insofar as the material process of production is that inherited from the past, and merely formally subsumed under capital's categories. However, as Marx has shown, the process of production becomes really subsumed under capital when it is no longer possible for it to recover its pre-capitalist form; when the formerly independent artisan is reduced to a functional role within the 'collective labourer' organised by capital, and when the scale and intensity of production become determined by the requirements of big industry. In sum capital as form (self-valorising value) now produces from within itself a content adequate to it: the factory system. The key is its subordination of the workers through a reorganisation of the division of labour and the construction of a hierarchy of control. Only when form and content of a mode of production perfectly complement one another can one speak of an 'organic system',[9] of a *'social metabolism'* (something that will be important when we assess Mészáros's contribution). If they come into conflict it spells decline and the objective necessity for a supersession.

Let us now investigate what Marx had to say about the notion of 'metabolism', starting with the simplest idea, introduced by Marx right at the beginning of *Capital*: 'Labour . . . is an eternal natural necessity which mediates the metabolism [*Stoffwechsel*] between men and nature, and therefore human life itself.'[10] Not surprisingly the same theme is explored at greater length in the chapter on the labour process.[11] The idea here refers to the immediate material life of human beings working upon nature; and in the chapter on the labour process Marx considers it without references to social forms, such as exchange. However, exchange introduces a definite social dimension to *Stoffwechsel* because in commodity production no material consumption is possible unless products first change hands in the commodity *form*. Marx says 'We therefore have to consider the whole process in its formal aspect, that is to say, the change in form [*Formwechsel*] or the metamorphosis of commodities through which the social metabolism [*Stoffwechsel*] is mediated.'[12] And a little later he refers to the '*Formwechsel*' wherein the '*Stoffwechsel*' of the products of labour is accomplished.[13] The emphasis is here not on a relation between 'man and nature' but the exchange of products between 'man and man' mediated in the social form of circulation.

These two different aspects of *the social metabolism* are dialectically integrated in the process of capitalist production and circulation, a matter first explored in the *Grundrisse*: 'In the circulation of capital we have . . . a system of exchanges, exchange of matter [*Stoffwechsel*] if seen from the angle of use-value, a change of form [*Formwechsel*] if seen from the angle of value as such.'[14] In Volume Two of *Capital* Marx returns to this subject in the first part, on the Metamorphoses of Capital, in which he demonstrates that the unity of the change *in* matter effected in production with the exchange *of* matter in circulation is accomplished in the circuit of forms of capital, namely money capital, production capital, and commodity capital. It is 'within the circuit of capital . . . that the metabolism [*Stoffwechsel*] of social labour takes place.'[15] Finally in the last part of Volume Two Marx shows that the system of reproduction, embracing the formal and material interchanges between 'Departments', constitutes the social metabolism of the entire capitalist economy within which production, exchange and consumption are interior 'moments'.

The investigation of these coincident exchanges is crucial to the secret of value and use value, and their interpenetration. In particular, one must speak here of 'form-determination': capital goes beyond mere form in penetrating (rather than abstractly counterposing itself to) the matter it regulates in order to shape it into its own content (real subsumption of labour for example). Valorisation is something which can be discovered in a factory no more than can value in a commodity, but it is nevertheless the key to comprehending what is occurring.

The theoretical problem in rightly elucidating the effectivity of formal and material determination is to conceptualise how *Formwechsel* and *Stoffwechsel* work together in a unified system of capitalist social metabolism. This point is missed by those 'materialists' such as G. Stedman Jones, writing here in the *New Palgrave* article on 'Dialectical reasoning':

> The relationship between matter and form in Hegel is only one of apparent exteriority. Matter relates to form as other only because form is not yet posited within it. Once the terms are related, they are declared to be identical. Marx, on the other hand, insists upon the irreducible difference between matter and form, between the material and the social. . . . Not only are matter and form different, but the one determines the other: value is determined in relation to the material production of use value; the opposite is not true.[16]

There has to be something wrong with the last sentence of this passage. No amount of dissection of material use value or the process of its production will turn up value. So in what sense is value conceivably determined by it? Capital creates value in virtue of its *sui generis* form. Of course, for Marx, it is relative labour times that determine relative values but value as a form is clearly constituted in exchange and insofar as the Marxian point about relative magnitudes is accepted it is the value form of capital itself that determines that labour time is to be the necessary dimension of its content. What is missing in Stedman Jones is the concept of mediation, a unity of opposites that keeps the two sides distinct as he insists, but allows that they inform each other, not that one is either reducible to the other or else its mere epiphenomenon. The distinction between formal and material determination *and* their unity must be considered.[17] The former 'ideally' gives sense and purpose while the latter conditions the former by the potentials and limits of the matter concerned.

If it were not for the real historical existence of labour-power, and of the general framework of capitalist social relations which ensures its exploitation, then there would be no self-expansion of value. But Marx also investigates the logic of social forms such as exchange, money and capital. These real forms have a specific effectivity, whereas on Stedman Jones's account all the weight is given to the material content regulated and directed by such forms. While it is true that the forms cannot realise their logical potential unless materially supported (there is no surplus-value without the exploitation of labour), it is equally true that the material potential is not realised without the compulsion exercised by the social form. It is capital that demands the continual reduction of socially necessary labour time. In sum, a full account of valorisation requires *both* formal and material explanation.

The *key* point is that the form-determination of capital as infinitely self-expanding value means capitalism is utterly different from any other mode of production. In all modes of production it is possible to seek ways of improving the productivity of labour, and all exploitative modes rely on some form of 'pumping out' surplus labour. *Only* capital is *in point of form* as such *driven* by this interest under the necessity to accumulate 'wealth'. Capital is an original unity of form and content in the sense that form has a certain unique effectivity arising from its purely self-mediating character granted in circulation. The following quotation from Marx gives some sense of this in that what is emphasised in it is the value form rather than the so-called 'substance'.

> To develop the concept of capital it is necessary to begin not with labour but with value, and precisely, with exchange value in an already developed movement of circulation. It is just as impossible to make the transition directly from labour to capital as it is to go from the different human races to the banker....[18]

Of course, systematic valorisation depends upon capital sinking into production and appropriating labour; but value is not a form 'naturally' taken on by labour (hence the impossibility of starting from labour), it is rather a form arising elsewhere and imposed on it. In virtue of its form capital is embarked on an endless drive for accumulation, but its self-determination as accumulative is limited by its reliance on land and labour as inputs to the production process. But, as we know from Marx, capital first formally subsumes these factors under itself and then subordinates labour and machinery to its purposes through a material transformation of them and their organisation (real subsumption).

What is capital? It is value in process. It takes the form first of money, then of factors of production, then of commodities, then of more money. Whence this 'more'? – from the process of production where valorisation of capital takes place. At the ideal level capital is self-valorising value. At the material level it is the pumping out of surplus labour in the factory system. In a very real sense we may speak of the organisation established to accomplish this operation as the materialisation of capital. (Just as a chain-gang is the materialisation of slavery.)

Marx makes the point in his *Grundrisse*, using the language of matter and form we already discussed:

> In the machine, and even more in machinery as an automatic system, the use value, i.e. the material quality of the means of labour, is transformed into an existence adequate to fixed capital and to capital as such; and the form in which it was adopted into the production process of capital, the direct means of labour, is superseded by a form posited by capital itself and corresponding to it. . . .
>
> The appropriation of living labour by objectified labour – of the power or activity which creates value by value existing for-itself – which lies in the concept of capital, is posited, in production resting on machinery, as the character of the production process itself, including its material elements and its material motion. . . .
>
> The development of the means of labour into machinery is not an accidental moment of capital, but is rather the historical reshaping of the traditional, inherited means of labour into a form adequate to capital. . . .
>
> However, while capital gives itself its adequate form as use value within the production process only in the form of machinery and other material manifestations of fixed capital, such as railways etc., this in no way means that this use value – machinery as such – is capital, or that its existence as machinery is identical with its existence as capital.'[19]

Mark well! Just because it is impossible to understand the development of the factory system without grasping that it was shaped by capital, so as to become its adequate *content*, this does not make it *capital* itself.

The Soviet Union

Let us now turn to those post-revolutionary systems that claimed to have superseded capitalism, in brief to the 'Soviet model'.

As far as *social form* is concerned capitalism was destroyed in the USSR. It is not meaningful to speak of the system as having had value, surplus-value, or capital accumulation (it should go without saying that development of heavy industry is not itself any sign of capital accumulation). There was the price form, and the wage form, but this in no way represented some appearance-form of value, since they were fixed within a totally administered system (although of course such forms provide a point of transition to capitalism when political conditions put this on the agenda, as we see today).

What remained, however, was the *materialisation of capital*, namely the factory system. For various historical reasons this was never questioned: socialism was proclaimed without radically overcoming the material embodiment of capital. Hence the global factory in the USSR started from this capitalist model, of which the key element is the hierarchical division of labour, from those at the bottom who execute orders of others, up to those involved in the five-year plan process. The entire human/material configuration of capital's technique was replicated. But without the objective economic regulator of value measures. A factory is not a mode of production. It has to be specified further by what social form regulates it. Since the factory system was laid down through capital's own development it followed that, once separated from capital itself as a social form, this content lost the character precisely of being a content and became a material foundation of the new order. The great difference with capitalism is that the lack of an objective value regulator leaves the mechanism without a spring, i.e. there is no drive for capital accumulation. Furthermore, without being continually regulated by capital this material presupposition ceased to be posited by capital as its presupposition and hence became subject to a kind of 'drift' – the Soviet factory became *unlike* capitalist factories in many respects.[20]

What was this new social form? It was certainly not socialism. Rather, the requirements of the inherited material basis for some kind of *direction* led with extraordinary rapidity to a bureaucratic dictatorship. As Ticktin has pointed out, to speak here of a 'planned economy' is wildly inaccurate, for the basic information and monitoring systems were not in place because of the antagonism between planners and planned; at most one can speak of an administered economy within which enterprise managers and workers survived as best they could. If it *had* been planned there would have been a good 'fit' between form and content and it would have survived. The trouble arose precisely because the materialisation of capital was freed from capital's controlling form but without another organic system of social metabolism taking root and transforming more or less rapidly and radically the material basis of the economy. Being neither capitalism nor socialism the USSR lacked organic coherence. According to Ticktin 'there are only capitalism and its essence, the law of value, and socialism with its essence, the law of planning; anything in between . . . has no essence, no laws except ones of formation and decay.'[21] This paradoxical character is expressed by Ticktin when he says it was not a mode of production at all (*a fortiori* neither 'state capitalism' nor 'bureaucratic collectivism'). The politically enforced directives were incapable of controlling the factories in such a manner as to promote the development of the productive forces in a stable and permanent fashion.

Lenin (surprisingly for such a political thinker) was enthusiastic about the 'scientific management' pioneered theoretically by Taylor and practically by Ford. But the truth is that Taylorism was never applied in the USSR! (Stakhanovism, besides being purely a publicity stunt, was not scientific in Taylor's sense.) The Soviets had no theoretical objection to it; they *wanted* to apply scientific management; but they were unable to do so because production was governed by a non-capitalist social form. It could not be applied in the USSR because it was tailor-made for capitalism; it is not, as Lenin seemed to imagine, a socially neutral body of knowledge. Moreover, Taylor would roll in his grave if anyone dared to associate him with the gross overmanning characteristic of Soviet industry. Fiat built a factory for the Soviets: it took four times as many workers to run as exactly the same factory in Italy.

The Soviet system was not a labour-saving system but a labour-hoarding one. Clearly where it was illegal to fire workers managers had not much interest in saving labour time. Furthermore they could not organise a just-in-time system because in the USSR supply was never in time. Hence it was important to build up and hoard stocks against such a drying up of supply for more or less long periods. Thus Soviet production worked on the 'never-in-time' system; it took most of the month to get the machinery in order and the inputs delivered, then to meet the monthly targets the factory engaged in a process known as 'storming' when everyone available worked until they dropped; then another hiatus occurred, and so on. In fact managers hoarded labour in case a period of 'storming' to meet a plan deadline is required. I do not think Taylor would call this scientific management! Certainly the workers did not like the hanging about or the storming. And the consumer discovers the products of storming are defective. In sum Taylorism makes no sense when workers jobs are guaranteed.

The inefficiency of the central planning system, combined with the absence of a proper market, resulted in a paradoxical retrogression in the social division of labour. Füredi explains: 'The response of individual production units to the problem caused by the absence of economic regulation is to strive for a measure of self-sufficiency. Thus instead of a mutually beneficial division of labour *between* enterprises, industries and regions, the pattern is for the division of labour to be reproduced *within* each sector of the economy.'[22] Hence there was a fragmentation of the economy and inefficiency. Because 'the goal of any enterprise manager is to reduce his reliance on the overall division of labour to a minimum, to give the best chance of reaching centrally imposed performance targets,'[23] resources were kept hidden from the planners and thus they could not effectively plan for they did not know where the resources were.

I have said, following Hillel Ticktin, that there was no mode of production in the USSR. This purely negative definition does not mean much, except as a promissory note on its collapse. Let me try to give the theory more substance. What is a mode of production? It is a stable, relatively harmonious, combination of a social form and a material content. In Marx's glib aphorism, 'the handmill gives us society with the feudal lord, the steam mill society with the industrial capitalist'. It must be understood that, in the combination, the elements are not indifferent to one another, nor do they exhibit a one-way determination (the Marx passage has been misread as a technological determinism), rather they are dialectically interrelated. Just this form shapes and develops just this content; just this content embodies and reproduces materially just this form. Thus it is the social form of capital that, through its tendency towards competition and enlarged production, brought forth the steam engine; and it was the enormous boost to labour productivity occasioned by it that enabled capitalism to stomp all over pre-capitalist forms. If the social form and material content come into contradiction this spells trouble. For example Marx believed that the increasing socialisation of the productive forces, and associated labour processes, will prove incompatible with their capitalist integument.

What I argue is that the relations of production in the USSR always suffered from an incoherence of form and content. It was a self-aborting montrosity. The matter is not unrelated to its inauspicious beginnings. Apart from the much canvassed political dimensions, the isolated USSR had not the human and technical resources to avoid copying capitalist technique. But when the factory is brought under a quite different social form characterised by the absence of capital's logic, and by employment guarantees, productivity goes out of the window, exploitation is inefficient, and control must be exercised in a new way, i.e. by a bureaucratic apparatus backed up by a police state. This was then reinforced and reproduced as the emerging bureaucracy opted for maintaining their own position at the head of a hierarchical command structure.

The interests of the capitalist are congruent with the growth of social wealth, but the individual interest of the bureaucrat is not. This is why there was no new mode of production. Adam Smith showed long ago that the capitalist benefitted society simply in pursuit of his own interest. The interest of the worker however, was not so self-evidently connected with social wealth; for doubling productivity is immediately in the interests of the capitalist but leaves up to half the workforce unemployed. Now bourgeois apologists may argue that the increase in social wealth will somehow generate new industries to re-employ these people, but this is a very indirect link and the workers may be forgiven for trying to hold on to the jobs they have. The argument for socialism has always appealed to the idea that when the workers work 'for themselves' they will become interested in increasing production and it will be possible to reorganise the technology of the factory to gain the full benefit of this. But in the USSR the factory provided no avenue for workers' initiative and in any case their exclusion from control over the surplus gave them no guarantee that such efforts would benefit themselves or their families. Thus far not much different from capitalism: but in fact worse than capitalism for the individual bureaucrat had no immediate interest of his own in increasing social wealth either. Remember they were not stock holders in the industries under their control. Their rewards depended upon political favour. Hence the resistance to innovation, the tendency to pass the buck and blame others when things went wrong, the hoarding of labour and materials against a future episode of 'storming'. What a bureaucrat wants is above all a quiet life. The reason for what happened was not 'the adoption of

Taylorism' but the necessity to maintain distinctions to justify bureaucratic privilege and prevent the self-organisation of the workers.

If we return to basics we must start the social analysis not from the form of state but from the form of production. It was not production for profit; it was not production for need; it was production for targets laid down external to the logic of the production process itself. In the case of capitalism we know that the law of value transmits from factory to factory the socially necessary labour times for any item, and that capital flows and technological innovation are mutually reinforcing. In the case of production for need we might imagine some mutually informative institutionalisation of producer/consumer relations. But the USSR had no such feed back loops! The targets had no relation to real needs, nor, more importantly, to the real resources and the real capabilites of the factories. No five year plan ever succeeded but had to be drastically reworked year on year. The so-called plans were meaningless because the information available was so corrupted by the political distortions of the system. And where the plan was fulfilled it was often only in the letter and not the substance. The state interfered in the economy, but the system did not regulate itself in accordance with some inherent logic of its productive capacity. Thus I would argue that the well-known phenomenon of a rapid expansion of basic factors of production, followed by chronic paralysis when diverse sophisticated products were required, should not be interpreted as effects of some economic law but as a sign of a lack of law. A combination of political factors (coercion and voluntarist enthusiasm) got things off the ground, but because no new mode of production was stabilised the system could not run itself when these political pressures diminished.[24]

Although the general run of commodites were defective the system was capable of prioritising allocation of materials, machinery and men to certain uses. That is why it worked in war, and why the concentration of scarce resouces, and the best talent, in the armament sector could produce Sputnik. (Of course the presence of imperialism forced this priority on the system which otherwise might have been more rewarding for certain layers of the population.) While there was considerable extensive growth this process itself was enormously wasteful; but the crucial problem was the retardation of intensive growth. Just to cite one problem here; how can the intellectual productive forces be developed on a broad scale when the rulers did not trust people with photocopiers?

In order to make more plausible the claim that no mode of production existed in the USSR let us observe that Ernest Mandel distinguished between specific relations of production, which must characterise any social formation, and a mode of production. This is 'one of the essential distinctions between periods of transition and the great "progressive stages" of history outlined by Marx.'[25] A mode of production is an organic whole that reproduces itself almost automatically. It can only be replaced by violent social revolution. 'On the other hand, precisely because of their generally hybrid character the relations of production of a society in transition between two modes of production can decompose of their own accord, evolve in various directions without necessarily experiencing revolutionary perturbations of the same type as the social revolutions necessary for the passage from one mode of production to another.'[26] So there were certainly relations of production of a sort but no organic system of social metabolism.

The whole experience demonstrates the wisdom of Marx's insight that economics is decisive over politics. The elite wanted to be a true ruling class, and it seemed they had all the power anyone could wish for, with the KGB, the GULAG and the house-trained party milllions; but they could not ground themselves on production; they poured our 'plans', 'decrees', 'orders', 'reforms', but they could not deliver the goods. It was as simple as that.

To summarise this sketch of history: in the pre-capitalist period the *form* of capital emerged; in the capitalist period it seized hold of production and shaped this matter into a *content* adequate to it; in the post-capitalist period this form of capital was extinguished but its material presuppositions were not radically transformed but merely administered within new social relations, resulting in an uncontrolled process of deformation of the material basis in the context of a continued failure for the form and matter to achieve a new organicity.[27]

Beyond Capital

In the final part of this paper I look closely at an impressively argued new book by István Mészáros, which contains a theory of transition worth discussing on its own account, and also for the purpose of further illuminating my own view of the Soviet Union, which overlaps with his. While the necessity of the socialist alternative is reasserted, Mészáros also investigates the reasons for the collapse of the USSR. As the title, *Beyond Capital*, indicates, central to the book is the thesis that it is necessary not merely to go beyond 'capitalism' but beyond 'capital' itself. A lot hangs on the coherence of this distinction, therefore. In particular it is used to characterise Soviet-type régimes of production as being 'post-capitalist' yet still under the sway of 'capital'. He says 'the tragedy of Soviet-type post-capitalist societies was that they followed the line of least resistance by positing socialism without radically overcoming the *material presuppositions* of the capital system'.[28] This is outlined in a fascinating chapter on 'changing forms of the rule of capital'. Capital's metabolism, based on its domination of alienated labour, on the predominance of exchange over use value, and on a hierarchical division of labour, is driven by the imperative of expansion. As a system with its own logic and coherence it cannot be changed without tackling this central metabolic order and replacing it; tinkering with surface phenomena (e.g. juridical arrangements) will not change such fundamentals. Thus Mészáros argues that without the *positive transcendence* of capital's metabolic functioning 'labour itself self-defeatingly continues to reproduce the power of capital over against itself'.[29]

Mészáros concludes that 'the real target of emancipatory transformation is the complete eradication of capital as a totalising mode of control from the social reproductive metabolism itself, and not simply the displacement of the capitalist as the historically specific "personification of capital".'[30] In an interview he expanded on this: 'The bureaucracy is a function of this command structure under the changed circumstances where in the absence of the private capitalist you have to find an equivalent to that control.'[31]

In one version the distinction between capital and capitalism is already familiar to us; for it is a commonplace that merchants and usurers employed money as capital long before capital seized hold of production and established the modern system of industrial capitalism. But it is novel to argue that capital may *survive* capitalism. So let us look first at his definition of capitalism: he argues that the capitalist formation extends over only that particular phase of capital production in which:

(1) production for exchange is all pervasive; (2) labour-power itself is a commodity; (3) the drive for profit is the fundamental regulator; (4) the vital mechanism for the extraction of surplus-value, the radical separation of the means of production from the producers, assumes an inherently economic form; (5) surplus-value is privately appropriated by the members of the capitalist class; (6) following its economic imperative of growth and expansion capital production tends towards a global integration.[32]

It follows from this definition, according to Mészáros, that one cannot speak of 'capitalism' in post-capitalist societies as we have known them.[33] Yet at the same time he argues that 'capital' maintains its rule in such societies. What then is the definition of 'capital' that would be consistent with this survival? He says the necessary conditions of all conceivable forms of the capital relation – including the post-capitalist forms – are:

(1) the separation and alienation of the objective conditions of the labour process from labour itself; (2) the superimposition of such alienated conditions over the workers as a separate power exercising command over labour; (3) the personification of capital as 'egotistic value'[34] pursuing its own self-expansion – the bureaucrat is the post-capitalist equivalent of the private capitalist; (4) the equivalent personification of labour whether as wage-labourer under capitalism or as the norm-fulfilling 'socialist worker' under the post-capitalist system.

'Capital can change the *form of its rule* as long as these four basic conditions – which are constitutive of its "organic system" – are not radically superseded', he concludes.[35]

The key conceptual innovation introduced by Mészáros, then, is a distinction between capital and capitalism. Let us now examine Mészáros's definitions of these. The five point definition of capitalism he gives is generally plausible, but I would challenge it at what might seem its strongest point, namely the criterion that surplus-value is privately appropriated by the members of the capitalist class. Capitalism does not at all refer essentially to such personal appropriation in any simple sense. It is well-known that for Marx the enemy is capital itself, the capitalist featuring merely as 'capital personified'. If capital originally took the shape of such a 'capitalist' this is not definitional of the capital relation, which is purely a matter of capitals being individuated from one another as value bodies and of the subordination of living labour by dead labour. Marx made an error in Volume III when he spoke of the joint stock company (made necessary by the increasing scale of the social productive forces) as the negation of capitalism within capitalism.[36] On the contrary, the elimination of any idiosyncrasy, which the person of an individual capitalist may introduce, when he is replaced by the corporate person (which in law is solely concerned with protecting the investments of the shareholders), results in a *purer* form of capital. It is even possible as an imaginary experiment to see that capital can survive the elimination of the capitalist class. Already the institutions, such as pension funds and insurance companies, have a preponderant role in shareholdings; it is only necessary to imagine that as a result of a punitive inheritance tax the individual capitalists are driven out and the slack taken up by these institutions. But if the corporations were all owned by pension funds this would change nothing about the fundamental metabolism (just as in feudalism Church estates, the beneficiaries of which owned no property, were generally run in the same way as those of the Lords temporal).

Now let us turn to Mészáros's definition of capital. It is a structural requirement of his argument that the criteria be more abstract than those for capitalism so that capitalism may be relegated to one form of the capital system, but it must not be so abstract as to comprehend systems in which no capital relation could plausibly be said to exist. I think this remit is impossible to fulfil and is not in truth fulfilled by Mészáros. His four part definition of capital may be reduced to a two part one because items 1, 2 & 4 are all about the alienation of the labourer, while only point 3 refers to the presence of capital which is defined here as 'egotistic value pursuing its own self-expansion'. However it is unclear how seriously we are meant to take the term 'value' here because Mészáros generally talks not of surplus-value but of surplus labour, for example he says 'capital accumulation' in the USSR was 'secured by means of politically controlled extraction of surplus labour'.[37] But it is impermissible to play fast and loose with 'surplus-value' and 'surplus labour' – the existence of the latter (as it is common to all exploitative modes of production) does not at all prove the existence of capital which is accumulated value via profit on any reasonable reading of Marx.

What on earth is his concept of capital if it has no reference to value, sur-plus-value, or profit?

It can only relate to the so-called organic system of metabolic control under-stood in *use value* terms, that the very organisation of material production qualifies here as capital and that in virtue of that material organisation it sub-ordinates labour to its purpose of uncontrolled self-expansion in which the latter must be understood not as valorisation, but as expansion of physical plant. There are two things wrong here. Such a system would not constitute capital accumulation which is necessarily a value form; and there was in the USSR no immanent tendency to self-expansion. But everyone would agree that capital is inherently accumulation driven. Indeed Mészáros goes out of his way to argue that this was still true of the USSR:

> The imperative of accumulation driven expansion can be satisfied under changed economic circumstances not only without the subjective 'profit motive' but even without the objective requirement of profit, which hap-pens to be an absolute necessity only in the capitalist variety of the capital system.... During several decades of Soviet economic development high levels of capital accumulation [were] secured by means of the politically controlled extraction of surplus labour, without remotely resembling the capitalist system in its necessary orientation towards profit.[38]

This seems very odd to me; in capitalism we see the hegemony over pro-duction of value forms including, especially, capital – not production for pro-duction's sake but for the sake of *profit*. Capital as a subject is essentially a value form and cannot survive the abolition of profit. What was accumulated in the USSR, however, was not capital but means of production lacking the form of capital. Moreover the accumulation-fetish was not rooted in 'the meta-bolic order' but in the hopes of the controllers, who imposed external 'tar-gets', terroristically driven. If the USSR as a 'capital' system was really expansion orientated, how is that compatible with the failure to innovate which led to permanent stagnation? No matter how the political authority, for external reasons of state, tried to coerce or stimulate the producers, the economy responded only sluggishly in quantitative terms, and innovation became completely bogged down.[39] This was crucial politically; for the fail-ure to 'catch up' with the West, and the failure to achieve real growth in the

Brezhnev years, stripped the system of legitimacy, even in the eyes of its beneficiaries, and brought about the implosion. Mészáros argues in his point 3 that the bureaucrat is the post-capitalist equivalent of the private capitalist as the representative of capital. The bureaucrat is certainly the representative of a material metabolism so structured as to expropriate the subjectivity of the workers; but his interest in controlling the workers is not in expansion per se but simply in meeting externally imposed targets; hence neither capital nor any new personification of it (the bureaucracy) can be present. What is true is that, as it inherited the materialisation of capital, the Soviet factory was characterised by a hierarchical division of labour and the subordination of the immediate producer to alien purposes. Saying this we have now reduced Mészáros's definition effectively to the other three points to do with the claim the USSR, like capitalism, rested on the exploitation of alienated labour.

Let us examine Mészáros's claims in relation to this other part of his core definition of capital namely the following: 'the *separation* and *alienation* of the objective conditions of the labour process from labour itself'; 'the superimposition of such objectified and alienated conditions over the workers as a separate power exercising *command over labour*'; for the sake of the pursuit of 'self-expansion'. Clearly there is considerable room for discussion about such a definition of capital. As I have already argued, without the drive of self-valorisation infusing the conditions of production there is no immanent tendency to expansion. On the other hand it is true that the organisation of labour both materially and socially is at first sight directed towards exercising 'command over labour'; however the empirical record (see books cited earlier) shows that this failed miserably to achieve its objectives precisely because the 'mode of production' within which the factories were now set was radically changed.

There is an interesting contrast between the Marx of 1844 who assimilated feudalism and capitalism under the general category of alienation of the conditions of labour from the worker, and the Marx of 1857 who was concerned to sharply demarcate capitalist from pre-capitalist forms on the grounds that in capitalism the worker was at the mercy of the decisions of the private owner in finding work, whereas in feudalism the communal system of production was prior to and included the immediate producer. Now if we think about this distinction of 1857 then we can see that in the USSR the 'community' was also prior to labour in that, just as in feudalism, the worker must work but cannot be fired. Therefore Mészáros's inclusion of the term 'separation' in the above definition is mistaken. Strictly speaking there was no separation of workers from the conditions of production – the Soviet manager was stuck with the workers just as the feudal estate carried its complement of serfs. The Marx of 1844 read feudalism as another system in which the conditions of labour are dominant over the workers; the Marx of 1857 insists that capitalism is different from feudalism in that in feudalism the worker is presupposed as in unity with the conditions whereas in capitalism he is separated from them and 'seeking work'. Now it is obvious that the USSR conforms to the feudal model. Even if the conditions are dominant over the worker it is still true that there is the presupposed community which both forces people to work and supposedly guarantees work. Just as in feudalism, the powerlessness of the immediate producer was politically grounded in the USSR, rather than on the economic 'separation' from the conditions of production; if anything they were *part* of these conditions.

Mészáros's strongest argument is that real subsumption of labour under capital was retained in the USSR. Originally this was organised in capital's interest to produce value: hence capital's obsession with time saving and the expropriation of control over the production process from the immediate producer. But when the factory is detached from the value regulator and enters into a new relation of production there is a significant loss of such 'command' as the empirical studies show; yet Mészáros rightly includes 'command' as a *sine qua non* of the capital relation, and hopes for 'the total eradication of capital from the social metabolism as *command over labour*'.[40] He supports himself with a couple of quotations which do lend some colour to his position, in particular a passage from the *Grundrisse* in which Marx speaks of 'the monstrous objective power' belonging to 'the personified conditions of production. i.e. to capital'.[41] This is key to Mészáros's whole position. My own position is the converse: that the monstrous power of the conditions of production over labour is due to its being the materialisation of the capital form where capital's personification arises from the acquired independence of value and more specifically the domination of self-valorising value as a form, the objective conditions being shaped into its content. The 'monstrous power' of the factory organisation is shaped by the imperative of valorisation and is hence the materialisation of capital. Although the factory system is tailor-made to expropriate the subjectivity of the worker the counter-subject that exercises command is self-valorising value not its material integument. To identify the source of the problem with the factories, rather than their social form, is an easy mistake when the conditions of labour are form-determined by capital. But that organisation extracted from its social form has no inherent drive to expand. This view falsely assumes the *only* way it can function is as it was designed to do, and hence calls forth for its appropriate personification a replacement for the private capitalist. So if it functions in the same way as in capitalism we might as well say it is capital. This is what Mészáros seems to imagine.

At the deepest philosophical level Mészáros overgeneralises the notion of a subject-object reversal. 'Originally' the subject is the producer and the object is the conditions of production, including the tools wielded by the worker. If one simply inverts this then the worker becomes the object to be 'commanded' and the subject becomes 'the personified conditions of production' – which is clearly how Mészáros understands capital. But, even though Marx gives warrant for this reading in some of his remarks, this is a wrong-headed account of what actually occurs in capitalism. For what it is worth, in 1867 Marx defines capital as a 'subject'[42] long before he discusses production; he clearly bases it on the 'developed movement of circulation' namely M-C-M.

In practice when Mészáros discusses in detail how exactly capital has established itself he concentrates not on the forms of circulation but on the level of production. Even though it is true that the worker experiences the conditions of production as an alien power, indeed he experiences even his own labour as alien, this is misleading, for the true subject, namely capital, is not the personified conditions of production but self-valorising value defined by the formula M-C-M; when this circuit sinks into production, and becomes M-C . . . P . . . C-M, it constitutes the conditions of labour as alien to the worker.

Mészáros tries to go from labour (that is alienated labour) to capital without taking seriously 'developed circulation'; thus the way is open for him to identify alienated labour in the Soviet Union with the rule of capital for he takes capital as identical with the estrangement of the material conditions of labour from the worker. Since such alienation continued in the USSR he misidentifies it as founded on capital. He thinks that in capital it is the autonomy of the material conditions of production that is the problem, whereas in fact it is the autonomy of value and the imposition on production of self-valorising value that is the root of the problem, the factory organisation being the materialisation of capital.

Time and again Mészáros argues that capital continues in being until replaced by *another organic system* namely socialism.[43] What is missed here is the possibility of something stalled, the negation of capital which is not yet the supersession of capital, an existent contradiction therefore, thus precisely a system not organically coherent and therefore lacking any immanent motor of reproduction. But a negation of capital that fails to go beyond capital is necessarily a negation of capital that falls behind capital. (Hence the perception of Soviet workers that they were serfs and their initial enthusiasm for the market as a liberation.)

Mészáros is clearly right to argue that socialist revolution is not merely a matter of a transfer of political power, or of redistribution, but of changing the fundamental social metabolism established by capital; it means transforming the very structure of material production and abolishing the hierarchical division of labour. He is clearly right that post-capitalist social formations failed to achieve this positive transcendence; and the emergence of 'the bureaucracy' is explicable primarily on that basis. His conceptualisation of the problem in terms of the survival of 'capital' beyond 'capitalism' is most interesting; but although we both see 'the moment of capital' in the USSR, what I call the materialisation of capital Mészáros identifies with capital itself. In the sense that something survives from the previous period our views overlap; my difference with his account relates to what survives. This raises interesting issues about the *concepts* involved. Mészáros identifies capital's social metabolism with the system of material interchanges; he focusses on the factory system. This sounds thoroughly materialist, but in my view this level of the social metabolism cannot be understood as having its own organic coherence and dynamic. It is only comprehensible as the bearer of, and subordinated to, an ideal metabolism, the interchange of values constitutive of the life of capital. Thus the general line of my critique of Mészáros is that he pays insufficient attention to the *value form* of capital, and the positing of expansion inherent in its search for profit.

Does this difference between my claim that the materialisation of capital survives, and the view of Mészáros that capital survives, amount to no more than semantics? No, because my view gives a better explanation of collapse.

Conclusion

I argue that in the Soviet Union capital's metabolism was disrupted without an alternative being established; lacking organic coherence, the system could not survive once the exceptional conditions of revolutionary mobilisation, of terror, and of war, passed. The USSR has to be seen as the negation of socialism within socialism, and tendentially refounding capitalism as indeed occurred. This is because the benefits of social ownership are only possible with self-management; but where materialised capital remained, without the capitalist economic form to direct it, there was nothing to motivate efficiency; voluntarism, coercion, incentives, all failed. Hence the chronic crisis of under-utilisation of resources, massive waste, defective products, and final collapse. Certainly, if the factory system in which capital materialised itself remains, then one cannot speak of socialism; but, conversely, if the law of value enforced through capitalist competition is no longer operative we have a clock without a spring.

[1] The first such attempt was Leon Trotsky's *Revolution Betrayed* (1936). For a critique of Trotsky see: Arthur, C. J. 1972 'The Coming Soviet Revolution'.
[2] The form-matter distinction is not absolute; there is no such thing as completely formless matter. It is more a question of the reforming of matter that is at issue.
[3] Marx, K. 1988 'Economic Manuscript of 1861–63', p. 32.
[4] For more on this see Arthur, C. J. 2000 'From the Critique of Hegel to the Critique of Capital'.
[5] Marx, K. 1988 'Economic Manuscript of 1861–63' p. 428; Marx, K. 1994 'Economic Manuscript of 1861–63' pp. 117–121.
[6] Marx, K. 1994 'Economic Manuscript of 1861–63' p. 424.
[7] Marx, K. 1994 'Economic Manuscript of 1861–63' p. 426.
[8] Marx, K. 1994 'Economic Manuscript of 1861–63', p. 426.
[9] For Marx on the nature of an 'organic system' see Marx, K. 1973 *Grundrisse*, p. 278 and p. 100.
[10] Marx, K. 1976 *Capital* Volume I, p. 133; Marx, K. 1962 *Das Kapital: Erster Band* p. 57.
[11] Marx, K. 1976 *Capital* Volume I, p. 283, and p. 290.

[12] Marx, K. 1976 *Capital* Volume I, pp. 198–9; Marx, K. 1962 *Das Kapital: Erster Band* p. 119. Contrary to the Penguin translator Ben Fowkes (p. 198n), this was not the first place Marx uses the term *Stoffwechsel*: we have seen it earlier in *Capital* itself (p. 133), and it was first employed ten years before in Marx's *Grundrisse* as we shall see below.

[13] Marx, K. 1976 *Capital* Volume I, p. 210; Marx, K. 1962 *Das Kapital: Erster Band*, p. 128.

[14] Marx, K. 1987 'Economic Manuscripts of 1857–58' p. 25. In German: *'Ein System von Austauschen, Stoffwechsel, so weit der Gebrauchswerth betrachtet, Formwechsel, so weit der Werth als solcher betrachtet wird.'* Marx, K. 1981 *Ökonomische Manuskripte 1857/58* p. 522. (For some reason Nicolaus gets it the wrong way round: Marx, K. 1973 *Grundrisse* p. 637.)

[15] Marx, K. 1978 *Capital* Volume II, p. 226 The translator's note referring us back to the chapter on the labour process is in my view slightly inaccurate; the context seems to indicate Marx was thinking more of the exchange of products discussed in *Capital* Volume 1, pp. 198–9.

[16] Stedman Jones, G. 1990, 'Dialectical reasoning' p. 127.

[17] A good analogy is computing. There is the software logic, which is here the demand of valorisation flowing from the form, and the firing sequence in the hardware, which is here the production process. The question is how far the hardware *supports* the software. One could argue that at a minimum it must have the labour-power chip in it.

[18] Marx, K. 1973 *Grundrisse* p. 259.

[19] Marx, K. 1973 *Grundrisse* p. 692, p. 693, p. 694, p. 699.

[20] See these informative studies: Filtzer, D. 1986 *Soviet Workers and Stalinist Industrialisation*; Füredi, F. 1986 *The Soviet Union demystified*; Ticktin, H. 1992 *Origins of the Crisis in the USSR*; Arnot, B. 1988 *Controlling Soviet Labour*.

[21] Ticktin, H. 1992 *Origins of the Crisis in the USSR* p. 14. The 'law of planning' does not necessarily mean *central* planning of all details. Local self-management is necessary in order to integrate what Hilary Wainwright has called 'tacit knowledge' possessed by the workers of a given enterprise founded in experience and a tradition of 'know-how'.

[22] Füredi, F. 1986 *The Soviet Union demystified,* p. 103.

[23] Füredi, F. 1986 *The Soviet Union demystified* p. 124.

[24] A fascinating, but imponderable, question (asked of me by Riccardo Bellofiore) is whether or not, if there had been no more advanced external world competing with it, the USSR could have carried on indefinitely absorbing its own inefficiencies. One recalls that it took war with superior economies to break down Tsarism.

[25] Mandel, E. 1978 'On the Nature of the Soviet State' p. 28.

[26] Mandel, E. 1978 'On the Nature of the Soviet State' p. 29.

[27] Of course a more or less long period of transition to socialism is inevitable, but it can be argued that things would be very different if a transition were to occur with an educated work-force and a democratic tradition; then self-management and political progress could be a real possibility.

[28] Mészáros, I 1995 *Beyond Capital,* p. 621.

[29] Mészáros, I 1995 *Beyond Capital,* p. 494.

[30] Mészáros, I 1995 *Beyond Capital,* p. 369.

[31] Mészáros, I 1995 *Beyond Capital,* p. 981.

[32] Mészáros, I 1995 *Beyond Capital,* p. 630.

[33] Mészáros, I 1995 *Beyond Capital,* p. 631.

[34] Marx, K. 1973 *Grundrisse,* p. 303.

[35] Mészáros, I 1995 *Beyond Capital,* p. 617.

[36] Marx, K. 1981 *Capital* Volume III pp. 567–69.

[37] Mészáros, I 1995 *Beyond Capital,* p. 780.

[38] Mészáros, I 1995 *Beyond Capital,*p. 780.

[39] An important technical point is that where relative surplus-value is concerned this is premised on competition between capitals. Without this the relations of domination may well promote absolute surplus-value production, and extensive growth, but this is insufficient to power dynamic growth intensively.

[40] Mészáros, I 1995 *Beyond Capital,* p. 619.

[41] Marx, K. 1973 *Grundrisse,* p. 831, quoted Mészáros, I 1995 *Beyond Capital,* p. 620.

[42] *Capital* Volume 1, p. 255, and Marx, K. 1973 *Grundrisse,* p. 266.

[43] Mészáros, I 1995 *Beyond Capital,* p. 617, p. 622.

Chapter Eleven
Whose Reason? and Whose Revolution?

'Reason' with a capital 'R' does nothing; it fights no fights; it produces no actions, arguments, explanations or justifications; reason is exercised by a material subject: it is the latter who reasons, acts, etc., and whose rationality, in thought and deed, is assessed by other rational beings. Thus the philosophical problems that arise here are not only the formal ones dealt with by logic, but also the ontological ones, concerned with the nature and situation of the being who reasons, or from whose standpoint reason is being exercised (for example I shall argue that Marx reasons from the standpoint of the proletariat), and their relation to other such subjects. Here I am concerned with practical reason, which poses particularly acute problems; that is, I am concerned with the problem of identifying a material subject able to decide rationally what to do. Is it, or is it not, equally as sensible to ask what it is rational for *us* to do as to ask what it is rational for *me* to do? The ramifications of this issue will be explored in the case of the socialist project. To begin with, I look at the situation of an individual having to act within a set of social institutions, and I argue that reason cannot speak with a single voice wherever the norms enjoining conformity with the system conflict with elementary self-assertion on the part of disadvantaged sections of society whose needs it meets only minimally and insecurely. Such a system might be said to be 'irrational'. So I then raise the question of the status of judgments about the rationality or irrationality of the system as a whole (that is, as opposed to judgments about the rationality of acts defined within it). Distinguishing between concrete reason and abstract reason, I maintain that such a standpoint (that is, of the totality) can be concretely rational only in unity with the practice of a class subject. I consider the conditions that give historical form and validity to the interests and practice of the revolutionary class. Finally I address the mediations that secure its class identity.

The Individual and Institutions

Where a range of actions are identified by reference to a pre-existing institutional practice an action can be justified by reference to that practice: 'I paid the money because I owe it to him' make sense, and can be accepted as a complete explanation, given various credit institutions. The justification of the practice itself is another problem however.

In so far as social institutions make available certain ends and means, by that very fact they will be structured in such a way as to exclude other means and ends; an individual can live by Stock Exchange speculation only if there is a Stock Exchange. We can thus refer to the 'rationality of the system' as short-hand for this feature; that is, the rationality of the system is a description of the ends and means it permits, the way it structures interests and provides avenues for their satisfaction. The model of 'rational economic man' exemplifies this in the case of capitalist rationality. Capitalist rationality enjoins one to speculate against the pound regardless of the Government's view that this is unpatriotic. Another example: an old-age pensioner may need a television set but the need will not be recognised at all by the commodity system unless it can be translated into (money) 'demand'.

Before moving to my main problem, I would like to consider the rationality of individual transgression of the rules of social life. When individuals seek to meet their needs in the context of a certain set of social institutions these institutions determine the meaning of each person's behaviour independently of the description that may be chosen by the individual in question. Someone living in a certain property system may tell themselves that they have a fundamental need to read and describe a certain action of theirs as providing for that need; but in doing so they are abstracting from the institutional set-ting in which they met it. If in their action they fail to conform to the insti-tutional setting presently regulating the distribution of books they are liable to find their action defined as stealing, and they themselves as a book-thief. It is, of course, not possible to be described as a book-thief outside the con-text of an institution that regulates the distribution of books in a certain way; stealing from a library has a slightly different set of criteria than stealing from a bookshop.

The point I want to stress is that only the existing norms correlative with the rationality of the system are concretely universalisable. Kant was quite right to argue that a person lacks any moral integrity if their actions are unprin-cipled; but he was quite unable to establish which principles are the right ones. Of course there is something odd about a professional thief indignantly calling in the police when his own house is turned over; but there is noth-ing inconsistent about the idea of a complete absence of property right. The concrete content needed to supplement Kant's formal maxims is supplied by the 'reason' embodied in the customary forms of life of the community. Stealing is not wrong in the abstract; it is wrong because one lives in a community which reproduces itself in accordance with a framework of private property.

Now we can see straight away that this is not the whole story. Some social systems are so indifferent to the basic needs of sections of the population that the latter have no recourse but to become outlaws. In such a condition legal sanctions hold no terrors and moral imperatives seem empty and hypocrit-ical. Self-preservation is an unimpeachably good reason for action. But even if the extreme case is neglected, Reason cannot speak with a single voice whenever we can demonstrate that rational self-interest, and the public inter-est safe-guarded by social norms, are in conflict. This will be especially obvi-ous when the rationality of the system promotes inequality.

While accepting this duality, I would like to refute here one particular pseudo-revolutionary gloss on transgression. I return to the example of stealing books. I have often been frustrated in libraries and bookshops because the volumes I required had been stolen by people I call 'lumpen-revolutionaries'.[1] These people differ from ordinary thieves in that they describe their actions in pos-itive tones as 'ripping off the system'. They do not excuse it as due to some personal difficulty they were in, thus implicitly accepting the legitimacy of the norms enshrined in the present practices regulating the distribution of goods. Rather, they deny any wrong-doing and invite praise for their revolutionary defiance of existing norms.

I think there is something very abstract about this reasoning. It is one thing to say that the private property system is an irrational and unfair way of distributing goods, to argue that needs are only inefficiently and unevenly satisfied in the present system of ownership and exchange; it is another thing to take books from a bookshop without paying for them *in* the present system. To advance beliefs about the relative merits of alternative systems as a *direct* justification for actions within the present is to behave as if actions can be isolated from their institutional setting and evaluated by freely chosen norms. The book-thief cannot get around the fact that the social context of such behaviour constitutes it as stealing. The action, although a form of negation of property, does not amount to a reconstruction of the property system; it is an *abstract negation* of social rules. As such its social meaning is determined by the system as it is. To defend it is therefore to defend the proposition that 'Stealing is right'. Now the usual Kantian argument applies: not everyone can live by stealing because then nobody would be producing anything to steal. Stealing does not transform social reality, rather it is logically and materially parasitic on the existing institutions. As well as being impossible to justify rationally in the manner cited, the anti-social consequences of such an act cannot be ignored. A bookstore may be forced to close altogether to the net loss of everybody. Whatever grounds for each offence there may have been the overall effect is to promote insecurity. Even where the institutions survive, the necessary security measures degrade the quality of the service.

I have said that one cannot justify directly an infringement of an existing social practice by reference to the allegedly superior quality of non-existent alternative practices, because, for practical purposes, it is the meaning of the action within the existing system that determines the kind of act that it is. However, it is perfectly reasonable to make *indirect* connections between the ideal and such infringements, along the lines of the end justifying the means. Occasional exploits such as the mass expropriation of goods, and their subsequent distribution to the poor, may have a propaganda value in drawing attention to the failure of the existing system to meet needs equitably. *Collective refusal to pay rent, or fares, combined with the propagation of an alternative* programme for meeting social needs increases the confidence of people in their power to change the system.

To return to the main point: I have shown that obedience to the rationality of the system on the one hand, and particular negations of its norms (constituted by acts of self-assertion on the part of disadvantaged sections) on the other, are both equally valid, that this contradiction cannot be resolved in theory if it expresses the structure of a material situation. It follows that only a practical transformation of that reality is capable of resolving it.[2] In the next section therefore I raise the problem of whose 'reason' it is that is embodied in such a transformative practice.

The Individual and the Class

Considering matters from the standpoint of the standards of rationality implicit in it, the actions of an individual within the system have to be judged in terms of their efficacy *in the system*, how closely they fit its rationality: the 'done thing' is both *descriptive* and *prescriptive*. Yet at the same time, in view of the possibility of other arrangements, it may be said that the existing social institutions are themselves 'irrational' from some 'larger' standpoint. This brings up a crucial point, namely what problems are involved in condemning a whole social structure as irrational, and advocating its transformation?

The difficulties inherent in this sort of judgment constitute the problem of this section. At this point, too, there is a 'change of gear' in that I leave behind the level of abstraction of the first section. From here on I am going to work with the concrete case in which I am especially interested, namely the socialist project, and, in doing so, taking as premises such substantive claims of Marx's analysis as that capitalist society is inherently exploitative.

Consider the contradictory behaviour of someone without property, specifically without means of production, in a society based on private property. The rationality of the system enjoins one to sell one's labour-power to the capitalists (who monopolise the means of production) simply in order to live. Yet, insofar as one thus alienates one's labour, the surplus-value created by it only serves to expand the power of capital, reinforcing one's subordination to it. The system which oppresses workers by systematically excluding them from the wealth created by labour could not exist without the continual exploitation of labourers. In a sense therefore it is disadvantageous for them to participate in such a system. Yet daily they do so in order to survive. If there is anything worse than being exploited it is not being exploited!

The behaviour of such workers is capable of alternative evaluations. In terms of the rationality of the system they are good utilitarians, preferring half a loaf rather than no bread. In so far as they desire a whole loaf the rationality of the system enjoins each of them to be a 'blue-eyed boy' in search of promotion, to be thrifty, and to be enterprising enough to join the democracy of property owners. But this solution is for some individuals only; it is presupposed that only some can succeed. From another point of view each worker is a wage-slave, a member of a class of such wage-slaves, which can be emancipated as a class only by means of a total restructuring of society involving the abolition of wage slavery.

The latter way of talking poses problems: from what standpoint can the judgment be made that the situation of the class as a whole is unacceptable? In the first place it is clear that, although it is not much a choice, selling one's labour and starving are both specifiable in terms available within capitalist rationality. But the choice between wage-slavery, and revolution, requires reasoning at the level of the totality of the institutional structure and its potential for retotalisation; the object with which reason works is not a particular nexus of the system but the totality itself. Bearing in mind the ontological principle mentioned in our opening remarks, the question arises: whose 'reason' is operative here? Can the standpoint expressed in such judgments as 'wage-slavery ought to be abolished' be ascribed to a concrete subject?

In order to illuminate the importance of this problem I make a distinction between abstract reason and concrete reason. Briefly, the point of the distinction lies in the failure of abstract reason to relate to practice, but there may be several ways in which this can occur. An example of concrete reasoning is 'If I keep reading Hegel I will eventually understand him'; for, although possibly false, this judgment is concretely unified with my practice, namely my present and future studies. Karl Popper, on the other hand, is a splendid example of an abstract reasoner. In arguing against the Marxist account of the relative priority of economics over politics, he simplifies this to a straw-man theory of the impotence of politics,[3] and then says:

Political power is fundamental. . . . We can, for instance, develop a rational political programme for the protection of the economically weak. . . . And when we are able by law to guarantee a livelihood to everybody willing to work, and there is no reason why we should not achieve that, then the protection of the freedom of the citizen from economic fear and economic intimidation will approach completeness. . . . Economic power must not be permitted to dominate political power; if necessary, it must be fought and brought under control by political power.[4]

But who is the 'we' postulated in this morality play? Presumably it is not so comprehensive as to include a government intent on crippling workers' organisations. In the last sentence Popper even hypostatises the abstract concept of political power and charges it with the task of doing all the fighting. All the problems about the relationship of forces in society, about the power of the State machine, about ideology and the development of class-consciousness, about the role and organisation of parties and other sociopolitical formations, about mass mobilisation and parliamentarism, which have defeated many of the best brains in the socialist movement, are ignored by Popper with his touching faith in the abstract entities 'we' and 'political power'. Popper's whole construction falls to the ground if 'we' is replaced with 'each of us' or something similar. If, by such constructions as 'we can use our political power to make laws' etc., Popper simply means that each of us has the possibility of participating in politics, at least in a 'democracy', then the question as to the relation of economics and politics that he avoids by saying 'we can make laws' is opened. For instead of talking about the things 'we' might take it into its head to do, one would have to start from concrete individuals, with particular problems, class interests, religious affiliation, level of education, occupation, and position in the existing social hierarchy. One would have to discuss ways in which different individual's ideas are formed, how realistic they are, the opportunities and difficulties they have in propagating them and combining with others to implement them; this political problematic is conditioned, whether those involved realise it or not, by the class structure and the underlying economic development. Most importantly, from the point of view of our argument here, the very question of the constitution of a historical subject capable of theoretically and practically intervening in society is kept out of sight by Popper.

To return to the main argument: it is clear that an individual thinker can argue that 'wage-slavery ought to be abolished' only abstractly, because simply as such the judgment remains isolated from practice. If it is possible for the judgment to be unified with the practice of a material subject then it becomes concrete. How could this happen? On the one hand strict limitations are inherent in the standpoint of individualism, which must view the social structure as a 'given' basis delimiting the options open to individuals. Yet, on the other hand, it is clear that these structures are not given like the climatic and geographical bases of activity; they owe their genesis to history, that is to say, to the activity of 'humanity' (as a whole). However, the concept of 'humanity' cannot provide a practical attitude to the given reality for the opposite reason to that which rules out the individual; the individual is a concrete subject of activity, but too limited in its powers; 'humanity' seems all powerful but it is not possible to posit the unity and consciousness necessary to flesh out this abstraction. Such a standpoint can only be that of some shadowy Hegelian 'spirit of the time', sufficiently exploded by Marx's trenchant critique in *The German Ideology* and elsewhere.

For Marx the problem of historical genesis is solved by reference to class action. The class is *particular* enough to have the necessary unity of interest, and solidarity in action, while powerful enough to envisage a *universal* mission and to realise it through revolutionary practice. It is not the individual wage-labourer, but the class of wage-labourers embarked on class struggle, that provides a material basis for the abolition of wage slavery.

It will now be clear that when we were earlier contrasting two ways of talking about the situation of the proletarian (namely the one in terms of the rationality of the system and the other formulated in terms of the totality of the institutional structures, or social relations) we were not comparing alternative strategies and finding one more rational than the other. Rather we were comparing two standpoints. The objects with which reason worked differed in nature because they constituted the appropriate fields for the concrete reason of two different *subjects*. (Although we should add, to avoid the charge of dualism, that these subjects are dialectically related in that they arise – both conceptually and materially – out of the contradictions in the social existence of the proletarians.) For an individual proletarian, as such, the objective situation in which they are placed makes only one strategy rational (namely to seek advancement within the system) because the alternative, given by the second way of talking, cannot be posed as a real choice for an individual as an individual, but only for a class-member considering matters from a class standpoint.

Individual consciousness of the possibility of overcoming wage-slavery could only take the form of an abstract utopian moralising. ('Wage-slavery is bad; socialism would be good.') An unbridgeable gap appears between the way things are and the way they ought to be. The gap is not so much logical as ontological; it results from the limitations inherent in the practical being of the individualistic standpoint. In order to avoid the charge that the standpoint of totality degenerates into abstract moralising and utopian dreaming, it is essential to show that this standpoint can provide a guide to action by a material subject, not simply an ideal to contemplate. But only the class can relate to the whole of reality in a practical revolutionary way. What does Marx have to say about conditions for class-consciousness? In the case of the proletariat he says:

> Economic conditions had first transformed the mass of the people of the country into workers. The domination of capital has created for this mass a common situation, common interests. This mass is thus already a class as against capital but not yet a class for itself. In the struggle . . . this mass becomes united, and constitutes itself as a class for itself. The interests it defends become class interests. But the struggle of class against class is a political struggle.[5]

It is necessary to stress that, in addition to the proletariat's numerical weight and key position in the productive process, its special relation to the historically determined problems of the age must be considered. For effective class-consciousness to form, it is by no means sufficient that we have a group of people in a similar social situation, if they are unable to act on this basis. Marx says of the French peasantry:

> The great mass of the French nation is formed by simple addition of homologous magnitudes, much as potatoes in a sack form a sack of potatoes. Insofar as millions of families live under economic conditions of existence that separate their mode of life, their interests, and their culture from those of the other classes, and put them in hostile opposition to the latter, they form a

class. Insofar as there is merely a local interconnection among these small-holding peasants, and the identity of their interests begets no community, no national bond and no political organisation among them, they do not form a class.[6]

According to Marx the mode of insertion of the French peasantry in the social structure does not provide a basis for independent action. They are incapable of acting in their own name and must be represented by others. The proletariat however is supposed to be different. Marx again:

> It is not a question of what this or that proletarian, or even the whole proletariat, at the moment *regards* as its aim. It is a question of *what the proletariat is*, and what, in accordance with this *being*, it will historically be compelled to do. Its aim and historical action is visible and irrevocably *foreshadowed* in its own life situation as well as in the whole organisation of bourgeois society today. There is no need to explain here that a large part of the English and French proletariat is already *conscious* of its historic task and is constantly working to develop that consciousness into complete clarity.[7]

We see here that Marx thinks there is something about the organisation of bourgeois society itself which gives sense to the notion of the proletariat being more than a group within that society but of having a special 'historic task' to perform in relation to it. As he explicitly allows, this proletarian standpoint has to be identified independently of what actual workers at any given moment take to be their aim.

At the same time Marx is interested in the empirical conditions within which consciousness develops. Here the proletariat 'disciplined, united, organised by the very mechanism of the process of capitalist production itself'[8] is more favourably placed than the peasantry whose mode of production isolates them from one another. However, the revolutionary aim Marx ascribes to the proletariat cannot be derived, inductively, or in any other way, simply from the existence of conditions of work favouring group solidarity. Group solidarity can perfectly well be articulated within the conceptual framework provided by capitalist rationality. A wage worker can recognise similarities with other such workers, and they can form a Trade Union to defend common interests, even though it is difficult to supersede their competitive situation in the labour market. (The Trade Union is 'a school for socialism' simply in the sense that it overcomes atomism through a limited generalisation of interests.) It is even possible for them to intervene in politics by mounting pressure for Factory Acts and the like. However, such group consciousness does not put the wage-system itself into question. A clear distinction must be drawn between activity designed to protect and advance the position of labour within the system and revolutionary action to change the system. The latter cannot be derived by studying the situation of the workers defined by the social structure of capitalism and its associated capitalist rationality, but only by relating the standpoint of the workers to the movement of history and the historically meaningful alternatives to capitalism. It is only because the dialectic of capital's own development implicitly puts socialism on the agenda that the revolutionary potential of the proletariat can be posited.

To put it negatively, it was not only the isolation of the French peasants from one another that prevented them from playing an independent historical role, and delivered them to the demagogy of Louis Bonaparte; it was also the lack of an historically grounded political programme. The peasants could complain of 'abuses', and suggest reforms, but they could not envisage a social transformation of the situation that ineluctably generated 'abuses' and the need for reforms.

Marx believed that the class interests of the proletariat lead to the class constituting itself on the basis of a self-transcending practice, i.e. one which envisages its final emancipation through a transformation of the structures defining its subordination. All this makes it clear that the class-consciousness (in the fullest sense) of the proletariat has to be identified in a rather recondite way. The immediacy of class existence, i.e. labour-power as a commodity, must be distinguished from a form of consciousness situating the class in the structured totality of social relations underlying commodity exchange. Only the latter form of consciousness provides the class with the possibility of a dialectical negation of capitalism. Luddism provides an example of a form of very militant action which remained stuck at the level of immediacy. Instead of grasping capitalism as a structured totality which must be reconstituted as a whole, the Luddites perceived it only in terms of the face it presented to them. They depended for their daily survival on the sale of labour. Their immediate enemies were the machines which threatened to deprive them of their jobs. They tried to oppose this alarming development in an equally immediate way by breaking the machines. Such a negation of capital may be called an 'abstract negation' in so far as it is not founded on an intervention in the inner development of capitalism. It fails to resolve the conflict through a synthesis which take up what was positive in capitalism's achievement, and instead it abstracts one element (the machine) from the total picture and attempts to destroy it in isolation. Even if the Luddites were continually successful this would only mean that capitalism remained stalled; the dialectical negation, by contrast, negates the negation between living labour and dead labour by addressing the relation between them.

In this section I have argued that the putative revolutionary agent is the exploited class. Only the class as a whole, not the individual, has a potential for retotalisation; only reasoning from its standpoint is concretely unified with practice. Nonetheless the class is made up of individuals: how can their class identity come to the fore? This is the final problem I address.

Class Identity and its Mediations

Lukács famously defined class consciousness as follows:

> Class consciousness consists in fact of the appropriate and rational reactions "imputed" to a particular typical position in the process of production. This consciousness is, therefore, neither the sum nor the average of what is thought or felt by the single individuals who make up the class.[9]

It might seem, then, that Marxists such as Lukács try to foist their own agenda ('imputed class consciousness') onto the proletariat at the expense of the aims the individuals might adopt. However I do not think it is fair here to speak of some substitutionist option: 'It would be nice if the class thought as we do, so let us impute such a content to their "true" consciousness'. The necessity of this consciousness is founded on a scientific study of capitalist society which reveals the structural antagonism inherent in it. This result allows us to infer two complementary conclusions.

First, that only classes defined by this structural antagonism can be expected to be practically effective in relation to the organisation of the sum of inter-human relationships; Kant and Hegel reasoned from the standpoint of the existing whole to argue against transgressions of bourgeois norms; but in the case of the proletariat Marx assigns it the project of a revolutionary reconstitution of social relationships. Secondly, it is also true that only through revolutionary action against capital can the proletariat *constitute* itself as a class for itself.

It is of course already constituted as a class in relation to capital but, given that along with material dominance goes ideological dominance, it is difficult for workers not to accept the definition of themselves, and their situation, provided by bourgeois ideology, and hence to act in any other way than in terms of the rationality of the system. It is often possible for an individual proletarian to seek to improve their position in the existing hierarchy; they may even decide to secure their position through betraying other members of the class. Quite large groups of workers may secure an improvement in their conditions through collective action which presupposes the existing structure of particular interest groups. Moreover white workers may find it in their interest to exclude coloureds, Protestants to exclude Catholics, men to exclude women, and so on. But if we are talking of action by the proletariat as a whole, as a collective subject, then the only material basis for this is its objectively given relation to capital, informed by the historical destiny before mentioned. The overthrow of capital is the only general interest capable of superseding the aforementioned particular interests; and furthermore it is the only permanent reality, for the emergence of a labour aristocracy, and other cases of special treatment mentioned, depend on particular conjunctures in the development of capitalism.

The reality of class does not depend on mere similarity of social situation: it is an effect of a structure of opposition. Marx says: 'The separate individuals form a class only insofar as they have to carry on a common battle against another class; in other respects they are on hostile terms with each other as competitors.'[10] So both dimensions are active at the same time, both unity and competition.

It is because class identity is realised only at the moment of revolution and is otherwise compromised by difference and opposition that political parties endeavouring to articulate the general and long-term interest of the class have to 'stand-in' for the posited identity, working to *make* it actual.

Moreover, besides political mediations, moral imperatives also have a place. If workers are class-conscious this by no means abolishes individual interests. Game theory has shown it is often impossible to reduce common action for common benefit to the rational self-interest of each individual taken separately. 'Selling out' often presents itself as a preferred option. Hence the need for mediation by proletarian morality expressed in such terms as 'solidarity', 'class loyalty', 'revolutionary duty'; and the inculcation of contempt for ratebusters, scabs, 'blue-eyed boys' and the like. The contradiction between class interest and individual interest is a lived experience that cannot be abolished in thought but only as a result of practical action to change the situation.

Marx worried that morality, as an ideological superstructure, was a bourgeois ambush tying the workers to a fake universal; he wanted to rely on class interest alone. It is interesting that when he was forced to include in the Rules of the WMIA phrases about 'duty', 'right' 'truth', 'justice', and 'morality',[11] he wrote to Engels that they were so placed as to 'do no harm'.[12] When this 'place' is examined the context is in the first instance that of members' 'conduct towards each other'; and in any event it is clear that such notions are subordinate to the struggle against class rule. Marx here as elsewhere failed to grasp that the necessary loyalty of individuals to their class cannot be reduced to a purely prudential calculation; the individual's identity as a class warrior has to be socially constituted, and instrumental in this is the inculcation of the appropriate values.

Marx only dimly perceived that class interest as a universal stands over against the members and hence needs ethical mediation. This universal – the class interest as distinct from the particular interest of a worker – must be actualised theoretically and practically for effective action against capital. But what sort of universal is this? It is not to be conceptualised *abstractly*, that is to say as transcending difference, but *concretely* as including difference, and responding to the specific experience of various sections of the class, skilled and unskilled, men and women, etc. It is necessary for the movement to take bases of oppression other than class seriously, not just because people suffer discrimination additional to class oppression but because their experience of class oppression is itself mediated in this specificity.

Beside the usual tensions of ethnicity, sex, skill, etc., there is the *structural* problem of the enormous extension since Marx's day of public sector work, and the resulting problem of the division of the working class between those who are directly and immediately in conflict with capital and those who are only indirectly so through the mediation of the capitalist state. One expression of this division is that we have seen in the last fifty years the social-democratic parties becoming the representatives of the public sector and losing the support of the exploited in industry around different attitudes to tax cuts. Paradoxically it is now in the public sector that the density of Trade Union membership is greatest, while workers in the private sector are ever more atomised. It is the need to unite the class across these divisions that makes a revolutionary party necessary.

The idea that identities such as 'class' are 'discursively constituted' is evident nonsense. Class is rooted in objective social structures. But what is true is that, if these same structures fragment and atomise the proletariat, this contradiction has to be addressed in a political way. Class identity is an achievement, as much as it is a presupposition, of revolutionary politics. It has often been observed that, in contrast to the way the bourgeois revolution could 'muddle through' with an extremely ideological self-understanding, the proletariat not only can but must achieve a degree of genuine knowledge of its situation and revolutionary tasks. What has not been stressed (except by Lukács) is that such knowledge is not merely technical (on the analogy that bridge-building requires a science of engineering) it is self-understanding that has to be achieved. It is in this sense that theory and practice are united. The very achievement by the class of its understanding of itself as a class *changes* it so that it becomes practically effective in class struggle.

Conclusion

Let us sum up the main points. The revolutionary destiny of the proletariat is no mechanical inevitability which happens to the proletariat, but its necessity is the outcome of dialectical reasoning from the standpoint of the proletariat defined by its objectively given identity. The rationality of the system faces individuals, or even groups, with choices specified in terms of prevailing institutionalised options, or piece-meal reforms of these. Dialectical reason takes the totality as its object and has as its practical standpoint a class with a potential for retotalisation. The only appropriate and rational consciousness of the proletariat, as a class, is a revolutionary one. However, the class achieves its identity as a class, not simply in virtue of its historical destiny, but on the ground of political, moral, and theoretical, mediations. Marx's position is, for me, 'the critically adopted standpoint of labour'[13] in that it identifies the class of wage labourers as a class driven to revolt against wage labour. Marx stated that his critique of political economy represented the standpoint of 'the class whose historical vocation is the overthrow of the capitalist mode of production and the final abolition of all classes – the proletariat'.[14] The point of Marxist theory is not the academic one of observation and prediction, but lies in the contribution it makes to bringing the proletariat to the consciousness of its task.

[1] This is no new problem: Kropotkin had to write a sermon on 'Anarchist Morality' because an anarchist who ran a store in England found that his comrades in the movement, all dedicated opponents of private property, regarded it as perfectly all right to take goods without paying for them.

[2] When Stirner counterposed (his) egoism to (communist) selflessness, Marx and Engels replied that communism recognises that egoism is sometimes a necessary form of self-assertion. The material basis of the conflict between self-assertion and self-sacrifice must be understood, they say, and they look to a material, rather than speculative, supersession of such oppositions. Marx, K. and F. Engels 1976 *The German Ideology*, p. 247.

[3] Popper, K. 1945 *The Open Society and its Enemies*, Volume 2, p. 119. Engels already replied to a proto-Popper called Paul Barth:
'If Barth supposes that we deny any and every reaction of the political, etc., reflexes of the economic movement upon the movement itself, he is simply tilting at windmills. He has only got to look at Marx's *Eighteenth Brumaire*. . . . Or *Capital*, the section on the working day, for instance. . . . Or why do we fight for the political dictatorship of the proletariat if political power is economically impotent?' Engels to Schmidt, October 27, 1890, Marx, K. and F.. Engels 1965 *Selected Correspondence*, p. 424.

[4] Popper, K. 1945 *The Open Society and its Enemies*, Volume 2, p. 126.

[5] Marx, K. 1976 *Poverty of Philosophy* p. 211.

[6] Marx, K. 1979 *The Eighteenth Brumaire of Louis Bonaparte*, p. 187.

[7] Marx, K. and F. Engels 1975 'The Holy Family', p. 37.

[8] Marx, K. 1996 *Capital* Vol. I, p. 750.

[9] Lukács, G. 1971 *History and Class Consciousness*, p. 51.

[10] Marx, K. and F. Engels 1976 *The German Ideology*, p. 77.

[11] Marx, K. 1985 'Provisional Rules of the Association' p. 15.

[12] Marx to Engels, Nov. 4 1864: Marx, K. and F. Engels 1965 *Selected Correspondence*, p. 148.

[13] Arthur, C. J. 1986 *Dialectics of Labour*, p. 145. A recent book, *Time, Labor, and Social*

Domination by Moishe Postone, 1993, claims the working class is '*integral to*' capitalism and its development, rather than 'the embodiment of its negation'. Since I have contributed to a special issue on Postone of *Historical Materialism* I do not further reply here.

[14] Marx, K. 1996 *Capital* Volume I, p. 16.

Chapter Twelve
Conclusion

In this book a prominent role has been played by the concepts 'systematic dialectic', 'inversion', and 'totality'. The various chapters have demonstrated the fruitfulness of systematic dialectic in comprehending capitalism. Because capital as a totality given to us cannot be known by a linear logic, only a systematic development of categories can demonstrate the grounding of its abstract moments in the whole. But the entire sphere of the value forms totalised as capital posits itself only in negating that which is other than capital: centrally, living labour. Nonetheless, it is essential, before turning to this, to understand the *inner* structure of capital as a *system*. In this we have deployed the Hegelian logical categories, because capital itself has an ideal aspect in the value form.

These findings of ours illustrate a striking feature of capital, that it has a certain *conceptuality* to it. Adorno was one of the few to have understood this: he spoke of 'a conceptuality which holds sway in reality [*Sache*] itself', a conceptuality 'independent both of the consciousness of the human beings subjected to it and of the consciousness of the scientists.'[1] This ideal aspect springs from the *inversion* characteristic of the system of production for exchange, as we have argued throughout. The result is a peculiar interpenetration of 'ideality' and 'materiality' situating 'a contradiction in essence', which we have shown comes up whenever we try to locate 'productive power' in capitalism; it cannot be unequivocally assigned either to capital or labour.[2] This develops from the more basic contradiction between value and use value, extremes whose dialectic achieves ever more concrete mediatedness without ever reaching a final resolution.

I have presented an original interpretation of capital as an *ideal totality* that takes possession – like a malevolent spirit – of the material world of labour and goods. It attempts to subsume within its own form-determinations all otherness, including living labour and natural forces. Its claims in this respect may ultimately be false. Nevertheless, epochally it has made good these claims in developing its wealth and power, humbling even governments that dare to buck the market. In situating all otherness merely as a moment of its own absolute reality, capital achieves a self-identical totality. 'Post-modernists' deny the validity of the category of totality, as if Hegel and Marx were at fault for using it, whereas they reflect (Hegel uncritically and Marx critically) the totalising logic of the value form which really imposes itself in such a manner that all relationships become inscribed within it. All that is not itself 'conceptual' is degraded to its bearer. But capital contracts an unacknowl-edged debt for this; in totalising labours only as abstractions of themselves, it cannot account for what is in excess of its concept of itself, the concrete richness of social labour.

In revolt against such a 'concept' Adorno declared 'the whole is false'.[3] But it did not need Margaret Thatcher to remind us that 'there is no alternative' to capital, its power, its law, its truth. To think against capital's regime of truth requires a peculiar ability: to grasp that in an inverted world 'the true is a moment of the false' (Guy Debord[4]); but, it should be added, it *is* true all the same; when Marx retails such 'truths' in *Capital* his discourse thus characteristically takes the shape of a biting irony.

We take our stand with what escapes the totality, yet supports it, social labour, the exploited source of capital's accumulated power, no matter that this is denied. We saw, with Marx, that (form determined as wage labour) living labour realises itself only by its de-realising itself, producing 'the being of its non-being', capital. Only through the negation of this its negation can labour liberate itself, humanity and Nature, from the succubus of capital. The real-ity of this standpoint is still historically open-ended. Without it, our critique of capital's one-dimensionality would be utopian in the scientific sense of *unlocated* or even *dislocated*. Only revolutionary practice can 'prove the truth' of this critique.

[1]   Adorno, T. W. 1976 'Sociology and Empirical Research' p. 80.
[2]   Horrified by such consequences of the Marxian diagnosis of inversion (which he himself had earlier done much to elucidate) Colletti abandoned the field, declaring as his reason that Hegel's dialectic is there in *Capital* and that '*one cannot do science with dialectic*'. Colletti, L. 1998 'Value and Dialectic in Marx' p. 80.
[3]   Adorno, T. W. 1978 *Minima Moralia*, p. 50.
[4]   Debord, G. 1977 *Society of the Spectacle*, §9.

Bibliography

Adorno, Theodor W. 1976 'Sociology and Empirical Research' [1957] in *The Positivist Dispute in German Sociology* by T. W. Adorno *et al.*, trans. G. Adey and D. Frisby, London: Heinemann.

Adorno, Theodor W. 1978 *Minima Moralia*, trans. E. F. N. Jephcott, London: Verso.

Albritton, Robert 1986 *A Japanese Reconstruction of Marxist Theory* Basingstoke: Macmillan, and New York: St. Martin's.

Albritton, Robert 1999 *Dialectics and Deconstruction in Political Economy*, Basingstoke: Macmillan, and New York: St. Martin's.

Albritton, Robert 2003 (ed) *New Dialectics and Political Economy* Basingstoke: Palgrave.

Althusser, Louis 1969 *For Marx*, Trans. B. Brewster, London: Allen Lane The Penguin Press.

Arnot, Bob 1988 *Controlling Soviet Labour* Basingstoke: Macmillan.

Arthur, Christopher J. 1972 'The Coming Soviet Revolution' in *Trotsky: The Great Debate Renewed* edited by N. Krasso, St. Louis: New Critics Press.

Arthur, Christopher J. 1979 'Dialectics and Labour' in *Issues in Marxist Philosophy* (Volume 1 Dialectics and Method) edited by J. Mepham and D.H. Ruben, Brighton: Harvester.

Arthur, Christopher J. 1986 'Marx and Engels: *The German Ideology*' in *Philosophers Ancient and Modern*, edited by G. Vesey, Cambridge: Cambridge University Press.

Arthur, Christopher J. 1986 *Dialectics of Labour,* Oxford: Basil Blackwell.

Arthur, Christopher J. 1996 'Engels as Interpreter of Marx's Economics' in *Engels Today: A Centenary Appreciation* edited by C. J. Arthur, Basingstoke: Macmillan.

Arthur, Christopher J. 1998 'Engels, Logic and History' in *Marxian Economics: A Reappraisal* (Volume 1 Method, Value and Money) edited by R. Bellofiore, Basingstoke: Macmillan and New York: St. Martin's.

Arthur, Christopher J. 1998 'The Fluidity of Capital and the Logic of the Concept' in *The Circulation of Capital* edited by C. J. Arthur and G. Reuten, Basingstoke: Macmillan.

Arthur, Christopher J. 1999 'Napoleoni on Labour and Exploitation', in Baldassarri, M. and R. Bellofiore (eds) *Classical and Marxian Political Economy: A Debate on Claudio Napoleoni's Views*, special issue of *Rivista di Politica Economica*, IV–V April-May 1999 (English and Italian editions).

Arthur, Christopher J. 2000 'From the Critique of Hegel to the Critique of Capital', in *The Hegel-Marx Connection*, edited by T. Burns and I. Fraser, Basingstoke: Macmillan.

Arthur, Christopher J. 2002 'Capital in General and Marx's Capital' in *The Culmination of Capital* edited by M. Campbell and G. Reuten, Basingstoke: Palgrave.

Arthur, Christopher J. 2003 'The Problem of Use Value for a Dialectic of Capital' in *New Dialectics and Political Economy* edited by Robert Albritton, Basingstoke: Palgrave.

Backhaus, Hans-Georg 1992 'Between Philosophy and Science: Marxian Social Economy as Critical Theory', in *Open Marxism: Volume I Dialectics and History*, edited by W. Bonefeld *et al.*, London: Pluto.

Bailey, Samuel 1967 *A Critical Dissertation on the Nature, Measure, and Causes, of Value* [1825], Reprinted, London: Frank Cass.

Baldassarri, Mario and Riccardo Bellofiore 1999 (eds) *Classical and Marxian Political Economy: A Debate on Claudio Napoleoni's Views*, special issue of *Rivista di Politica Economica*, IV–V April-May 1999 (English and Italian editions).

Banaji, Jairus 1979 'From the Commodity to Capital: Hegel's Dialectic in Marx's *Capital*' in *Value: The Representation of Labour in Capitalism*, edited by D. Elson, London: CSE Books.

Bellofiore, Riccardo 1999 'The Value of Labour Value. The Italian Debate on Marx: 1968–1976' in Baldassarri, M. and R. Bellofiore (eds) *Classical and Marxian Political Economy: A Debate on Claudio Napoleoni's Views*, special issue of *Rivista di Politica Economica*, IV–V April-May 1999 (English and Italian editions).

Bellofiore, Riccardo and Roberto Finelli 1998 'Capital, Labour and Time' in *Marxian Economics: A Reappraisal* (Volume 1 Method, Value and Money) edited by R. Bellofiore, Basingstoke: Macmillan and New York: St. Martin's.

Benhabib, Seyla 1984 'Obligation, contract and exchange' in Pelczynski, Z. A. (ed.) *The State and Civil Society: Studies in Hegel's Political Philosophy*, Cambridge: Cambridge University Press.

Bhaskar, Roy 1991 'Dialectics', in *A Dictionary of Marxist Thought*, 2nd edition, edited by Tom Bottomore, Oxford: Basil Blackwell.

Bhaskar, Roy 1993 *Dialectic: The Pulse of freedom*, London: Verso.

Böhm-Bawerk, Eugen von 1975 *Karl Marx and the Close of his System,* London: Merlin Press.

Braverman, Harry 1974 *Labor and Monopoly Capital,* New York and London: Monthly Review Press.

Browning, Gary K. 1999 *Hegel and the History of Political Philosophy,* Basingstoke: Macmillan.

Cohen, G. A. 1981 'The labour theory of value and the concept of exploitation' in *The Value Controversy* by Ian Steedman *et al.,* London, Verso.

Colletti, Lucio 1973 *Marxism and Hegel,* London: NLB.

Colletti, Lucio 1998 'Value and Dialectic in Marx' (from 'Valore e dialettica in Marx' *Rinascita,* no. 18, 5th May, 1978) in *International Journal of Political Economy* 28.3 Fall.

Debord, Guy 1977 *Society of the Spectacle* [1967] Detroit: Black & Red.

Della Volpe, Galvano 1980 *Logic as a positive science,* London: NLB.

Derrida, Jacques 1994 *Specters of Marx,* New York: Routledge.

Dussel, Enrique 2001 *Towards an Unknown Marx,* London: Routledge.

Eldred, Michael and Mike Roth 1978 *Guide to Marx's 'Capital'* London: CSE Books.

Elster, John 1986 *An Introduction to Karl Marx,* Cambridge: Cambridge University Press.

Engels, Frederick 1954 *Dialectics of Nature,* trans. C. Dutt, Moscow: Progress Publishers, 2nd ed.

Engels, Frederick 1962 *Anti-Dühring,* Moscow: Foreign Languages Publishing House.

Engels, Frederick 1969 'Karl Marx, *A Contribution to the Critique of Political Economy'* in Karl Marx and Frederick Engels *Selected Works* Volume One, Moscow: Progress Publishers.

Engels, Frederick 1981 'Supplement to Volume 3 of *Capital'* in Marx, K. 1981 *Capital* Volume III, trans. D. Fernbach, Harmondsworth: Penguin.

Filtzer, Don 1986 *Soviet Workers and Stalinist Industrialisation,* London: Pluto Press.

Füredi, Frank 1986 *The Soviet Union demystified: a materialist analysis,* London: Junius Publications.

Gleicher, David 1994 'A Historical Approach to the Question of Abstract Labour' in *Debates in Value Theory,* edited by S. Mohun, Basingstoke: Macmillan & New York: St. Martin's.

Gunn, Richard 1992 'Against Historical Materialism' in *Open Marxism*, Volume II Theory and Practice, edited by W. Bonefeld, R. Gunn and K. Psychopedis, London: Pluto Press.

Habermas, Jürgen 1974 *Theory and Practice*, trans. J. Viertel London: Heinemann.

Hartmann, Klaus 1972 'Hegel: A Non-Metaphysical View' in *Hegel*, edited by A. MacIntyre, Garden City N. Y.: Doubleday Anchor.

Hegel, G. W. F. 1949 *Phenomenology of Mind*, trans. J. B. Baillie, London: George Allen & Unwin.

Hegel, G. W. F. 1967 *Grundlinien der Philosophie des Rechts*, [1821] ed. J. Hoffmeister Hamburg: Felix Meiner Verlag.

Hegel, G. W. F. 1967 *The Philosophy of Right* trans. T. M. Knox [1942], Oxford: Oxford University Press.

Hegel, G. W. F. 1969 *The Science of Logic*, trans. A. V. Miller, London: George Allen & Unwin.

Hegel, G. W. F. 1971 *Hegel's Philosophy of Mind* (Being part three of *The Encyclopaedia of the Philosophical Sciences*), trans. W. Wallace and A.V. Miller, Oxford: Oxford University Press.

Hegel, G. W. F. 1975 *Hegel's Logic* (Being part one of *The Encyclopaedia of the Philosophical Sciences*) trans. W. Wallace Oxford: Oxford University Press.

Hegel, G. W. F. 1977 *Phenomenology of Spirit*, trans. A. V. Miller, Oxford: Oxford University Press.

Hegel, G. W. F. 1979 '*Fragmente aus Vorleslungsmanuskripte zur Philosophie der Natur und des Geistes*' (1803/4): *Gesammelte Werke, Band 6, Jenaer Systementwürfe* I (Hamburg: Felix Meiner Verlag, 1975), trans. H. S. Harris and T. M. Knox, 1979 *Hegel, System of Ethical Life and First Philosophy of Spirit* Albany, N. Y.: State University of New York Press.

Hegel, G. W. F. 1979 '*System der Sittlichkeit*' (1802/3) in *Schriften zur Politik und Rechtsphilosophie* edited by G. Lasson (Leipzig: Felix Meiner 1923); trans. H. S. Harris and T. M. Knox, 1979 *Hegel, System of Ethical Life and First Philosophy of Spirit* Albany, N. Y.: State University of New York Press.

Hegel, G. W. F. 1983 '*Vorlesungsmanuskript zur Realphilosophie*' (1805/6) *Gesammelte Werke, Band 8, Jenaer Systementwürfe* III. I (Hamburg: Felix Meiner Verlag, 1976); trans. in Leo Rauch, 1983 *Hegel and the Human Spirit* Detroit: Wayne State University Press.

Hegel, G. W. F. 1985 *Hegel's Introduction to the Lectures on the History of Philosophy*, trans. T. M. Knox and A. V. Miller, Oxford: Oxford University Press.

Hegel, G. W. F. 1991 *Elements of the Philosophy of Right*, Trans. H.B. Nisbet, ed. A. Wood. Cambridge: Cambridge University Press.

Hegel, G. W. F. 1991 *The Encyclopaedia Logic*, Trans. Geraets, T. F. *et al.* Indianapolis: Hackett.

Hegel, G. W. F. 1995 *Lectures on Natural Right and Political Science*, transcribed by Peter Wannenmann, Heidelberg 1817–19, Trans. J. M. Stewart and P. C. Hodgson, Berkeley/Los Angeles/London: University of California Press.

Hunt, Ian 1993 *Analytical and Dialectical Materialism*, Aldershot: Avebury.

Ilyenkov, E. V. 1982 *The Dialectic of the Abstract and the Concrete in Marx's 'Capital'*, Moscow: Progress Publishers.

Jameson, Fredric 1990 *Late Marxism: Adorno, or, the persistence of the dialectic*, London and New York: Verso.

Lebowitz, Michael A. 1992 *Beyond 'Capital'*, Basingstoke: Macmillan Press.

Lenin, V.I. 1961 ' Philosophical Notebooks' trans. C. Dutt, *Collected Works* Volume 38, London: Lawrence & Wishart.

Lukács, Georg 1971 *History and Class Consciousness*, trans. R. Livingstone, London: Merlin Press.

Lukács, Georg 1975 *The Young Hegel*, [1948] trans. Livingstone, R. London: Merlin Press.

Lukes, Steven 1977 'Methodological Individualism Reconsidered', in *Essays in Social Theory*, London: Macmillan.

Mandel, Ernest 1978 'On the Nature of the Soviet State' *New Left Review* 108.

Mandel, Ernest 1990 'Karl Marx' in *The New Palgrave: Marxian Economics*, edited by J. Eatwell *et al.*, London and Basingstoke: Macmillan.

Marcuse, Herbert 1954 *Reason and Revolution*, London: Routledge.

Marx, Karl 1962 *Das Kapital: Erster Band*, Karl Marx and Friedrich Engels *Werke*, *Band* 23, Berlin: Dietz Verlag.

Marx, Karl 1964 *Das Kapital: Dritter Band*, Karl Marx and Friedrich Engels *Werke*, *Band* 25, Berlin: Dietz Verlag.

Marx, Karl 1973 *Grundrisse der Kritik der Politischen Okonomie (Rohentwurf)*, Engl. trans. M. Nicolaus, Harmondsworth: Penguin/NLB.

Marx, Karl 1975 'Contribution to the Critique of Hegel's Philosophy of Law' in Marx, Karl and Frederick Engels *Collected Works* Volume 3, London: Lawrence and Wishart.

Marx, Karl 1975 *'Economic and Philosophic Manuscripts* of 1844' in Marx, Karl and Frederick Engels *Collected Works* Volume 3, London: Lawrence and Wishart.

Marx, Karl 1976 *Capital* Volume I, trans. B. Fowkes, Harmondsworth: Penguin.

Marx, Karl 1976 *Ökonomische Manuskripte 1857/58,* Karl Marx and Friedrich Engels *Gesamtausgabe* (MEGA) *Abteilung* II *Band* 1.1, Berlin, Dietz-Verlag.

Marx, Karl 1976 *Poverty of Philosophy*: Marx, Karl and Frederick Engels *Collected Works* Volume 6, London: Lawrence and Wishart.

Marx, Karl 1976 *Value: Studies by Karl Marx,* trans. A. Dragstedt, London: New Park.

Marx, Karl 1978 *Capital* Volume II, trans. D. Fernbach, Harmondsworth: Penguin.

Marx, Karl 1979 *The Eighteenth Brumaire of Louis Bonaparte*: Marx, Karl and Frederick Engels *Collected Works* Volume 11, London: Lawrence and Wishart.

Marx, Karl 1981 *Capital* Volume III, trans. D. Fernbach, Harmondsworth: Penguin.

Marx, Karl 1981 *Ökonomische Manuskripte 1857/58, Marx-Engels Gesamtausgabe* (MEGA) *Abteilung* II *Band* 1.2, Berlin, Dietz-Verlag.

Marx, Karl 1983 *Capital Volume One*, London: Lawrence and Wishart.

Marx, Karl 1983 *Das Kapital Erster Band* 1867: Karl Marx and Friedrich Engels *Gesamtausgabe* (MEGA), *Abteilung* II *Band* 5, Berlin, Dietz-Verlag.

Marx, Karl 1983 *Das Kapital Erster Band:* Marx, Karl and Friedrich Engels *Werke, Band* 23, Berlin, Dietz-Verlag.

Marx, Karl 1985 'Provisional Rules of the Association' in Marx, Karl and Frederick Engels *Collected Works* Volume 20, London: Lawrence and Wishart.

Marx, Karl 1986 'Economic Manuscripts of 1857–58' in Marx, Karl and Frederick Engels *Collected Works* Volume 28, London: Lawrence and Wishart.

Marx, Karl 1986. 'The Civil War in France', in Marx, Karl and Frederick Engels *Collected Works* Volume 22, London: Lawrence and Wishart.

Marx, Karl 1987 'Economic Manuscripts of 1857–58' in Marx, Karl and Frederick Engels *Collected Works* Volume 29, London: Lawrence and Wishart.

Marx, Karl 1987 'Original text of *A Contribution to a Critique . . .*' Marx, Karl and Frederick Engels *Collected Works* Volume 29, London: Lawrence and Wishart.

Marx, Karl 1987 *A Contribution to the Critique of Political Economy* [1859] Marx, Karl and Frederick Engels *Collected Works* Volume 29, London: Lawrence and Wishart.

Marx, Karl 1988 'Economic Manuscript of 1861–63': Marx, Karl and Frederick Engels *Collected Works* Volume 30, London: Lawrence and Wishart.

Marx, Karl 1989 'Economic Manuscript of 1861–63': Marx, Karl and Frederick Engels *Collected Works* Volume 32, London: Lawrence and Wishart.

Marx, Karl 1989 'On Wagner' in Marx, Karl and Frederick Engels *Collected Works* Volume 24, London: Lawrence and Wishart.

Marx, Karl 1989 *Das Kapital I 1883* Karl Marx and Friedrich Engels *Gesamtausgabe* (MEGA) *Abteilung* II, *Band* 8, Berlin, Dietz-Verlag.

Marx, Karl 1989 *Le Capital 1872–75,* Karl Marx and Friedrich Engels *Gesamtausgabe* (MEGA) *Abteilung* II, *Band* 7, Berlin, Dietz-Velag.

Marx, Karl 1990 *Capital 1887*: Karl Marx and Friedrich Engels *Gesamtausgabe* (MEGA) *Abteilung* II, *Band* 9, Berlin: Dietz Verlag.

Marx, Karl 1992 *Das Kapital. Drittes Buch. Die Gestaltungen des Gesamtprozesses,* in Karl Marx and Friedrich Engels *Gesamtausgabe* (MEGA) *Abteilung* II, *Band* 4.2 Berlin: Dietz Verlag.

Marx, Karl 1994 '*Capital First Edition* Appendix on the Value Form' in *Debates in Value Theory,* edited by S. Mohun Basingstoke: Macmillan & New York: St. Martin's.

Marx, Karl 1994 'Economic Manuscript of 1861–63': Marx, Karl and Frederick Engels *Collected Works* Volume 34, London: Lawrence and Wishart.

Marx, Karl 1994 'Results of the Direct Production Process' in Marx, Karl and Frederick Engels *Collected Works* Volume 34, London: Lawrence and Wishart.

Marx, Karl 1996 *Capital* Volume I in Marx, Karl and Frederick Engels *Collected Works* Volume 35, London: Lawrence and Wishart.

Marx, Karl and Frederick Engels 1965 *Selected Correspondence,* Moscow: Progress Publishers.

Marx, Karl and Frederick Engels 1975 'The Holy Family' in Marx, Karl and Frederick Engels *Collected Works* Volume 4, London: Lawrence and Wishart.

Marx, Karl and Frederick Engels 1976 *The German Ideology,* in Marx, Karl and Frederick Engels *Collected Works* Volume 5, London: Lawrence and Wishart.

Marx, Karl and Frederick Engels 1983 *Letters on 'Capital'* trans. Drummond, A., London: New Park Publications.

Marx, Karl and Frederick Engels, 1983, Letters 1856–59: Marx, Karl and Frederick Engels *Collected Works* Volume 40, London: Lawrence and Wishart.

McCarney, Joseph 2000 *Hegel and History,* London: Routledge.

McTaggart, J. M. E. 1922 *Studies in Hegelian Dialectic,* 2nd ed., reissued 1964, New York: Russell & Russell.

Meek, Ronald 1973 *Studies in the Labour Theory of Value,* 2nd ed., London: Lawrence & Wishart.

Mepham, John 1979 'From the Grundrisse to Capital' in *Issues in Marxist Philosophy* edited by J. Mepham and D.-H. Ruben, Volume One: *Dialectics and Method*, Brighton: Harvester Press.

Mészáros, István 1995 *Beyond Capital*, London: The Merlin Press; New York: Monthly Review Press,

Mohun, Simon 1994 'Value, Value-Form and Money' in *Debates in Value Theory,* edited by S. Mohun, Basingstoke: Macmillan and New York: St. Martin's.

Mohun, Simon 1994 (ed.) *Debates in Value Theory,* Basingstoke: Macmillan and New York: St. Martin's.

Murray, Patrick 1988 *Marx's Theory of Scientific Knowledge* Atlantic Highlands N. J.: Humanities Press.

Napoleoni, Claudio 1975 *Smith, Ricardo, Marx,* Oxford: Basil Blackwell.

Napoleoni, Claudio 1991 'Value and exploitation: Marx's economic theory and beyond' in *Marx and Modern Economic Analysis,* edited by G. A. Caravale, Aldershot: Edward Elgar.

Norman, Richard and Sean Sayers 1980 *Hegel, Marx and Dialectic*, Brighton: Harvester.

Ollman, Bertell 1993 *Dialectical Investigations*, London: Routledge.

Popper, Karl 1945 *The Open Society and its Enemies*, Volume 2, London: Routledge & Kegan Paul.

Postone, Moishe 1993 *Time, Labor, and Social Domination,* Cambridge: Cambridge University Press.

Reuten, Geert 2000 'The Interconnection of Systematic Dialectics and Historical Materialism' in *Historical Materialism* No. 7 Winter.

Reuten, Geert and Michael Williams 1989 *Value-Form and the State*, London: Routledge.

Rigby, S. H. 1992 *Engels and the Formation of Marxism*, Manchester: Manchester University Press.

Rodano, Giorgio 1999 'The Economic Thought of Claudio Napoleoni' in Baldassarri, M. and R. Bellofiore (eds) *Classical and Marxian Political Economy: A Debate on Claudio Napoleoni's Views*, special issue of *Rivista di Politica Economica*, IV–V April-May 1999 (English and Italian editions).

Rosenthal, John 1998 *The Myth of Dialectics*, Basingstoke: Macmillan.

Rubel, Maximilien 1981 'Plan and Method of the "Economics"' [1973] in *Rubel on Marx* edited by J. O'Malley & K. Algozin, Cambridge: Cambridge University Press.

Rubin, Isaak I. 1972 *Essays on Marx's Theory of Value* (trans. from 3rd ed. 1928) Detroit: Black and Red.

Rubin, Isaak I. 1994 'Abstract Labour and Value in Marx's System' [1927] in *Debates in Value Theory*, edited by S. Mohun, Basingstoke: Macmillan and New York: St. Martin's.

Screpanti, Ernesto 1998 'Towards a General Theory of Capitalism' in *Marxian Economics: A Reappraisal* (Volume 1 Method, Value and Money) edited by R. Bellofiore, Basingstoke: Macmillan and New York: St. Martin's.

Sekine, Tom 1998 'The Dialectic of Capital' in *Science & Society* 62.3.

Shamsavari, Ali 1991 *Dialectics and Social Theory* Braunton: Merlin Books.

Shortall, Felton C. 1994 *The Incomplete Marx* Aldershot: Avebury.

Smith, Adam 1976 *The Wealth of Nations* ed. E. Cannan [1904] reprinted Chicago: University of Chicago Press.

Smith, Tony 1990 *The Logic of Marx's 'Capital': Replies to Hegelian Objections*, Albany, N. Y.: State University of New York Press.

Smith, Tony 1993 *Dialectical Social Theory and its Critics*, Albany, N. Y.: State University of New York Press.

Sohn-Rethel, Alfred 1978 *Intellectual and Manual Labour*, London and Basingstoke: Macmillan Press.

Stalin, J. V. 1939 'Dialectical Materialism' in *History of the C.P.S.U (Bolsheviks): Short Course*, Moscow, FLPH.

Stedman Jones, Gareth 1990, 'Dialectical reasoning' in *The New Palgrave: Marxian Economics*, edited by J. Eatwell *et al.*, London and Basingstoke: Macmillan.

Stirner, Max 1995 *The Ego and Its Own*, Cambridge: Cambridge University Press.

Sweezy, Paul M. 1970 *The Theory of Capitalist Development*, [1942] New York, Monthly Review Press.

Ticktin, Hillel 1992 *Origins of the Crisis in the USSR: essays on the political economy of a disintegrating system*, New York: M. E. Sharpe.

Waszek, Norbert 1983 'The origins of Hegel's knowledge of English' (with a list of English books in Hegel's library extracted from the auction catalogue), *Bulletin of the Hegel Society of Great Britain*, 7.

Willett, Cynthia 1990 'The Shadow of Hegel's *Science of Logic'*, in *Essays on Hegel's Logic*, edited by G. di Giovanni, Albany, N. Y.: State University of New York Press.

Williams, Howard 1989 *Hegel, Heraclitus and Marx's Dialectic*, Hemel Hempstead: Harvester Wheatsheaf.

Williams, Michael 1988 (ed.) *Value, Social Form and the State*, Basingstoke: Macmillan.

Index

Wainwright, H.   223
Waszek, N.   197, 256
Weber, M.   152
Willett, C.   164, 256

Williams, H.   15, 256
Williams, M.   4, 5, 7, 12, 15, 77, 87, 255–6
working day   53–7, 75
World Spirit   6